Listening to the Sea

Pitt Series in Policy and Institutional Studies

Bert A. Rockman, Editor

Listening to the Sea

The Politics of Improving Environmental Protection

Robert Jay Wilder

UNIVERSITY OF PITTSBURGH PRESS

Published by the University of Pittsburgh Press, Pittsburgh, Pa. 15261
Copyright © 1998, University of Pittsburgh Press
Manufactured in the United States of America
Printed on acid-free paper
10 9 8 7 6 5 4 3 2 1

Library of Congress Cataloging-in-Publication Data
Wilder, Robert Jay.
    Listening to the sea : the politics of improving environmental
protection / Robert Jay Wilder.
        p. cm. — (Pitt series in policy and institutional studies)
    Includes bibliographical references and index.
    ISBN 0-8229-4059-0 (cloth)
    ISBN 0-8229-5663-2 (pbk.)
    1. Oceanography. 2. Marine resources. 3. Ocean engineering.
4. Marine ecology. I. Title. II. Series.
    GC11.2 .W55 1998
    333.91'6415—ddc21   98-8947
                                                              CIP

A CIP catalog record for this book is available from the British Library.

For Diana and Carson, Sophia, Emanuel, Betsy, and Rick;
and for the beauty of all marine ecosystems
throughout the world.

In the end we will conserve only what we love;
we will love only what we understand; and we
will understand only what we are taught.

Baba Dioum, Senegalese ecologist

Contents

Acknowledgments

My thinking across the fields of environmental law, marine policy, and conservation biology has been deeply informed by visionaries. Some I had the great pleasure to know personally or to work with closely, whereas a few I know solely through the lingering voice of the written word. These remarkable people include Stanley Anderson, Jack Archer, Tanya Atwater, Dave Brower, David Caron, Rachel Carson, Biliana Cicin-Sain, Barry Commoner, Robert Costanza, Jacques-Yves Cousteau, Sylvia Earle, Daniel Fiorino, Bob Friedheim, Dan Hauser, Tim Hennessey, Marc Hershman, Richard Hildreth, Ann Hollick, Jon Jacobson, Larry Juda, Herbert Kaufman, Richard Kenchington, Jim Kennett, John Kingdon, Bob Knecht, Amory Lovins, James Lovelock, Dean Mann, Lynn Margulis, Daniel Mazmanian, J. Marc McGinnes, Mary Morgan, Rod Nash, Elliott Norse, Orrin Pilkey, G. Carleton Ray, Paul Sabatier, Michael Soulé, Lewis Thomas, Jon Van Dyke, John Vasconcellos, E. O. Wilson, and George Woodwell. Many other people far too numerous to name here have helped as well, and I extend my deep gratitude to you all.

This book required many years of effort; therefore as a practical matter it would not have been possible without timely financial support. I am grateful to generous organizations that provided fellowships, grants, and practical experience, including a California Sea Grant Fellowship to work on ocean and coastal legislation in the California State Capitol; a grant from Institute of Marine Resources in the Scripps Institution of Oceanography at University of California at San Diego; a Fulbright Fellowship in the Ocean Resources Management Programme at the University of South Pacific in the Fiji Islands;

a National Academy of Sciences Joint U.S.-Russian Young Investigator Award
on Biodiversity; a National Academy of Sciences Young Investigator Award
on Coastal Ecology; a grant from the National Science Foundation; a grant
from the Marine Science Institute at University of California at Santa Barbara;
and an American Association for the Advancement of Science/Environmental
Protection Agency Fellowship in Environmental Science and Engineering,
which took me to Washington, D.C. These opportunities helped to refine my
understanding of policy making and taught me to appreciate practical issues
faced in day-to-day ocean management.

During the thirteen years that I spent growing up and learning at the Park
School in Brooklandville, Maryland, a wonderful group of teachers showed
that critical thinking and imagination are critical to understanding the world.
Later on, two essential inspirations, Sarah Katherine Cooper and Kimberly
Kotnik, helped me to grow in many ways. I also appreciate the support I re-
ceived from Bob Hackey, Clyde Barrow, Jean Doyle, and Peter Cressy at the
University of Massachusetts at Dartmouth. Other help has come from the
Political Science Department, the Environmental Studies Program, and the
Donald Bren School of Environmental Science and Management at the Uni-
versity of California at Santa Barbara.

Government agency staff members, representatives of nongovernmental organizations, members of Congress, academics, and others selflessly gave me interviews: my thanks to you all. In particular I would like to acknowledge the
many interviews provided by Brian Hoyle, Davis Colson, Tom Kitsos, Bob
Lagomarsino, David Hardy, Bruce Mead, Charles Bennett, Michael Poling,
Pete DeWitt, Jack Rigg, James Lawless, Martin Finerty, Peter Bernhardt,
Ashe Roach, Gary Magnuson, and Joan Bondareff. I appreciate the invaluable
comments on early draft portions of this book that were offered by Lynton K.
Caldwell, Gerard Mangone, Milner Ball, and Shirley Taylor, among others;
I clearly also owe an intellectual debt for the exceptionally helpful comments
offered by several anonymous reviewers along the way. And my thanks to
Cynthia Miller, who as director of the University of Pittsburgh Press had the
requisite faith that a book idea on environmental policy for the oceans could
be a worthwhile project. I am also indebted to Jane Flanders for her indis-
pensable and valorous copy editing—as well as to Eileen Kiley, Colleen
Salcius, Kathy Meyer, and Jennifer Flanagan for helping bring this work to
its fruition. My thanks extend as well to Jill Perry Townsend for her artistic
aplomb in penning the illustrations. The Santa Barbara Historical Society provided the photographs used in chapter 2.

Selected portions of this book appeared in the *Virginia Journal of International Law* 32 (1992): 681–746; *UCLA Journal of Environmental Law and Policy* 11 (1993): 131–73; and as a chapter in *Ocean Yearbook* 12, edited by Elizabeth Mann Borgese, Norton Ginsberg, and Joseph Morgan (Chicago: University of Chicago Press, 1996), 207–22. Permission to reproduce these portions here as updated text is gratefully acknowledged.

Long ago, Diana Lee Francis persuaded me to abandon my Luddite ways and to embrace the Macintosh computer. In so many things, her gentle persuasion, support and guidance were all spot on. She has shown me new worlds, introduced me to exciting possibilities, and made much possible; thank you for everything, Diana. And while the selfless efforts of the above-mentioned people have all improved this work immeasurably, I must proclaim that all the opinions offered here, as well as any errors or omissions, are my responsibility alone.

The unique physical environment that surrounds University of California at Santa Barbara greatly influenced this project. Many singular places near there, like Campus Point, Rincon, and the Los Padres Mountains, made years of writing not toil but a joy—as did a good deal of surfing, diving, biking, and the spirit of place. I am forever in awe of the Pacific Ocean and am indebted to the poetry of its fertile seas and marine ecosystems. Finally, the Marine Science Institute there, like the broader academic community, proved mentally invigorating. But most of all I give this book to my father, mother, brother, wife Diana, and son Carson. It is my fervent hope that this book makes a contribution, however modest, to enhancing appreciation of the marine environment.

Preface

This book is about opportunities to create a more ecologically sensible relationship between humankind and the sea. There are many incentives to begin undertaking this task. Modern governance of the oceans and coasts is excessively fragmented and piecemeal. Policies continue to be divisive or focus exclusively on one resource, and in that way are quite unlike the highly interconnected life of the sea. Only if we act in ways that are more ecologically aware, prune ossified regulations, and learn from our mistakes can we make ocean and coastal protection work in ways that are smarter, cheaper, and more effective to boot. The time is ripe for improved governance; moreover, given the ongoing degradation of the marine environment, there is little alternative.

It is thus useful to begin by considering how modern problems in ocean governance initially arose. A keen sense of history is vital. Chapter 1 begins by tracing the origins of the three-mile territorial sea. That legal limit, which long defined the public order of the oceans, first arose from a colorful history of bold pretensions to ownership of the seas. Surprisingly, it had its origins in quirks of history and coincidences having no connection to either modern maritime issues or the physical nature of marine ecosystems.

Chapter 2 addresses the sharp divisions in domestic ocean jurisdiction by returning to the Tidelands Debate of the mid-twentieth century. With protection of marine ecosystems not yet a matter for attention and conservation of natural resources still only a budding concern, an outline of governance was shaped that continues to dominate the United States today. Chapter 3 completes the historical survey by describing events of the later twentieth century, then discusses the ecology of the seas and concepts like biological diversity, highlighting the discrepancies between actual ecosystem processes—and the present state of ocean and coastal governance, both at the state and federal levels.

Chapter 4, on the management of offshore oil and gas, reviews current policies for regulating the extraction of offshore oil—a case in which management is failing badly. It discusses severe policy breakdowns caused by a distant federal bureaucracy that pursues one-size-fits-all thinking. Many solutions are suggested, such as devolving some federal authority to the states. Other options include narrowly amending existing legislation. The chapter highlights fiscally prudent and profitable means to reduce U.S. demand for oil, with an emphasis on increasing energy efficiency and promoting conservation.

Chapter 5 suggests how to achieve better energy efficiency—as well as to become more ecologically aware. It offers fresh ways of improving the bottom line for industry while reducing harm to the marine environment. The path forward is clear. To combat harm to ecosystems, government usually mandates command-and-control, "end-of-pipe" approaches to curbing pollution. That thinking has gone about as far as logic dictates. Because of the great expense of control technologies, without a reasonable return in environmental benefits, it is smarter to prevent pollution in the first place. The new precautionary principle and pollution prevention depend on new thinking as well as nimble-footed government agencies in which continuous adaptation and change—in short, the acquisition of wisdom—are integral. That sort of flexibility will demand a rather sharp departure from traditional practices.

Precautionary action is increasingly evident in international law. Although still evolving, this concept shifts the burden of proof to those who propose potentially dangerous activities—such as when substances to be released are persistent and toxic and will bioaccumulate. This precautionary concept avoids the harms caused by overfishing, for example, and it minimizes bycatch and destruction of habitat. By looking upstream to activities on land that will ultimately degrade marine ecosystems, the precautionary principle emphasizes prevention rather than cure.

Chapter 6 addresses the important obstacles that confound efforts to integrate science and policy in decision making about the protection of ocean resources. Chief among these is inertia. Coastal and ocean policy is still reductionist by design; it is bureaucratically compartmentalized, and so the sea is similarly approached as a mass of unrelated domains. The unsurprising result is that "first-generation" marine policy sacrifices biodiversity in genetic terms and promotes the loss of species and habitat. For instance, although land-based sources of pollution are now known to cause most contamination of the sea, until recently the nexus between land-based sources of pollution and the state of the seas was ignored in policy.

New knowledge brings opportunity. The nature of marine ecology and the linkages that tie humankind to the sea are lately being uncovered at an unprecedented rate. To be sure, there are still immense gaps in our understanding of the seas and still greater research is needed. Nonetheless, exciting paths are opening up for preventing pollution, improving fishery management, preserving the integrity of ecosystems, minimizing coastal pollution, and enhancing energy efficiency. But with new knowledge comes a fresh responsibility: we must now learn to listen to the sea. Because this book is written from a political science viewpoint, it is concerned with marine law and improving policy. However, I have a broader goal: to integrate disciplines in pursuit of better environmental protection and to be a blueprint for wiser ocean policy.

Listening to the Sea

By the Middle Ages, the Roman Empire was in decline. As its supremacy eroded, so too did its ability to prohibit other claims to the sea, bringing to an end the only era in which a formalized *mare liberum* (open seas regime) had prevailed. Various powers soon began competing vigorously for control of the waters off their shores. In the vacuum left by the demise of that first liberal regime, little law prevailed. The seas, like the land, were now susceptible to any number of claims to exclusive jurisdiction, and these pretensions were often backed up by force. The dangers of formalized warfare and pirate attacks became indistinguishable; once a ship set sail, human threats were added to the natural perils of the sea.[2]

By the late Middle Ages, various powers began to make vaguely defined claims to control of the Mediterranean and the Atlantic. Pirates grew more bold, often supported by rulers eager to capture foreign ships laden with goods and treasure. Acts of piracy sponsored by sovereigns gave rise to privateering (a word that first appeared in the thirteenth century), whereby rulers commissioned private ships to plunder the vessels of hostile nations. Scandinavian rovers attacked in the Baltic, the North Sea, and the English Channel, while Mediterranean trade was disrupted by Saracen and Greek raiders.[3]

An assortment of kings, queens, and princes who ruled coastal lands responded by expanding their spheres of authority seaward, if only for the sake of security and to protect their own vessels and those of their allies. In Jessup's words, "Working out from shore with claims of varying intensity and extent, it soon developed that no expanse of ocean was too vast to evade national pretension to exclusive control thereof."[4] Claims over adjacent waters continued to be vaguely defined, yet given the navigational standards of the day, it was impossible to offer measured distances.[5]

In retrospect, certain claims from that era of turmoil are noteworthy as much for their relative clarity as their impact. Among the most significant pretensions was that asserted by the Republic of Venice, which had begun commanding fees from vessels sailing the Adriatic as early as 1269. A unique ceremony symbolically reaffirmed Venice's claims to sovereignty and, over time, no doubt added to the legitimacy of its claim. Each Ascension Day, a lavish barge was rowed through the Channel of Lido, accompanied by music. A ring was thrown onto the waters, with the proclamation, "De-

1

New Light on an Old Limit

> A lawyer without history or literature is a mechanic, a
> mere working mason; if he possesses some knowledge of
> these, he may venture to call himself an architect.
>
> *Sir Walter Scott, 1815*

TWO MILLENNIA AGO Roman jurists offered the first view on the proprietorship of the seas when they formally pronounced the marine realm
and fish in it as the common property of all. Under that regime, sovereignty
over land could not be extended beyond the high-tide mark. The Roman
jurist Marcianus offered perhaps the first legal pronouncement on the legal
status of the sea in the second century, and Justinian I (483–565) later
codified Roman law and the notion of open seas in *Corpus Juris Civilis*, a body
of law issued between 529 and 535 A.D. It is impossible to imagine a more
liberal view, yet that open-seas philosophy was not especially remarkable,
since Rome enjoyed uncontested control of the Mediterranean. One cannot characterize this doctrine as defending true freedom of the seas, because non-Romans were effectively barred from exploiting these "open"
waters.[1]

I

The Past

sponsamus the mare in signum veri perpetuique dominii" (We espouse thee, O sea, in sign of a real and perpetual dominion). The papal nuncio and ambassadors took part in the ceremony of "espousing" the sea.[6] Venice was able to enforce its demands for tribute from ships on the Adriatic long past the duration of its military power, showing the growing impact of legal precedent.[7]

Venice's ability to exert respected seaward authority beyond its military prime largely reflects the efforts of its legal scholars.[8] Best known and most frequently quoted was Bartolus de Sassoferrato (1314–1357),[9] who introduced the novel idea that jurisdiction and control over adjacent waters extended for a measured hundred miles.[10] This was the first time that a published work offered a specific range defining a sovereign's offshore jurisdiction.[11] In defending his claim, Bartolus wrote that a hundred miles was a reasonable distance, corresponding to something less than a two-day journey over land.[12] Conveniently, this zone rendered the narrow Adriatic an Italian sea.

The idea of offering a specific distance for seaward jurisdiction was seconded in the works of Baldus de Ubaldis (1327–1400), who favored a limit of sixty miles.[13] Yet for some time the distances offered by Bartolus and Baldus remained as exceptions to a wide variety of hazily defined claims to coastal waters. Amid this cacophony, claims to seaward authority expanded widely in the coming centuries.[14]

The Ascendance of Iberia: Toward Closed Seas

By the fifteenth and sixteenth centuries, Portugal and Spain were asserting wildly extravagant pretensions to sovereignty over the seas. Great differences in geography help to explain this leap from the narrow claims of fourteenth-century Venice. For seasoned fourteenth-century Italian sailors, the Mediterranean was fairly well charted. In contrast, Portugal and Spain sat on a peninsula jutting into a hostile Atlantic, an incredibly vast and unknown realm to sailors of the day. Unlike the mercantilist Italians, who engaged in sedate nearshore trade, Iberian explorers sailed countless leagues over uncharted waters. The extravagance of Iberian claims reflects in part a unique geographic and psychological outlook. While Mediterranean lawyers were facing finer points such as the legal status of Venice's nearshore seas, fourteenth-century Portuguese and Spanish sailors were exploring the coastlines of Africa and beyond.[15]

Fifteenth-century Portugal's exploratory zeal was supported by the Catholic church. Seeking to bring Christianity to "heathen" souls, church leaders realized that they could accomplish their goal more expeditiously by promoting the conquest of an empire. Pope Nicholas V, pleased with Portuguese efforts to explore the west coast of Africa, issued the papal bull *Romanus Pontifex* in 1455. "Seeking and desiring the salvation of all," the pontiff gave Portugal exclusive control over Africa, stretching from Cueta to Guinea and "beyond towards that southern shore."[16] Although it was unclear where that southern tip was, at the pope's generous invitation, the Portuguese swiftly went about creating an empire born of seagoing prowess. Portugal's influence soon stretched across the known world. Its powers were broadened when Vasco de Gama navigated around the Cape of Good Hope in 1488, opening a sea route to the Orient.[17]

With Columbus's voyages to the New World in 1492, Spain acquired a maritime status that rivaled Portugal's. By the late fifteenth century and into the sixteenth, the two nations were locked in a struggle for maritime superiority. In heated confrontations, each power sought to counter the advances of the other. Not long after Columbus's voyage, Portugal's king made it known that he considered the New World to be part of his realm, as conveyed in *Romanus Pontifex*, and he began preparing an armada to try to seize the New World lands claimed by Spain. Hearing of this development, Spain's Ferdinand and Isabella appealed to Pope Alexander VI for an immediate decision that would divide this largely unknown territory to the west.[18]

In response, Pope Rodrigo Borgia (a Spaniard) issued a papal bull, *Inter Cetaera*, on 4 May 1493. The bull issued by Borgia, "one of the most corrupt and unscrupulous Pontiffs," strongly favored Spanish interests. It gave Spain exclusive rights over all lands and seas lying westward of a line drawn "from the Arctic Pole, namely the North, to the Antarctic Pole, namely the South . . . the line to be distant one hundred leagues (or 345 miles) towards the west and south from any of the islands commonly known as the Azores and Cape Verde."[19] (A marine league measures 3 nautical miles, or 3.45 statute miles).[20]

In deceptively simple language, *Inter Cetaera* awarded almost all of the New World to Spain. It forbade anyone but the Spanish, for whatever reason and on pain of excommunication, to cross a line drawn at 35 degrees west meridian. This boundary line meant that Portuguese ships first had to obtain Spain's permission to sail more than 345 statute miles west of their possessions in the Azores and Cape Verde Islands. Frustrated by the pope's decision, the Portuguese at once rejected it and appealed to Spain for a new dividing line farther to the east, claiming that they needed much greater leeway to maneuver near their oft-visited island possessions. But Portugal's King John secretly wanted a new dividing line even farther west, for he suspected that "within those limits famous lands and things must be found." He was indeed prescient. Discovery of what would be known as Brazil gave that rich find to Portugal, not Spain. Spain was eager to obtain Portugal's recognition of its New World claims and thus agreed to this compromise.[21]

The resulting Treaty of Tordesillas, concluded in June 1494, has had an incalculable impact on the political outline of the Western Hemisphere. It placed a newly revised demarcation meridian separating the Spanish from Portuguese territories at about 45 degrees west longitude, about 1,250 statute miles west of the Cape Verde Islands.[22] This treaty gave Spain exclusive navigational rights over the western Atlantic, the Gulf of Mexico, and the Pacific. Portugal in turn won exclusive navigational rights over the Atlantic south of Morocco and the Indian Ocean.[23]

The extravagance of this claim is startling, but there it is: two European nations, in conjunction with the Catholic church, sought to divide most of the known world between them. Despite the church's ostensible propaganda motive, their claims were mostly based on naked worldly desires for wealth and territory. The equitable and wise governance of the oceans was simply never an issue. Rather, the stark division was built upon an emerging philosophy of closed seas (*mare clausum*). It was the very antipode of the open seas (*mare liberum*) philosophy that prevailed under the Justinian Code of Rome.

This Treaty of Tordesillas also contained novel language implying that

Spain and Portugal not only had mere control over their respective seas, but also were sovereign owners. While the subtle legal distinction between having full sovereignty versus mere jurisdiction would later become vital, these early pretensions were vague as to the exact jurisdiction being claimed. (Only a claim to sovereignty, meaning full ownership or supremacy of rule, could be a claim to a territorial sea. Yet that concept was not fully developed until the early seventeenth century.)[24] "'Sovereignty' connotes a freedom to perform governmental acts to the exclusion of all other authority," observes Jessup, "subject to such limitations as are self-imposed or imposed by international law."[25] However, there is no evidence that the sovereignty prescribed by Baldus ever found its way into the general practice of nations.[26]

The idea of a closed sea was surprisingly unsophisticated; on the contrary, open seas work to the greatest benefit of seafaring powers. The Roman Empire understood long ago that given their de facto maritime preeminence, the greatest benefits and opportunities flowed from free and open seas.

The Pendulum Swings Back Toward Open Seas

A modicum of legitimacy was attached to the closed seas idea as long as Spain and Portugal possessed the maritime assets to enforce it. Then by the close of the sixteenth century, English, Dutch, and French maritime forces were mounting increasingly effective raids on Iberian interests.[27] These victories soon proved the frailty of Iberian pretensions to dominion of the seas. Privateers like Francis Drake and Thomas Cavendish famously overcame idle Iberian boasts of supremacy, and a crucial event in this struggle was the defeat of the Spanish Armada by the English in 1588. Thus the stage was set for new approaches to defining the legal status of the seas.[28]

England, and to a lesser extent Holland, France, and the Scandinavian countries, were the great maritime powers at the start of the seventeenth century.[29] Yet Great Britain was particularly schizophrenic in its policies. The Crown laid vigorous claims to closed seas, especially around the British Isles, where foreign ships were prohibited from fishing in protected waters. Hence, Britain asserted dominion (closed seas) over portions of the North

Sea, the Bay of Biscay, and the Atlantic from Cape Finisterre, Spain, to Stadland, Norway. But in more distant waters Britain refused to recognize foreign claims and so "argued by force the freedom of the seas where it suited her purpose."[30] Other seafaring nations naturally opposed these actions, unwilling to exchange the maritime tyranny of Spain and Portugal for that of Britain.

Holland, on the other hand, favored open seas and opposed Britain's claim to dominance. In particular, the brilliant Dutch lawyer, Hugo Grotius (1583–1645), became the champion of freedom of navigation. King Henry IV of France described Grotius as the "miracle of Holland"; at age fifteen he graduated from the University of Leiden and only a year later received the Doctor of Laws Degree from the University of Orleans.[31] While employed by the Dutch East India Company, which engaged in an extensive trade in Far East waters claimed by Portugal, Grotius was asked to defend the lawfulness of the capture of merchant ships. One chapter of the legal brief, "On the Laws of Prize and Booty," was published in 1609 as *Mare Liberum*.[32]

In arguing for open seas available to all, *Mare Liberum* justified the Dutch East India Company's mercantilist trade across waters claimed by the Portuguese. It was also used against Britain's prohibition of foreign fishing off the coasts of England, Scotland, and Ireland, so the British felt the sting of Grotius's argument more than the Spanish or Portuguese.[33] Grotius argued that the Portuguese claim to title over the oceans as decided by the pope was founded on mere exploration, not possession, and possession was required for good title:

> Since the sea is just as insusceptible of physical appropriation as the air, it cannot be attached to the possession of any nation. But if the Portuguese call *occupying* the sea merely to have sailed over it before other people, and to have, as it were, opened the way, would any thing in the world be more ridiculous? . . . There is not a single person in the world who does not know that a ship sailing through the sea leaves behind it no more legal right than it does track.[34]

Regarding the papal grant that had conveyed the East Indies to Portugal, Grotius declared, "Trade with the East Indies does not belong to the Portuguese by virtue of title based on the Papal Donation . . . for no one can give away what he does not himself possess." Grotius buttressed his position: "The Lord Jesus Christ when he said 'My Kingdom is not of this world,' thereby renounced all earthly power."[35] As advocate for a nation with no rights under the papal bulls, Grotius argued frankly that the sea and the "right of navigating it, are concerned only with money and profits, not with piety; surely everyone with any brains at all will agree that the Pope has no jurisdiction here."[36]

In making the case for open seas, Grotius clearly took the position of Holland (and the rich Dutch East India Company), which stood to benefit significantly from navigational freedom. The Dutch were great merchants, but they lacked military power and a large navy. In arguing for open seas, Grotius chose a tack that allowed Holland to dominate commerce more effectively than was possible under a *mare clausum*. Of course, he was merely echoing the Roman open seas philosophy in the Code of Justinian, placed in the context of seventeenth-century mercantile interests and trade.[37]

The prolific Grotius refined his theories in *On the Law of War and Peace* (1625), where he links the possible extent of a nation's seaward claims to the actual control it could assert by artillery from a land-based army. This connection between the breadth of a nation's seaward jurisdiction and the presence of land-based forces was a new concept.[38]

Grotius did not elaborate his views on the legal nature of jurisdiction, such as whether it constituted full sovereignty to govern an area of sea for virtually any purpose, or some lesser degree of control (a subtle legal issue that later became critically important).[39] Nor did he suggest a standardized offshore distance like the hundred miles offered by Bartolus. Nonetheless, Grotius introduced the intuitively appealing concept of a nation's right to control a narrow strip of water off its shores, while maintaining the idea of open seas.[40] The description of jurisdiction as a "function of the effective extent of control from the land," Swartztrauber comments, captured "the fancy of statesmen for the next 300 years."[41]

England responded to Grotius with a stellar legal advocate of its own. To counter foreign (i.e., Iberian, Dutch) opposition to its claims, the Crown assigned the renowned scholar John Selden the task of defending Britain's claim to closed seas. The result was Selden's landmark treatise, *Mare Clausum, Seu de Dominio Maris* (1635). But Selden's well-documented reasoning was out of step with the times. Not only was he defending the status quo in an age of widespread liberalization, but also he was handicapped by the inconsistencies in Britain's position—claiming closed seas in nearby waters and open seas where it preferred freedom of navigation. (Britain later reversed itself to become the staunchest defender of navigational freedoms and a narrow three-mile sea, but over the next few decades, Selden's work provided the legal basis for Britain's claim to closed seas).[42]

This idea that a nation should control a narrow belt of water off its coast eventually led to a basic principle in ocean governance: the three-mile limit of territorial sea. Its antecedents are (1) the four-mile Scandinavian league, (2) the line-of-sight doctrine, and (3) the cannon-shot rule. Although these claims have faded away, the three-mile limit they spawned continues to define much of U.S. ocean governance to this day.

Origins of the Three-Mile Limit

The seventeenth century witnessed a fresh set of claims over the coastal oceans. Some were modest, others very selective in their purpose. One type of claim might only establish a neutrality zone near the coast where ships of warring nations were not permitted to engage in hostilities. Another might reserve an exclusive zone for protecting fisheries. Various methods for claiming jurisdiction were becoming legally precise and were applied to specific purposes.[43]

One influential claim made by the Dano-Norwegians (Denmark ruled Norway from 1397 to 1814 and ruled both Norway and Sweden from 1397 to 1523) was to an exclusive fisheries protection zone of two Scandinavian leagues in breadth (roughly eight nautical miles).[44] First announced in the early seventeenth century, it was unusual in that it was measurable.[45] The Italian jurists Bartolus and Baldus had suggested zones of a hundred miles and sixty miles, respectively. But the more modest Dano-Norwegian claim was more easily measured, was narrow enough to be enforceable, and thus was consistent with a philosophy of freedom of the seas.[46]

This claim over fisheries was understood not to confer sovereignty, that is, unlimited authority. Rather, given the vital importance of fishery resources, the Danes prudently sought a more limited (eight-mile) jurisdiction for the sole purpose of excluding foreign fishing. Because fishing grounds off Denmark's Icelandic possessions were being exploited by the British, Denmark hoped that by claiming this "narrow defensible belt," it could at least preserve in-shore fishing for its own nationals.[47] Patently unable to enforce a *dominium maris*, the Dano-Norwegians chose narrow, measurable limits so that their claims might be easily upheld.

The modest size of the Scandinavian fishing zone suggests that a nation's image of itself and its vision of the oceans plays an important role in shaping the regime it creates. When a nation wishes to exploit largely unknown lands beyond the horizon, it prefers vast claims that will lock out competing nations. But a mid-range mercantile power has a different concept of the legal status of the seas.[48] Hence, just as geography plays an important part in shaping offshore claims, the military and economic strength of a nation are also relevant to the marine jurisdiction it asserts. In 1779, a royal decree narrowed the Danish-Norwegian fishing claims to a single Scandinavian league, and thus Sweden adopted a uniform claim of four miles for protecting fisheries.[49]

The Line-of-Sight Doctrine

Unlike the Scandinavian league, the line-of-sight doctrine—whereby a sovereign claimed jurisdiction as far as the visible edge of the horizon—was flexible. The simplicity of this idea is intuitively very attractive. A populace might readily feel they "own" the seas for a distance stretching to the horizon. But this form of measurement led to many thorny difficulties. A nation with high coastal cliffs could claim a broad coastal sea; someone standing at sea level can see about three nautical miles, while at a height of thirty-three feet an observer sees about twice as far, and from a hundred-foot cliff one can see more than twelve nautical miles. The height of the object viewed is another variable. A passing ship carrying a hundred-foot mast can be spotted eleven miles at sea even by one standing at sea level. So in practice this line-of-sight principle was used to justify coastal sea claims ranging anywhere from zero to fifty miles.[50]

As with claims based on the Scandinavian league, line-of-sight did provide the coastal sovereign with an unbroken belt of authority that followed

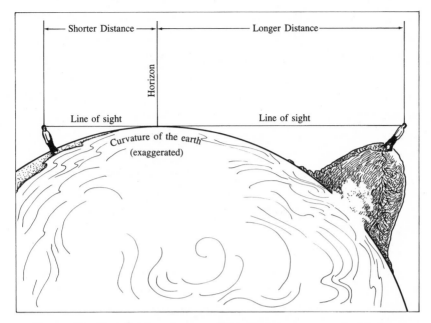

Figure 1. The line of sight rule assumed that lookouts were stationed along a coastline, so the height of the coast largely determined the extent of seaward control. *Artist: Jill Townsend*

the sinuosities of the coastline. (See figure 1.) It assumed that lookouts placed along the shore would alert the populace to the approach of a ship. The purpose of the rule was to provide an offshore security belt closed to vessels of hostile intent. While the Scandinavian league was designed only to protect coastal fisheries, the often broader line-of-sight boundary was designed as a shield.[51] But because of so many variables in defining this limit, it never found much scholarly support.[52]

A partial solution was reached when a nation's jurisdiction was assumed to extend as far as a person standing at sea level could see: roughly three miles. For this reason, some scholars point to the line-of-sight principle as a chief precursor of the three-mile limit.[53] Hence, a sovereign who sought both to protect fisheries and to assure coastal security could assert claims based on the Scandinavian league as well as line of sight.[54] These were two major precedents for the three-mile limit. A third was the cannon-shot rule.

The Cannon-Shot Rule

The cannon-shot principle was first noted in a Dutch document from 1610. (See figure 2.) Its specific purpose was to prevent the outbreak of hostilities between belligerent ships sailing within range of cannon on neutral shores. The cannon-shot rule codified a real control asserted within the range of shore-based artillery. This rule helped to prevent neutral nations from being drawn into hostilities by prohibiting warlike actions (like taking prize) within reach of cannon on neutral shores. Its enclaves of neutrality were determined by firing actual cannon and roughly measuring the distance to the splash. Because this rule first appeared around the time of *Mare Liberum* (1609), Grotius is sometimes thought to be responsible for it, and indeed he introduced the idea of jurisdiction enforced by land-based defenses. But while Grotius probably did not originate the cannon-shot rule, his writings suggest that he would have favored the notion.[55]

Because it conjures up images of the roar of cannon and clash of battle, the cannon-shot idea fits preconceptions of what an eighteenth-century territorial sea should look like. In fact, a number of commentators have mistakenly pointed to the cannot-shot rule as the sole origin of the three-mile limit.[56] Yet the better view is that while cannon varied enormously in caliber, their practical range grew from only about one mile to two miles over the course of the century and did not reach three miles until the end of the Napoleonic Wars, after the introduction of the three-mile limit. Thus it is a misconception that the cannon-shot principle was the sole origin of the three-mile limit, but there are certain connections between them.[57]

Early Links Between the Cannon-Shot Rule and the Three-Mile Limit

Cornelius Von Bynkershoek (1673–1743) did much to popularize the cannon-shot principle as the basis for a three-mile limit. In *De Dominio Maris* (Dominion of the Sea, 1702) he challenged British claims to control the seas. As a champion of an open seas philosophy, Bynkershoek advocated the cannon-shot rule because it neatly restricted claims to a narrow belt

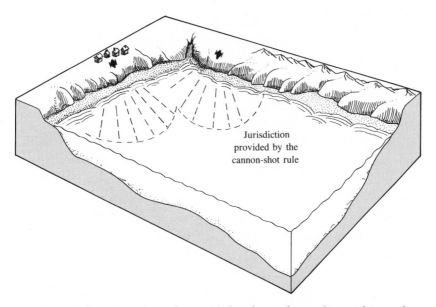

Jurisdiction
provided by the
cannon-shot rule

Figure 2. The cannon-shot rule provided enclaves of neutrality within reach of actual shore-based cannon. *Artist: Jill Townsend*

offshore. He points to the weaknesses of other methods of jurisdiction but does not mention the three-mile limit.[58]

The modern three-mile territorial limit idea did not formally appear until 1793, when the United States first made such a claim in identical notes sent to England and France. An earlier proposal of a three-mile limit was made in 1761, following the capture of two British ships, the *Ellen* and the *Squirrel*, by French privateers in 1761. They were seized in waters claimed by Denmark, a neutral power during the Seven Years' War (1756–1763) between England and France. Denmark claimed a neutral zone of one Scandinavian league. However, because France declared that claims to neutrality had to adhere to a standard cannon-shot rule, it held that its own privateers could capture as prize any ship caught near the shores of a neutral country if the action took place outside the range of shore-based cannon.[59]

Hence a conflicts of law issue arose when France recognized the capture of these two British ships off Denmark's coast. Under Danish law, the seizure of any ship within its neutral waters was illegal. The dispute was brought before the French Conseil des Prises, which rejected the complaints of Denmark and Britain and held in favor of France. Yet the ruling showed a willingness to refine France's previous position by recognizing a uniform belt of waters such as that asserted by the Scandinavians.[60] Although the French felt that the four-mile Scandinavian league was too wide, they suggested they might accept a zone of three miles.[61]

This French proposal was remarkable. Although only a suggestion and viewed with skepticism by the British, it marked the first judicial linkage between the three-mile limit and the cannon-shot rule. (Of course, cannon of the period were incapable a three-mile range, so the French may have implied a compromise between the two measures.) Whatever the cause, an important early blending to create a continuous three-mile offshore belt had occurred. The idea then fell into disuse and was not heard of for two decades. In 1782 the equation of the cannon-shot principle and the three-mile zone for neutrality again appeared in a monograph by Ferdinando Galiani (1728–1787), *The Duties of Neutral Princes Towards Belligerent Princes*. Galiani links the two with this reasoning:

> Without waiting to see if the territorial sovereign actually erects some fortifications, and what calibre of guns he might mount therein, we should fix, finally, and all along the coast, the distance of three miles, as that which surely is the utmost range that a shell might be projected with hitherto known gun powder.[62]

Galiani had served in Paris as secretary and chargé d'affaires at the embassy of the Kingdom of the Two Sicilies from 1759 to 1769. No doubt he was aware of France's three-mile proposal in the cases of the *Ellen* and the *Squirrel*, and he took a position consistent with the 1761 compromise offered by France. Yet by advancing a three-mile limit, Galiani may have been simply offering a compromise between range of cannon (then about two miles) and the Scandinavian league (four miles). Galiani's advocacy of the three-mile limit profoundly influenced the future practice of the law of the sea. After Galiani, scholars began to closely identify the rule of cannon shot with the popular three-mile limit.[63] Thus by the end of the 1780s, Galiani's works were disseminating a linkage between the range of cannon and the three-mile distance for coastal authority. However, a uniform three-mile neutrality belt was not yet popularly accepted.

Early American Claims to Jurisdiction Offshore

The three-mile limit was not the only seaward zone claimed in early U.S. ocean policy. In 1782 Congress agreed that American fisheries might extend three leagues from shore (or nine miles), while in 1783 sovereignty was acknowledged to include islands within twenty leagues (sixty miles). (Twenty leagues may be a distant echo of Baldus's fourteenth-century writings.) A third type of claim is found in a 1787 Treaty with Morocco that recognizes range of cannon for neutrality purposes.[64] The Founding Fathers were picking and choosing from many possibilities. Even if the notion of a three-mile limit existed at the time of Independence, Swartztrauber writes, it's likely that "the idea of a three-mile zone for fishing or customs would have been repugnant to American statesmen at the time."[65]

Although the new nation was an ocean away from the Old World, President Washington was caught in the turmoil of the war between England and France. As an ally, France insisted that the United States quickly settle on a claim for neutral waters. Faced with more pressing matters, Washington found it hard to give this question the attention it deserved. Yet fixing a neutrality zone was essential. France, Britain, and Spain were all engaged in hostile actions just off the American coast but were unsure of U.S. laws on prize. The young nation had to struggle to stay detached from the hostilities.[66]

By not asserting a neutral zone, the United States had hoped to avoid antagonizing Europe's major powers. But a prompt decision was unavoidable following the capture of the British ship *Grange* by the French frigate *L'Embuscade* in Delaware Bay. In May 1793, the U.S. attorney general reported to Secretary of State Jefferson that the range of cannon might be a justifiable measure for a neutral zone. However, since Delaware Bay was entirely within U.S. territory, the seizure was illegal on its face.[67] Thus the rules for taking prize off American shores remained uncertain.

On 13 September 1793, French Foreign Minister Genet urgently appealed to Jefferson for a decision.[68] Despite French threats and warnings, however, neither Washington nor Jefferson was ready to establish an official U.S. position. Jefferson would have preferred to claim a neutrality zone using a boundary marked by the Gulf Stream, which he felt was a natural limit; in this he anticipates ecosystems management wherein natural processes help determine legal boundaries. President Washington wished to postpone the matter, because other nations had yet to establish their own areas of dominion: "The extent of Territorial jurisdiction at Sea, has not yet been fixed," he wrote, "on account of some difficulties which occur in not being able to ascertain with precision what the general practice of Nations in this case has been."[69] Yet Genet's insistence forced the announcement of a tentative U.S. claim. On 8 November 1793, Jefferson sent nearly identical notes to Britain's Minister Hammond and France's Minister Genet:

SIR: The President of the United States, thinking that, before it shall be finally decided to what distance from our seashores the territorial protection of the United States shall be exercised, it will be proper to enter into friendly conferences and explanations with the powers chiefly interested in the navigation of the seas on our coasts, and relying that convenient occasions may be taken for these hereafter, finds it necessary in the meantime to fix provisionally on some distance for the present government of these questions. You are sensible that very different opinions and claims have been heretofore advanced on the subject. The greatest distance to which any respectable assent among nations has been at any time given, has been the extent of human sight, estimated at upwards of 20 miles, and the smallest distance, I believe, claimed by any nation whatever is the utmost range of a cannon ball, usually stated at a sea league. Some intermediate distances have also been insisted on, and that of three sea leagues has some authority in its favor. The character of our coast, remarkable in considerable parts of it for admitting no vessel of size to pass near the shores, would entitle us, in reason, to as broad a margin of protected navigation as any nation whatever. Reserving, however, the ultimate extent of this for future deliberation, the President gives instructions to the officers acting under his authority to consider those heretofore given them as restrained for the present to the distance of one sea league, or three geographical miles, from the seashores. This distance can admit of no opposition, as it is recognized by treaties between some of the powers with whom we are connected in commerce and navigation and is as little, or less, than is claimed by any of them on their own coasts.[70]

Jefferson's note contains the first unambiguous statement of the three-mile limit. However, by its own terms the zone was intended as only temporary, was the narrowest feasible breadth so as not to engender oppo-

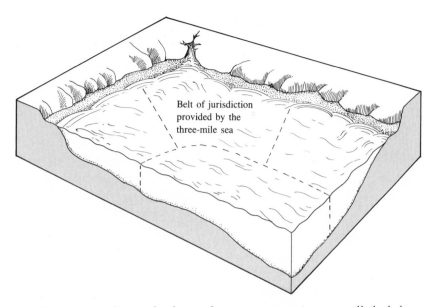

Figure 3. According to the three-mile sea concept, nations controlled a belt that followed the sinuosities of a coastline. *Artist: Jill Townsend*

sition, and was asserted for the sole purpose of protecting navigation. In creating this three-mile belt, the United States apparently combined aspects of the Scandinavian league, the line-of-sight doctrine, and the cannon-shot rule.[71] (See figure 3.)

Moreover, this neutral zone coexisted with other claims that were far broader than three miles. American leaders in the late eighteenth century would have found three miles too narrow for defining other key U.S. claims —such as for customs purposes or fisheries. Nonetheless a three-mile limit ripened into the globally accepted standard over which a nation could assert ownership of the seas; it was this sovereign belt that eventually evolved into the territorial sea.

In sum, this measure was adopted as a compromise. There is no evidence to suggest that important future implications, such as the crucial question of state versus federal control of marine resources, were even considered. In 1794 Congress passed legislation prohibiting "captures made within the waters of the United States or within a marine league [three miles] of the coasts."[72] This unpretentious act made the fledgling United States the first nation to establish by statute a three-mile neutrality belt. Yet it did not become an active proponent of this idea until the twentieth century; that role fell instead to the British.

Britain Popularizes the Three-Mile Limit

Unlike Spain and Portugal, Britain foresaw the advantages her powerful fleet might enjoy by paring back maritime claims around the globe and thus became the leading champion of a three-mile limit. That the British should adopt this exceptionally narrow breadth for territorial seas was no small matter. Following the defeat of Napoleon and the Congress of Vienna, Britain's vast naval assets made it the predominant European imperial power. The three-mile limit of jurisdiction was strengthened via several treaties signed by Britain. Three miles became attached to the idea of ownership of marine resources, and that principle acted as both a de jure and a de facto constraint on future fisheries claims.[73] This can be seen in legal decisions of that period, where in case after case British courts proclaimed the three-mile rule supreme.[74]

Over the nineteenth century, Britain systematically enshrined this rule across its far-flung empire. A series of enactments officially adopted three miles as the standard for instance in Canada (1852), Britain's Pacific Island possessions (1877), Australia (1881), and Cyprus (1882).[75] The impressive Royal Navy did its part to ensure that other nations regarded this rule as having the status of customary international law of the sea—something that all were obliged to follow.

Nineteenth-century British legal publicists endorsed the three-mile idea. Of course, they had to reject the earlier closed sea principle enunciated by John Selden, but that proved to be no problem. Sir Travers Twiss (1809–1897), William Hall (1836–1894), and Thomas Lawrence (1849–1919) felt the three-mile limit had now matured into a formal principle of international law fully divorced from the cannon-shot measure, which was constantly enlarging as cannon achieved greater range. Their view, which fit Britain's needs of the day, was that nations should be regarded as owning the sea and all resources for a fixed three miles (emphasizing the new idea of a territorial sea).[76] The rising dominance of their writings also strengthened the implicit idea that broader claims such as for fisheries or customs purposes should be restrained.

(Note that the three-mile sea is measured in nautical miles rather than statute miles. A statute mile [a term derived from the Latin for 1,000 paces] measures 1,609 meters, or 5,280 feet, whereas the nautical mile is an arc on the earth's surface equal to one minute of latitude, 1,852 meters, or 6,076 feet. The two are similar in length; the nautical mile is equal to about 1.15 statute miles. Both are referred to as *miles*, unless the distinction is material.)

More than anything, it was Britain's struggle to halt smuggling that made this measure an international standard. Well before the eighteenth century, contraband goods like peppers, raisins, mace, and coffee were being smuggled into England to avoid customs duties. Other dutiable items included tobacco, alcoholic beverages, and tea.[77] In response, Parliament passed a "Hovering Act" in 1736 that was meant to improve the enforcement of customs laws and tax collection. It prohibited ships, ostensibly bound for foreign ports, from hovering near English shores. The law at first established a zone of six miles and authorized British agents to board those vessels for inspection.

This measure was inadequate, however, so Parliament passed another Hovering Act in 1765 extending the zone to nine miles, but smugglers were resilient. Avoiding import duties was a business between armed gangs on land and ships hovering just beyond Britain's expanding customs limits, waiting for a chance to unload their goods unmolested. Parliament extended the zone to twelve miles in 1784, and twenty-four miles in 1802. All in vain. That too proved to be insufficent, and a "golden age of smuggling" erupted. In desperation, Parliament in 1805 extended the zone to 300 miles.[78]

This vast zone was favored by the Lords of the Treasury, even if only for enforcing customs laws, but it was troubling to bureaucrats in the British Foreign Office. Those officials charged with foreign relations and matters of reciprocity rightly feared that other nations might demand to search British ships more than three miles from their shores. Indeed, when other nations began pressing such claims, the Foreign Office sought to reduce the British zone to three miles. Fortunately, by the middle of the nineteenth century Britain's Coast Guard was having more success in combating smuggling.

Moreover, the Foreign Office won support from the Advocate General's Office. After a ship bearing French smugglers narrowly escaped capture following a heated battle some twenty-five miles off the shore of England, the advocate general advised the Treasury that apprehending and prosecuting that French crew was illegal, since English jurisdiction ended at three miles seaward.[79] The matter was finally decided in favor of the Foreign Office in an opinion favoring the three-mile limit.

Eventually smuggling was largely defeated, and in 1876 the British Parliament felt secure enough to pass a Customs Consolidation Act that repealed all previous claims to broader customs zones. In their place it created a uniform and narrow three-mile British customs zone applicable to all nations. Subsequently Parliament passed the Territorial Waters Act of 1878 and the Sea Fisheries Act of 1883, which conspicuously limited jurisdictional claims to a uniform three miles. From that time, Britain's advocacy of this standard firmly fixed the three-mile territorial sea as a global rule of law.[80]

Early Efforts to Conserve Marine Resources

Parliament also faced domestic questions created by the rise of the three-mile sea. A prominent question—which level of government owned offshore resources—raised vexing issues that anticipated the United States' Tidelands Debate of a hundred years later. Vast amounts of underground minerals, including copper and tin, had been extensively mined on the coast of Cornwall since the Bronze Age. Over the years, some of the mine tunnels extended under tidal beaches, and still others projected beneath the sea for considerable distances.[81]

Thus a unique issue arose when the Crown challenged a claim by the Duchy of Cornwall (and the Prince of Wales) to ownership of minerals below tidal flats and for distances offshore. Arbitration by the Court of Queen's Bench eventually resolved this novel domestic dispute by holding that rights to subsoil minerals beneath County Cornwall, including the area between high and low tide, were held by the Prince of Wales, but all minerals taken seaward of the low-water mark belonged to the queen. As an international matter, this did nothing to resolve the question of whether the Crown owned mineral deposits further than three miles offshore. However, coal mines elsewhere on the English coast did extend beyond three miles, and those resources were regarded as Crown property because the mines had been created by British industry.[82]

Early Conservation of Living Marine Resources

During this period, the sea was primarily useful for navigation, fisheries, and warfare; little attention was given to the conservation of living marine resources. It is difficult to imagine the attitudes of earlier centuries, when the sea was regarded as inexhaustible and when so little was known about the nature of that foreign realm. Yet what is clear today is that few early claims to jurisdiction over marine resources were made in the interest of preserving what we now recognize as biological diversity.

An illustrative tale is that of Steller's Sea Cow. This slow-moving sea mammal, weighing four to ten tons, grazed on seaweed—making it perhaps the largest herbivore on earth. Russian sailors who were stranded on Bering Island, in the cold North Pacific, first happened on the sea cow in 1741. The animal was easy prey for the hungry men, who found its meat delicious. When on their return home they informed others of their luck, the fate of the sea cow was essentially sealed. Their countrymen came back in large numbers to hunt the beast until the last one was killed in 1768. It took only twenty-seven years from initial discovery to the complete extinction of this once abundant sea mammal.[83] (See figure 4.)

Among Western nations, which have had such an influence on the evolution of the law of the sea, history shows that claims made for conservation purposes were the exception rather than the rule. Conservationist thinking was overshadowed by commercial interests, specifically freedom of navigation. There were, however, some broad claims designed to protect marine resources from exploitation by foreigners. One was the (al-

Figure 4. Steller's Sea Cow, rendered extinct only a few decades after its discovery. *Artist: Jill Townsend*

ready mentioned) four-mile fisheries belt off the shores of Scandinavia, as well as an 1829 ordinance restricting harmful trawling during certain months within nine miles of the coast of France. In the eighteenth century, Britain also restricted, over various broad distances, foreign oyster dredging off the Irish coast, beam and otter trawling off the coast of Scotland, pearl and chank fishing off Ceylon, and taking pearls, coral, and bêche-de-mer from its colonial waters around the world.[84] Yet truly conservationist claims were sparse. Those that succeeded in becoming law were often poorly enforced and in time eclipsed by the increasing supremacy of the three-mile sea.

A notable exception to this neglect of conservation interests is the case of the northern fur seal. This mammal was prized for its luxurious fur—so much so that by the early nineteenth century it was clear that without real efforts to protect it from hunters, the fur seal would go the way of the sea cow. Fur seals were found in great numbers along coasts claimed by Russia and could be protected by Russian law; however, officials had great difficulty in trying to protect them while they were in the open Bering Sea.

The problem was with the rapidly growing practice of pelagic (open-ocean) seal hunting on the high seas beyond Russian jurisdiction. Hunters knew that female fur seals spent much of their time searching for food for their pups in the surface waters of open ocean beyond three miles from shore—that is, beyond any nation's jurisdiction. Records from the period show that 80–90 percent of seals caught were females. The result was disastrous to the species: newborn, dependent young seals were doomed without their mothers. Thus pelagic fishing caused the seal population to drop precipitously in the Bering Sea.[85] Fearing a complete extinction of the species, Russia in 1835 passed a law prohibiting the taking of females at sea. However, because the law applied only to Russian nationals, it had no effect on the many U.S., Japanese, and British (that is, Canadian) hunters who vigorously continued to take seals in the Bering Sea.

The U.S. government continued to support commercial seal hunting on land. But pelagic methods that concentrated on pregnant and nursing females were drawing increasing opposition in the United States. Moreover, the practice was wasteful, since seals wounded or killed at sea were frequently lost below the surface. This meant that even when the pelt was not retrieved, the pups were still doomed.[86]

Events changed markedly following the Seward Convention of 1867 when Tsar Alexander II ceded to the United States all of Russia's North American territories, consisting of Alaska and its adjacent islands. The boundary line ran through the narrow Bering Strait and then southwesterly between Attu, at the tip of the Aleutian Island chain, and Russia's Komandorskie Islands.[87] In 1869 the United States passed a law prohibiting taking northern fur seals by pelagic methods, but like the Russian law this was domestic legislation that could apply only to American sealers. Great Britain continued to allow pelagic harvesting by its own fishermen; with no claims to Bering Sea rookeries, British seal hunters had no other way to catch these mammals other than outside the jurisdiction of other nations. Japanese fishermen also continued to use pelagic methods.

In 1881, in a remarkably bold stroke, the United States Treasury interpreted the 1867 law as applying not only to narrow U.S. territorial waters —but also all waters within the immense Bering Sea ceded by Russia. Thus the U.S. Treasury prohibited all pelagic fur seal hunting east of the U.S.-Russia dividing line and promptly dispatched U.S. Coast Guard vessels to enforce the ban.[88] At first they only issued warnings to foreign ships. But in 1886 coast guard cutters began to seize British-flagged sealers that violated U.S. conservation regulations. From 1886 to 1890, the United States seized fourteen vessels on the high seas, normally beyond any nation's jurisdiction. Such seizures, while conservationist in intent, were a flagrant violation of customary law of the sea. Because vessels on the high seas were considered to be outside national jurisdiction, they were free to operate as they saw fit. Nonetheless, extraordinary seizures occurred offshore at distances between 15 and 115 miles of land but within the United States's newly claimed portion of the Bering Sea. Britain of course protested vigorously when its ships on the high seas were confiscated and crews fined or imprisoned.[89]

A tentative agreement was reached in 1891 stating that Britain would no longer allow its pelagic sealing ships to enter the Bering Sea, and the United States would no longer arrest British vessels there. This agreement was extended a year to allow arbitration. A key question was whether the United States had "any right and if so, what [is the] right of protection or property in the fur seals frequenting the islands of the United States in the Bering Sea, when such seals are found outside the ordinary three-mile limit?"[90] An international tribunal in 1893 held against the United States by deciding that fur seals found outside the three-mile sea were beyond U.S. jurisdiction. Some minor conservation measures were recommended by that tribunal, but they had little impact. Swartztrauber describes the award as "at once a defeat for the Americans and for the fur seals, and a victorious step forward in the development of the three-mile rule."[91]

The saga of the fur seal does not end there. In 1911 a treaty was concluded among Russia, Japan, Great Britain, and the United States banning all pelagic sealing. That is not to say that all seal harvesting was ended; it was assumed that ample fur seal hunting should be maintained at various island rookeries supervised and controlled by the nations owning those islands.[92] Yet it was a step forward; the most wasteful pelagic methods were banned and a new goal was to maintain harvests at a maximum sustainable yield.

With rare exceptions, the early history of ocean resources governance is devoid of any concern for ecological complexity. It is now clear that government has a useful, at times essential, role to play in conserving marine resources. We are just beginning to understand this obligation. Our scientific knowledge of how marine ecosystems work has advanced considerably over the twentieth century, yet ocean governance has lagged behind:

domestic U.S. ocean governance still relies on archaic principles like the three-mile limit.

We are only just beginning to build marine policies that respond to threats to a "keystone species" such as the fur seal. When a species plays a functional role in an ecosystem greater than its abundance suggests, its removal can disturb the system in ways of ever expanding seriousness. Until recently that complex idea was overlooked in ocean management; the simple assumption was that a species was important to a system in direct proportion to its abundance. But this is not the case. For example, although the sea star is far from being the most common animal among a rocky shore community, its presence still has far-reaching impacts for species composition and even the physical structure of the marine environment. By consuming the mussels that otherwise would take up all available space on the rock face, the sea star allows many other species to colonize the rock's surface.[93] So extraordinarily complex are relationships of the sea.

Summary

The three-mile sea asserted by the United States as a neutral zone was remarkably narrow, particularly when compared to usual eighteenth-century international claims asserted for customs purposes or fisheries protection.[94] Indeed, statements made by American leaders at the time make it clear that they expected that a wider belt would be asserted once this pressing matter could be more thoroughly considered. As mentioned earlier, Jefferson felt that the U.S. neutral zone ought to be denoted not by a cannon shot but by the Gulf Stream, an interesting forerunner to the ecosystems management concept whereby natural processes help to delimit legal jurisdiction.[95] Yet the matter came up at a time when a weakened United States felt that it would be prudent to wait until it possessed the maritime assets sufficient to enforce a broader neutrality claim.[96]

Strangely, the issue did not come up again. Instead, the three-mile sea was immediately championed by the British Empire, which recognized that its authority as a sea power was enhanced in proportion to reduced jurisdictional constraints around the world. Unlike Spain and Portugal centuries earlier, Britain understood that the very narrowness of a three-mile sea conferred great advantages upon a global maritime leader. Thus over the nineteenth century the three-mile limit became accepted practice, and by the twentieth century was a conventional measure for sovereignty. Like so much else associated with the classic three-mile sea, the great popularity and tenacity associated with this measure were never anticipated by the rule's creators.[97]

In conclusion, the path taken in this early era contributed to very few conservatory measures, in part because the narrowness of the three-mile sea made protection of living marine resources like fisheries and fur seals difficult to realize. Yet that absence of robust conservatory measures was probably inevitable, given the thinking of the day when commerce and maintaining freedom of navigation were paramount concerns.

2

The Tidelands Debate

Carving Up the Sea

Nothing endures but change.

Heraclitus, 540–480 B.C.

For roughly one hundred fifty years following America's hastily made claim to a three-mile territorial sea, the internal matter of who owned these waters and their resources was of little domestic interest. Because of this lack of attention, some fundamental assumptions went unchecked. Most important was a continued understanding that coastal states alone owned the three-mile belt of waters contiguous to U.S. land territory. Hence states acting alone and without opposition from the federal government accepted full authority over the territorial sea and all resources in it.[1] Federal officials relied on the states to govern these waters; thus states regulated operations such as the floating canneries within this nearshore belt.[2]

Things changed rapidly in the early twentieth century. A discovery of valuable offshore oil under the shallow waters near Santa Barbara, California, caused this once minor question of ownership to grow into a topic of major economic importance. As a constitutional matter, it was clear from the start of this controversy that the federal government had paramount powers over this belt. Neither side disputed the claim that the federal government had paramount offshore rights regarding issues pertaining to commerce and defense—just as it was supreme in these matters on land. This battle was instead over ownership. The struggle between the states and the federal government would be played out in the Tidelands Debate, a major event of the first half of the twentieth century, which established the pattern of largely bifurcated ocean management that persists today.

Offshore Oil Gets Its Start

The modern story of oil begins in 1859, with a successful oil well sunk by Edwin Drake in Titusville, Pennsylvania. After that discovery, it did not take long for exploratory drilling rigs to spring up at the other end of the continent on the coast of California. A gusher in the town of Ojai in 1867 soon spurred oil fever there, while a very commercially profitable well in Los Angeles nine years later stimulated wider exploration throughout southern California. In 1889, more oil deposits were discovered in Summerland, a small seaside town founded one year earlier as a center for spiritualism, adjacent to the exclusive resort of Santa Barbara. The oil wells that sprouted in the streets of Summerland changed its character entirely. By the 1890s this town was more celebrated for the ample oil and gas being produced there than for its spiritual roots. While records from the period are sketchy, the U.S. Geological Survey estimates that 17,000 barrels of oil were produced in Summerland in 1895.[3]

Prospecting for oil and gas soon spread along the sandy shores of the Pacific. Drilling rigs were erected on private beaches, and from there entrepreneurial prospectors began to build drilling platforms atop specially built piers that extended into shallow ocean waters. The world's first offshore drilling began in Summerland in 1896.[4] (Offshore drilling was done from piers extending from land for some time to come; true stand-alone rigs did not appear off the California coast until after the Second World War). There were two powerful incentives to go offshore: first, all marine resources, whether fish or offshore oil and gas, were free for the taking; second, offshore activities were completely unregulated by the state.

All that was legally required was that a prospector—if he or she did not already own the land—should first negotiate an agreement with the owner of the ocean-front property from which the pier and drilling rig would extend.[5] The state had not yet moved to regulate this early offshore development, nor did it receive any royalties from the commonly owned oil and gas taken from submerged public lands.[6] Instead, California's Placer Mining Law simply gave oil and gas prospecting permits to all who applied, and these state permits were automatically converted into leases if prospectors found oil or gas beyond the shore edge.[7]

Despite the poor quality of sour Summerland crude, its value on the market tripled in the late 1890s, rising from $0.35 per barrel to $1.03 per barrel. Offshore exploration quickened. Ocean-front property owners rushed to get their own wells into production before neighbors could suck the black gold out from under their land. A brief Summerland oil war exhibited this passion. After a 1,200-foot wharf was built, with accompanying drilling platform and boat loading facilities, property owners on either side with smaller platforms contested the wharf builders' property rights. Armed guards (gun slingers, actually) were hired by all parties, and nighttime acts of vandalism became common. When each of their platforms was mysteriously damaged, owners erected formidable barbed-wire fortifications to protect their disputed oil platforms from further tampering.[8] (See figures 5 and 6.)

As prospectors rushed to be the first to extract offshore oil, considerable ecological harm was being inflicted on marine waters. Even though resources beyond the low-tide line belonged to no one (or perhaps precisely because of that fact), and since the state did not become involved, these waters were treated as dumping grounds. Production was typically a flat-out race to beat offsetting wells that might be built nearby to usurp the same valuable oil. Drilling was often rushed, ill-planned, and not surprisingly it typically was acutely destructive. The resulting wasteful practices reduced oil pressure, which allowed rich oil-bearing strata to become flooded by water, causing the loss of literally millions of barrels of oil. Once economically depleted, abandoned wells were often stuffed with old

Figures 5 & 6. Drilling rigs already dominated the coast of Summerland, California, in the early twentieth century. *Photos courtesy of the Santa Barbara Historical Society*

telephone poles or filled with junk and left to leak profusely.[9] (The cost of cleaning up the damage has already been massive, and millions of state tax dollars continue to be spent into the twenty-first century for retroactive cleanup of offshore wells abandoned before laws were passed requiring operators to cap their wells securely before abandoning them.)

Doubtless some operators acted during that time with care, but others, whether intentionally or out of negligence, spilled terrifying amounts of oil into coastal waters, thus contaminating the sea.[10] No state law had yet been written to prohibit spills of this type or to punish those responsible for them—such disasters were simply seen as part of the cost of doing business. Pollution included fouling the air. According to contemporary accounts, passengers on trains that ran near the coast were alerted to the oil platforms' presence as much by smell as by sight. The editor of the *San Jose Mercury News* lamented in 1901,

> Summerland is a very different sort of place now, for in a day fatal to its peace somebody struck oil; . . . even as the train whizzes by, one sees streams of black, syrupy looking oil pouring out from the pumps' mouths with the heavy flow and reluctant slowness of molasses running from a barrel on a cold morning. There are traces of Summerland's old character in the many pretty cottages about which the forest of "rigs" has grown up, but the general transformation is painful to look upon. The whole face of the townsite is aslime with oil leakages.[11]

In bucolic Santa Barbara just to the north, along a strikingly beautiful coast, prospectors' plans for expanded offshore drilling met with strong and united resistance. This included popular newspaper editorials calling for unified opposition to "force these unsightly creations from the shore" before they were established in the town.[12] One offensive exploratory derrick was mysteriously removed in the middle of the night. Treading a careful line, the Santa Barbara Chamber of Commerce supported existing oil and gas drilling rigs that were located on inland hills away from the ocean front—yet it pressed for a total ban on offshore drilling, citing the impact on the quality of life and on tourism. Plans for offshore drilling piers were thus abandoned in Santa Barbara, even as drilling continued in the waters off Summerland.[13]

The 1920s: California Attempts to Regulate Offshore Oil

In a scenario that might bring nostalgia to the wildcatter or oil executive, drilling for offshore oil in California continued for years without regulation from the state or the federal government. California had both the right and the duty to maintain open navigation in the three-mile sea claimed by the United States for international purposes, but no state law governed offshore activities. In retrospect, the state erred badly during these years of neglect. Because the valuable oil taken free of charge from beyond the high-tide line was publicly owned, and given the harm to coastal waters caused by drilling, the state should have swiftly crafted legislation claiming a reasonable royalty fee and addressing the environmental damage caused by drilling.

As with fishing, a prevailing "rule of capture" gave the operators legal possession of the offshore oil and gas seized by their drilling ventures. But unlike living creatures, oil resources could not be regenerated, while poor drilling practices were swiftly depleting and degrading the remaining supplies of oil and gas. Nonetheless, economic incentives made operators drill as quickly as possible without regard for the cumulative impact of their actions or the total productivity of the larger oil field.[14] Rigs atop private uplands along the beach front made this problem even worse, because oil lies in underground pools and tends to flow from untapped regions to areas tapped by productive wells.[15] So rigs on private land near the shore frequently drained offshore deposits, owned by the state, from oil-bearing strata that straddled coast and sea. Hence even more state oil was lost to prospectors who were enriched by it without paying any royalty charge.

In time, these alarming facts began to be widely reported in the news. Soon the outcry reached legislators in the state capital. The loss of a valuable public resource caused by unregulated drilling from piers beyond the low-tide line generated much popular opposition. Yet the California legislature struggled to draft the first framework of laws and policies governing the exploration and development of oil and gas in U.S. territorial waters.[16] As they set about creating a regulatory regime, California's lawmakers faced unprecedented problems. For instance, how stringently should offshore oil and gas be regulated? What was a fair royalty rate for these resources? For lack of a better course, lawmakers turned for guidance to the federal Mineral Leasing Act of 1920, which was designed to encourage mining prospectors, and largely duplicated provisions of that statute for the new state legislation.[17]

The new law, passed in 1921, proved to be in the same spirit as the 1920 federal mining act. It was extremely indulgent toward development and gave the state little real power to supervise drilling in a safe fashion. Reflecting the prevailing sentiments of the time, it was extremely indifferent to the public's right to fair compensation from offshore oil and gas profits. It established a meager royalty rate of just 5 percent. It also claimed, without federal objections, that the three-mile belt of offshore waters belonged to California.[18]

Following California's lenient regulatory legislation of 1921, a flood of applications for new offshore prospecting permits came before the state.[19] Permits were at once issued for portions of the Santa Barbara Channel, San Pedro Bay, and Santa Monica Bay. These events only exacerbated public opposition to the rapidly expanding, highly profitable rigs atop private coastal lands and on piers extending into the sea. Furthermore, adding to the appearance of unfairness, an entirely new event emboldened those calling for at least some governance over drilling. Many parties applying for offshore leases had neither the inclination nor the equipment to actually explore for oil. Instead, a novel breed of "prospectors" who succeeded in securing license permits found it profitable to sell their interests to individuals or corporations capable of drilling. To receive a permit from the state, one needed only to lodge a claim. Large sums of money stood to be made from the lax system of allocating state offshore permits, and the boom in offshore oil was on with a vengeance.

During this time, producing oil wells situated on hills hundreds of yards from the sea had continued to enjoy widespread support. Yet these popular inland sites had to compete directly with coastal rigs. This was because both types of rigs were extracting petroleum from the same underground pools, and under the "rule of capture," whoever got to the oil first got to keep it. Given the large size of California's oil fields, the state's surveyor general sought to protect oil tapped upland from being depleted by an ever increasing number of offshore wells. Seeking to curtail the leasing

of ocean tracts, Surveyor General Kingsbury ordered his office to stop issuing new offshore prospecting permits.[20] Thus, beginning in 1926, Kingsbury's office started denying hundreds of applications for new offshore
drilling.

That action was soon challenged in California's supreme court by offshore prospectors. Lawyers for Kingsbury argued that the legislature had
exceeded its authority by establishing such a lenient regulatory regime
in 1921. They failed to carry the day. On December 31, 1928, the state
supreme court handed down its decision in *Boone v. Kingsbury*, which upheld
the 1921 state law: "Minerals contained in the soil covered by tidal and
submerged lands belong to the state in its sovereign right."[21] As unpopular as that court ruling was with voters, the surveyor general was bound
by the decision. The next week a flood of permit applications came in.[22]
Surveyor General Kingsbury had wanted a much higher royalty rate than
the grossly inadequate 5 percent, but the court's decision made it clear that
he lacked authority to demand it. With charges of corruption flying, legislators needed some breathing room to reevaluate the equity and propri-
ety of the existing system.

Less than three weeks after the unpopular state supreme court ruling,
the state legislature responded. In January 1929 emergency legislation was
passed temporarily halting the issuance of new drilling permits.[23] The many
offshore wells that were producing under existing leases were mostly held
by a handful of large companies and were "grandfathered" in, that is, they
were allowed to continue operations unimpeded.[24] During this moratorium on new permits, state legislators began hearings on improving offshore governance.

It quickly became evident that California was still powerless to halt the
continued extraction of oil from beneath submerged public lands. There
were two reasons. First, the large companies that were operating wells on
piers or on privately owned lands were permitted to continue, which
meant allowing "adverse drainage" without compensation to the state. Second, extraction went on because of a new technology developed by industry called slant drilling. This novel technique made it possible to reach
even geologically distinct offshore pools by slanting wells from private
coastal strips. At Huntington Beach, California, the powerful Standard

Oil Company was draining significant quantities of oil by slant drilling. Ironically, Standard Oil faced no competition from the other large oil companies since the moratorium prevented any new offshore leasing. Seeing this, other companies took up slant drilling at existing sites elsewhere, and a new means of production known as whipstocking grew into a serious problem for the state. By the end of the 1920s, ongoing extraction from rigs on piers or the coastal strip was a pervasive problem, despite the ban on new leases. Moreover, the ban had unintentionally created an oil monopoly. By 1938, the Standard Oil Company had eighty-six "whipstock" wells draining oil from beneath state-owned submerged lands, and so despite attempts to ban the practice, offshore drilling continued.[25]

Confusion Prevents State Control

Whether owing to corruption, confusion, inertia, or some combination of the three, California was unable to halt the drainage of public offshore resources. During this infamous period, a handful of major corporations secured what amounted to a monopoly.[26] To some extent, the state's failure to regulate offshore oil extraction was the result of purposeful efforts by the major oil companies, which actively contributed to public confusion on the matter. They benefited from the ambiguous status of submerged lands, and they recognized that state regulation could end their stranglehold on offshore oil and could bring competition; even worse than higher royalty payments was the possibility of compensating the state for oil already taken.[27]

As smaller segments of the oil industry fought to reopen the coast to development, and the few large companies benefiting from moratoria struggled to preserve the status quo, the matter of assembling California's new ocean regime became mired in stalemate.[28] In time, a plan emerged to overcome the deadlock. Speculators, smaller oil interests, and others who were locked out hoped to gain better access to submerged lands under a brand-new system of federal control. More precisely, they sought to replace state ownership with a new system of federal control of offshore areas. Initially, federal officials offered no encouragement to those promoting such a dramatic change. High-ranking officials in the new Franklin Roosevelt administration, like Republican administrations before them, felt that submerged lands belonged to the states.

That was clearly stated in the "Proctor letter" of 1933.[29] In that letter, Roosevelt's colorful new secretary of the interior, Harold Ickes, unequivocally refused an applicant's request for a federal ocean prospecting permit.[30] Ickes's letter proclaimed that exclusive control belonged to the states—a view resurrected countless times by states' rights proponents as proof that federal officials had once believed that the states controlled the three-mile sea. That letter was clearly an embarrassment to Harold Ickes, and he later repudiated it. The secretary's change of heart was most significant, for more than anyone, it was Ickes who became a persistent champion of federal ownership offshore, and his views were crucial in the brewing Tidelands Controversy. (The term *Tidelands* was actually a misnomer, as control of the three-mile sea and beyond—not control of the much narrower area subject to the ebb and flow of tides—was at stake.)[31]

Secretary Ickes Rethinks Federal Ownership Offshore

This reversal in Ickes's thinking began with events of the early 1930s. At that time, a small but influential group of speculators, later known as claim jumpers, began an intense lobbying campaign of federal officials. They sought to have the administration reconsider its past acquiescence in California's declaration that it owned the sea just off its coast. However, these speculators advanced this unique position only after submitting numerous unsuccessful applications to the federal government for offshore prospecting permits. If federal officials could be convinced to assert a new form of ownership of offshore lands, they hoped to receive permits under the authority of the 1920 Federal Mineral Leasing Act, thereby making phenomenal profits. If state-issued permits were rendered worthless, the oil companies would have no alternative but to purchase permits from the claim jumpers (at exorbitant prices) for existing wells.[32]

Despite this assault upon the principle of state ownership, which escalated in the mid-1930s, applications for federal permits continued to be promptly rejected by the U.S. Department of Interior.[33] In rejecting the applications, the agency still maintained its position that states, not the federal government, were the true owners of submerged lands.[34] About this time, however, Interior Secretary Ickes began to rethink his position. He began to contemplate whether federal officials could—indeed, should— move to obtain the sole ownership of valuable resources offshore. Whether this critical reversal in Ickes's thinking was due to further reflection, his well-known drive for power, a personal friendship with an applicant, or some other factor is open to question. It seems likely that the secretary was principally interested in the conservation of oil,[35] but Ickes's own account implies that the persistence of a speculator may have contributed to his reconsideration:

> It developed that the Department of the Interior had accepted the view that the tidelands belonged to the State of California. The result was that subsequent applications for [federal] leases were turned down either by the Registrar of the Land Office or the Department of the Interior in Washington. No new Secretary taking over can review all of the decisions that have been made prior to his ascension. If he should undertake such a task, he could not possibly have time or energy for administration. This matter was not brought to my attention until a citizen of San Francisco, who was interested in an application for a lease that had been filed under the Federal Leasing Act, and who happened to know me personally, called on me in Washington. His lawyer had advised him that title to these lands belonged in the United States instead of in California, I asked for a full report on the case. . . . I further instructed that office [U.S. General Land Office] not to determine any question of title without first bringing the matter to me.
>
> When the files reached my desk, it seemed to me to be obvious that the United States at least had enough color of title so that the matter should be presented to the courts for final determination. . . . I regarded it as a question of law, that only the courts should pass on.[36]

While this passage throws the best possible light on the matter, it indicates that a speculator may have played a crucial role in changing Ickes's thinking. Likewise, in his testimony before Congress, Ickes again referred frequently to many conversations with speculators. Thus it may be that the Tidelands Controversy arose because of claim jumpers who initiated the federal government's interest in ownership of offshore areas.[37]

Other factors were also important, of course. The Roosevelt administration was committed to empowering national government—often at the expense of states. The Great Depression had made Washington bureaucrats and the president's cabinet more willing to adopt a strong approach to government. Harold Ickes himself was ready to enlarge the powers of his Interior Department. Moreover, Ickes, who was trained as a lawyer, probably realized that legal principles such as *laches* (a legal term regarding the need to take action without undue delay) would require the federal government to assert some claim to preserve whatever long-dormant rights it might possess, or it would forever lose its ability to pursue such a claim. Whatever the reason, in June 1937 Ickes ordered the Interior Department to begin placing all new applications for federal leases in abeyance, rather than to flatly deny them, as in the past.[38] This new and unprecedented policy was the earliest signal that federal officials were interested in obtaining control of resources in the three-mile sea.

Ickes's fateful decision had serious consequences. The federal government's new interest at once adversely affected numerous activities wholly unrelated to offshore oil. For instance, following Interior's refusal to flat-out deny applications for permits, the Port of New York was forced to halt its work on harbor improvements because of the possibility that they might be appropriated by the federal government.[39] The broad range of consequences flowing from the Interior Department's action soon became a rallying point for coastal states not directly affected by the decision on offshore oil. Even inland states supported California in its predicament because many believed that the federal government was unduly encroaching upon an area that should more properly come under the aegis of state sovereignty.

Legally speaking, the rights of both lessors and lessees with respect to offshore oil quickly became clouded and not just for seas off California. A nascent industry was at the time just getting off to a good start in state waters in the Gulf of Mexico, and the Interior Department's action, which clouded the issue of title, greatly dampened enthusiasm for development there. States bordering the Gulf of Mexico had always maintained much wider jurisdictional claims, such as three marine leagues (nine miles), due to their special historical circumstances and so felt especially aggrieved by federal action.[40] Consider also that as a geological matter offshore drilling was technologically feasible to a far greater distance in the Gulf than on the Pacific coast. The narrow continental shelf off California dropped off steeply, but in the Gulf of Mexico the continental shelf there was so broad and flat that it permitted oil production far out to sea.[41] Yet, to the dismay of oil companies and Gulf states like Texas and Louisiana, many promising state-owned portions in the Gulf had suddenly become of questionable value because of Ickes's new stance.

With a rapid increase in the demand for oil, this question of title could not be allowed to remain clouded for long. Because an authoritative decision on ownership of the coastal sea was urgently needed, the issue came before Congress. That body had to declare whether states were owners of the sea within three miles of their shores—or whether title resided with the federal government.

Congress Considers State versus Federal Control Offshore

The opening salvo came in April 1937, with the introduction of Senate Bill 2164 by Sen. Gerald Nye of North Dakota. Ickes was now convinced that the federal government had a potentially viable claim, so he personally asked Senator Nye to introduce legislation declaring submerged lands within a three-mile limit the domain of the federal government. By selecting a senator from an inland state to present the bill, Ickes showed much political acumen in orchestrating the federal assault upon state title.[42]

Senate Joint Resolution 208 was soon substituted for technical reasons and was then taken up by the House.[43] In February 1938, the House Judiciary Committee held a series of hearings on the joint resolution. The bill was amended so that rather than making a conventional claim to federal rights derived from title, it based the government's claims to authority on "paramount federal interests."[44] Moreover, this amended version was proclaimed a conservation measure that declared petroleum resources of the continental shelf to be reserved for use by the navy.[45] The specter of oil depletion, a warning heard since the nineteenth century, was a serious concern for the armed forces. The threat was especially disconcerting for the navy, since after World War I it had become almost entirely dependent on oil, not coal, to fuel its ships. Hence the attention given by the navy in establishing onshore petroleum reserves like those at Teapot Dome and Elk Hills. S.J.R. 208 passed favorably out of committee.

Strong opposition remained in the Senate, however. California may have been the only state at that time with significant offshore oil development, but other coastal states and especially those bordering the Gulf of Mexico saw their own inchoate interests in offshore oil deposits being nipped in the bud.[46] Many perceived S.J.R. 208 as just the beginning of a federal initiative that likely would not stop at offshore oil as the only marine resource claimed, nor be constrained to California waters. Hence a formidable coalition of opponents formed that included representatives from coastal states as well as interior states who opposed increased federal control. In response, supporters of the resolution scaled its language back farther by expressly limiting the federal claim to submerged lands off California. Despite these charges, proponents of federal control lost this round. The Resolution was voted out of the committee but it went no farther in the Seventy-fifth Congress.[47]

This defeat made it clear that legislation could not be passed in Congress declaring the federal government owner of submerged lands. Even the amended resolution met insurmountable opposition. But Secretary Ickes was not deterred. An entry in his diary from March 1938 indicates that while S.J.R. 208 was being considered in Congress, he was considering an alternative strategy whereby federal control might be obtained by a Supreme Court decision.[48]

Subtly the argument for federal control was being shifted away from naked ownership toward conserving an irreplaceable resource.[49] Proponents of federal ownership began to portray their position as essential to national defense: if the depletion of offshore oil reserves were allowed to continue due to lax control by California, the navy and its crucial Pacific fleet would be left without an adequate supply of petroleum during wartime.[50]

Ickes strengthened his case for federal control by allying his own goals with the needs of the navy. The Departments of Interior and Navy worked closely to coordinate their assault on state control. Only six days after the first introduction of the Nye resolution, the navy sent a letter to the Senate Public Lands Committee urging that submerged lands in the three-mile territorial sea be declared a federal "public domain." This would have brought resources of the seabed under the federal mineral laws, supposedly ensuring conservation.[51] However, the navy's argument for offshore reserves was not persuasive; it had an exceptionally poor record of managing inland oil reserves entrusted to it such as Teapot Dome. Doubts were also expressed regarding the navy's true intentions seeking federal control of submerged lands; whereas offshore oil production in California dated from 1897, the navy had suddenly taken an active interest in these lands.[52] The debate over offshore oil heated up further.

FDR Takes an Interest in Offshore Oil

In the late 1930s this dilemma broadened considerably to include not only domestic matters but the international sphere as well. Due to industry's growing interest in drilling for oil in the Gulf of Mexico with its wide continental shelf, it was feasible to produce oil from the Gulf of Mexico both within and outside the U.S. three-mile territorial limit. It was therefore necessary for federal officials to consider the legal ramifications should U.S. companies wish to explore beyond territorial waters.[53]

This unprecedented issue was thus brought to attention of administration officials in 1938 when the Independent Exploration Company sought federal permission to explore in the Gulf of Mexico outside the three-mile limit.[54] Lack of U.S. jurisdiction beyond three miles was clearly a problem. American companies could not reasonably invest in new offshore rigs —unless the United States first made a recognized claim over the seabed there. Requests to drill on what had been the unowned high seas presented a totally new question for the U.S. government. Oil had never been claimed beyond the three-mile sea.[55]

This unprecedented request raised immediate concerns in the Interior Department's legal section. The department's solicitor urged caution— there was no basis in international law to grant petroleum exploratory rights beyond U.S. territorial waters. The high seas are by definition considered incapable of ownership.[56] As noted by the director of the U.S. Geological Survey, "Under international law, the oceans beyond the three-mile limit are the common property of all nations, and no nation has exclusive jurisdiction over them." Not long after, the difficulties presented by lack of jurisdiction was brought to the president's attention.[57]

Roosevelt's response at once illustrated his enthusiasm for greatly expanding U.S. jurisdiction. In the summer of 1938, he asked Department of Interior Assistant Secretary Burlew to explore the feasibility of issuing an executive order that would establish "naval oil reserves on the coast beginning with the shore line and extending halfway across the oceans."[58] Such a request was characteristic of Roosevelt's attitude toward U.S. claims to the global ocean environment. His grandiose thinking merged the domestic issue of federal versus state ownership of offshore oil with a bid to greatly enlarge the nation's jurisdiction offshore.[59]

It was now apparent that the Roosevelt administration intended to usurp the coastal states' historic ownership within three miles. Not only was Interior holding applications for permits in abeyance while legislation was moving in Congress to grant federal ownership of the territorial sea, but also the president was considering an expansion of U.S. jurisdiction. The states quickly responded with actions of their own. Louisiana broadened its offshore claim to twenty-seven miles in 1938.[60]

At the president's request, the Interior Department studied the feasibility of extending U.S. jurisdiction offshore, but the result was not encouraging. While legal counsel believed that the Constitution did allow the president to claim federal control within three miles, outside territorial waters he was without "authority to promulgate the suggested [executive] order prior to the actual occupation of the lands by drilling or mining for oil."[61] But Roosevelt persisted. Like Harold Ickes, FDR demonstrated time and again that he was not deterred by adverse precedent. In July 1939, Roosevelt again broached an extension of national (federal) control seaward. He sent this memorandum to the secretaries of state, navy, and the interior:

> I am still convinced that: (a) Federal as opposed to State jurisdiction exists below the low-water mark . . . and that (b) Federal jurisdiction can well be exercised as far out into the ocean as it is mechanically possible to drill wells.
>
> I recognize that new principles of international law might have to be asserted but such principles would not in effect be wholly new, because they would be based on the consideration that inventive genius has moved jurisdiction out to sea to the limit of inventive genius.

I suggest, therefore, that this matter be studied by a joint interdepartmental committee of Justice, State, Navy, and Interior, with the Attorney General as Chairman.

I am, therefore, asking the Attorney General to undertake this task with your cooperation, with a view to the introduction of the necessary legislation at the next session.[62]

Roosevelt's enthusiasm to greatly expand federal control is clear from this memo, as is his determination not to be thwarted by principles of domestic or international law he considered outdated. In accordance with the president's wishes, an Interdepartmental Committee to Study Title to Submerged Oil Lands was formed to study ownership within the three-mile belt. In 1940 the committee concluded that federal interests inside the three-mile sea should first be defined through appropriate court proceedings and that the entire issue be referred "to the Attorney General with instructions to take all steps by way of judicial proceedings, or legislation, or both."[63]

This recommendation to proceed through the courts sat well with Interior Secretary Ickes. Having witnessed the futility of prior efforts to gain federal control through congressional action, Ickes saw a court case as the only possible means of overturning state ownership. But Acting Attorney General Francis Biddle seemed to be dragging his feet in commencing a test case. Biddle then informed Ickes that the president had ordered a change of plans after concluding (perhaps after conferring with Biddle) that legislation should first be passed by Congress.

Roosevelt was given a draft of the proposed legislation in 1940, but he evidently decided to put the matter on hold. Hollick suggests that he found it politically inappropriate because of the upcoming national election.[64] His Republican opponent Wendell Wilkie took a position favoring states' rights in submerged lands, and press leaks had revealed the president's contrary intentions. Thus in March 1942 Ickes learned that the president wished the matter to be considered dormant. Bills introduced to acquire federal authority offshore thus died with the Seventy-sixth Congress.

To sum up the 1930s, improvements in drilling technology together with a discovery of oil in the shallow Gulf of Mexico suddenly made it feasible to drill beyond the three-mile territorial sea. "Inventive genius," as FDR phrased it, was a new catalyst for federal officials to extend U.S. jurisdiction seaward. At about this time, the administration began to challenge traditional states' claims to ownership of the coastal sea, even envisioning a vast offshore zone of exclusive U.S. control. While it is not surprising that the federal government might assert some claim to marine resources offshore, it was never inevitable that this would be a claim for exclusive federal control. Within its territorial waters, as on land, the United States is a sovereign nation; thus the face of state-federal relations was an internal matter that could be decided more subtly within the framework of federalism.

It is regrettable that this contest over ocean governance between coastal states and federal officials was not resolved by some cooperative form of joint authority. However the mindset that would have allowed shared governance had not yet matured. From the beginning this was framed as a divisive debate, and control was seen as belonging exclusively to the federal government or the states. Outside three miles, in international waters, the United States should speak with a single voice. However, this does not preclude coastal states from at least sharing in the benefits (or the governance) within any broader U.S. claim. Federal officials apparently did not seriously contemplate establishing an integrated regime with the states. The struggle was a product of political tensions and had much to do with gaining advantage; protecting marine resources was relegated to lesser importance.

The U.S.-Japanese Dispute over Bristol Bay Salmon

The picture painted thus far has focused on offshore oil—but a controversy was also emerging over Pacific salmon. In the early 1930s, apprehensions surfaced in Alaska and the Pacific Northwest that Japan had entered the salmon fishery of Bristol Bay off the Alaskan coast.[65] Local passions were fanned by dire warnings that Japanese vessels would soon overfish this rich ocean area and destroy a precious resource that often spawned in fertile Alaskan streams. Chauvinistic reminders were aired in coastal communities that the salmon fishery had taken years to build. A memo from the Commerce Department to the State Department warned that "a difficult situation would be presented if Japanese vessels were to pack salmon in international waters off the coast of Alaska." Seeing a volatile situation, State Department officials "suggested to the Japanese Government that it withhold from Japanese fishing vessels licenses to fish for salmon in Bristol Bay."[66]

Japan acceded to this unusual request voluntarily by informally abstaining from the salmon fishery of Bristol Bay off the coast of Alaska.[67] It was in no way obligated to do so, since these were international waters freely available to all and Japan was unwilling to commit to a written agreement precluding its nationals from fishing on the high seas. Instead, informal assurances were given that it would not grant permits to fish salmon in the area without first notifying the United States.[68]

In the meantime, the Japanese continued to operate floating crab canneries outside U.S. territorial waters of the bay. Operations were generally limited to fishing for cod, halibut, and hake. Despite Japan's abstention from the salmon fishery, concerns continued to mount that a large Japanese salmon fishing fleet would invade Bristol Bay.[69] The Alaskan fishing community portrayed the situation as dire and declared a formal extension of U.S. jurisdiction as the only possible solution. However, the State Department faced a dilemma: lacking a supportive domestic clientele, it was torn between its mission of assuring that U.S. policy did not violate international law and domestic pressures to extend jurisdiction. Because a unilateral extension of jurisdiction was clearly inconsistent with international practice, the idea did meet strong resistance in the State Department.

On the other hand, Interior Department leaders were far less troubled by violations of international law. Interior saw its mission as developing natural resources. If recoverable oil lay outside territorial waters, it would urge the pursuit of new concepts of international law. Not shackled by the intricacies of law and diplomacy that proved so vexing for State, the Interior Department strongly favored expanded jurisdiction over fisheries.

The United States approached Japan in 1935 with a proposal to open formal negotiations. State hoped the problem could be solved at once through a bilateral agreement, but Japan first wished to complete three years of scientific research into the fishery resources of Bristol Bay.[70] U.S. anger was rekindled in mid-1937 by reports that the Japanese government was going to encourage resumption of salmon fishing off the coast of

Alaska.[71] Renewed prospects of a Japanese presence so inflamed local opinion that representatives from the Pacific Northwest and Alaska Territory proposed legislation in Congress to assert U.S. jurisdiction over Alaskan-hatched salmon, even if caught on the high seas. The bill, introduced by Senator Bone from Washington State, would declare all salmon hatched in Alaska the property of the United States, and these would fall under Department of Commerce regulation. It would also give the president the right to extend enforcement to a distance of twelve miles from shore, or to where the ocean's depth reached 100 fathoms (600 feet), whichever was greater.[72] Such a broad claim extending even over high seas was directly contrary to international law.

In response, in August 1937 Secretary of State Hull wrote to the Senate Commerce Committee that the bill's provisions might extend U.S. jurisdiction as far as 200 miles—an action without precedent.[73] He warned of "the dangers of international controversies and dissension inherent in such a proposal" and cautioned legislators in Congress that if the United States were to adopt extended jurisdiction over high seas fisheries "it would find it difficult to object to the application of the principle against our own nationals and vessels."[74] He acknowledged the need for some response but maintained that a true resolution would have to come through diplomatic negotiation; to lend some assurance, he noted the State Department was taking appropriate steps to this end.[75] Because of State's strong opposition, no hearings were ever held on the bill.[76]

Objections raised by Secretary Hull had a legitimate basis, yet this position was increasingly difficult to maintain in the face of mounting domestic political concerns. In November 1937 an alliance of powerful Pacific coast maritime interests formed that joined longshoremen with fishermen in a boycott of goods from Japan.[77] The unmistakable message was that salmon of Bristol Bay needed protection from foreign (Japanese) intrusion. The president apparently agreed. Internal memoranda of the period indicate that Roosevelt took a personal interest in seeing this marine resource conserved, even from U.S. overfishing.[78]

FDR looked for ways to better conserve Bristol Bay salmon. Significantly, he took note of a memo sent in November 1937 from Secretary of State

Cordell Hull to Ambassador Joseph Grew in Japan. It stated that, being an anadromous species, salmon spend most of their lives at sea but return to the inland rivers of their birth to spawn. These fish traverse a continental shelf adjacent to the coastline where they are taken, and this continental shelf "thus becomes *a kind of bridge* between the deep sea and the inland rivers and lakes where salmon spawn."[79] Roosevelt was clearly taken with the analogy of the continental shelf acting as a bridge from the shore, since this perspective seemed to offer a sound legal basis for actions designed to conserve valuable ocean resources. Thus in November 1937 he addressed the following brief memorandum to both Secretary of State Hull and his legal advisor:

> I am delighted with your memorandum in regard to Alaska salmon which you sent to Grew.
>
> You speak of the "shelf" extending as a kind of "bridge" from the shore line out to deep water.
>
> That gives me the thought that it might be possible, if the worst comes to the worst, to forbid fishing on this "shelf" and to a distance of perhaps twelve miles beyond it into real deep water.
>
> Could you:
>
> (1) Let me have a map showing the depth contours of the Alaskan Coast, and,
>
> (2) The estimate from the experts as to which contour depth could be chosen as affording complete protection.
>
> You are right in saying that far more than the Bristol Bay area is involved. Whatever we do should protect the entire shore line of the whole of Alaska.
>
> . . . I think it is well worthwhile to stress not only the investment in this American industry but also its relationship as a large factor in the American food supply.[80]

This suggestion was in many ways reminiscent of earlier legislation by Senator Bone of Washington which had likewise sought to claim jurisdiction over the shelf. The president again proved that he did not feel bound by the long-standing convention of a three-mile limit. His enthusiasm for extending U.S. jurisdiction was shared by Anthony Dimond, a delegate from Alaska to Congress. In February 1938 Dimond introduced a bill in the House of Representatives to prohibit foreign nationals from "engaging in salmon fishing in the waters adjacent to the coast of Alaska as far as the outer limit of the continental shelf."[81] Because he was regarded as the most knowledgeable person in Congress with respect to the salmon issue, legislation offered by Dimond carried substantial weight.[82] Thus both Dimond and the president favored extending jurisdiction for fisheries purposes; this put the State Department in a difficult position because it continued to adhere to a three-mile sea, entrenched in customary international law.[83]

Already accused of negligence for opposing bills designed to protect an important economic resource, State was now hard pressed to obtain assurances from Japan.[84] It achieved limited success in March 1938 when a joint statement was concluded whereby Japan agreed (albeit temporarily) to suspend survey activities in Bristol Bay.[85] But this carefully worded statement reserved Japan's right to exploit high seas fisheries. As expected, this was not enough to allay U.S. fears, and so in October 1938 the U.S. ambassador in Tokyo again sought formal recognition of U.S. interests in Bristol Bay salmon, but the Japanese refused to engage in further discussion. By now the salmon dispute was firmly mired in stalemate, and an acute worsening of U.S.-Japanese relations soon overshadowed the matter of Bristol Bay salmon.

The 1940s: Interior and State Develop a U.S. Ocean Policy

Even after the outbreak of the Second World War, struggles for authority continued inside the federal bureaucracy, among the three branches of government, and between the federal government and the states.[86] Within the Roosevelt administration, various officials benefited greatly from the additional powers afforded them as part of the war effort. Secretary of Interior Ickes successfully broadened his own base of authority. He was appointed petroleum coordinator for the war in 1941 and given emergency authority over state-owned submerged lands. The Interior Department thus gained broad new powers.

In May 1943, the General Lands Office (an Interior Department agency) advised Ickes that the time was ripe for the United States to assert jurisdiction over continental shelf resources. The memo noted that the war presented an excellent opportunity to at last strike "from our own thinking and international law the shackles of the three-mile limit for territorial waters"; in the "interest of national and domestic security" it would be wise for the nation to adopt a "line of 100 or 150 miles from our shores."[87] It urged the United States to assert exclusive jurisdiction over resources of the continental shelf, thus formally "reserving this valuable asset for the United States."[88] A letter containing similar language was submitted by Secretary Ickes to the president in June 1943. FDR had already expressed the sentiment, but it was now an official recommendation from Ickes and the Department of Interior.

My dear Mr. President:

The war has impressed us with the necessity for an augmented supply of natural resources. In this connection I draw your attention to the importance of the Continental Shelf not only to the defense of our country, but more particularly as a storehouse of natural resources. The extent of these resources can only be guessed at and needs careful investigating.

The Continental Shelf extending some 100 or 150 miles from our shores forms a fine breeding grounds for fish of all kinds; it is an excellent hiding place for submarines; and since it is a continuation of our continent, it probably contains oil and other resources similar to those found in our States.

I suggest the advisability of laying the groundwork for availing ourselves fully of the riches in this submerged land and in the waters over them. The legal and policy problems involved, both international and domestic, are many and complex. *In the international field, it may be necessary to evolve new concepts of maritime territorial limits beyond three miles; . . . in the domestic field, one of the perplexing questions would be that of the respective sovereign and proprietary roles of the Federal Government and of the several coastal States.*[89]

Ickes doubtless understood that declaring a single federal regime extending some 150 miles from shore was a radical departure from both domestic and international law.[90] Yet in floating this concept, Ickes continued to ignore the implications of extended U.S. jurisdiction; in doing so, he overlooked the fact that if other nations followed suit with similarly broad claims, then U.S. fishing vessels would find their operations vastly curtailed. But if Ickes did not fully realize the potential international repercussions resulting from unilateral extension of U.S. jurisdiction,[91] the Department of State did, so it opposed Interior's proposal. As both de-

partments accelerated their attempts to influence decision making, a bureaucratic turf war erupted for control of the emerging marine regime.[92]

By backing the concept of a single ocean area for national control of resources, Ickes may have sought to obtain a greater jurisdictional role for Interior in general. He was fortunate to find a kindred spirit in Franklin
Roosevelt. Displaying the same exuberance for extensive claims that he revealed in 1937, the president showed "no evidence that he had been persuaded [by State Department warnings] of the detrimental consequences
of unilateral claims to jurisdiction."[93] In June 1943, just four days after the
dispatch of Ickes's memorandum, Roosevelt sent the following to Secretary
of State Cordell Hull:

> I think Harold Ickes has the right slant on this. For many years, I have felt
> that the three-mile limit . . . should be superseded by a rule of common sense.
> For instance, the Gulf of Mexico is bounded on the south by Mexico and on
> the north by the United States. In parts of the Gulf, shallow water extends
> very many miles off shore. It seems to me that the Mexican Government
> should be entitled to drill for oil in the southern half of the Gulf and we in
> the northern half of the Gulf. That would be far more sensible than allow-
> ing some European nation, for example, to come in there and drill.[94]

Having gained presidential approval, Ickes next launched into a two-
pronged strategy: to gain a three-mile sea for the Department of Interior
and a broader continental shelf for the United States. To accomplish these
ends, Ickes still needed the cooperation of two reluctant departments—
State and Justice. Ickes already had the support of the president, but he
needed State to drop its opposition to the idea of expanding U.S. jurisdiction. Likewise, he needed Justice to drop its opposition to the proposed
federal court test case. Throughout the maneuvering, Ickes made the Department of Interior a pivotal player.[95] Thus Interior handled the "international phases of the problem" with State, even as it directed "domestic
phases" in conjunction with Justice.[96] It was thus assured a crucial role in
the formulation of any new U.S. offshore policy.

But Attorney General Biddle still opposed initiation of a suit, and in
June 1944 he told the president that the Justice Department felt a test case
should not be initiated until legislation was passed in Congress. He felt
that this was not an appropriate time to "inflame California, Louisiana,

Texas and the other oil states," and with a war on, it was essential to maintain an uninterrupted source of oil.[97] Roosevelt, presumably on Biddle's advice, ordered the planned suit dropped.

Another factor at play was that Roosevelt was facing immense political pressures regarding the Tidelands Controversy. Not only were large oil companies pressing the president to forgo the suit favored by Ickes, but even key administration insiders were urging the same. Edwin Pauley, the well-known treasurer of the Democratic National Committee and a man close to Roosevelt, allegedly told the president he "saw no reason for harassing the states and the oil companies forever."[98] Pauley is said to have told Ickes that big oil interests would make large contributions to the Democratic ticket if they were assured the federal government would drop its idea of a test suit. Conversely, Pauley allegedly warned FDR that if officials continued to pursue federal ownership, contributions would not be forthcoming.

Newspaper accounts show Roosevelt steering a middle ground by forestalling initiation of a test suit for the time being and avoiding "any political taint in connection with the controversy."[99] Whatever the cause, Roosevelt decided in mid-1944 to put Ickes's plan for a test case in the courts on hold. Thus with the domestic battle for the three-mile sea in a temporary remission, Ickes turned his attention to international matters and to breaking down the State Department's resistance to expanding U.S. jurisdiction offshore.

The Truman Proclamations: Interior and State Reach a Compromise

Apart from Interior's disagreement with Justice over the best procedure for gaining federal control, only State stood in the way of Ickes and his plans for the shelf. And State was now suddenly voicing a more cooperative position by designating Assistant Secretary Breckenridge Long to be its representative in the interdepartmental discussions. In a drastic turnaround from State's earlier position, the new representative actually agreed with Interior that the United States ought to assert jurisdiction over the shelf. Long felt that the traditional standards by which seaward boundaries had been fixed were no longer appropriate.[100] Thus State, in a major compromise, agreed to expand the nation's claims offshore, hoping that a carefully worded statement claiming jurisdiction over oil and the right to enter into international treaties to conserve fisheries would not cause foreign nations to use the U.S. extension as a pretext to extend their own claims seaward.

This new State Department position afforded common grounds for agreement. Yet Assistant Secretary Long still continued to oppose Interior's goal of a unified U.S. regime. State insisted that U.S. claims to oil beneath submerged lands and fisheries be asserted in two separate, limited statements, one to specified seabed resources like oil and gas, and the other a right to enter into treaties regarding conserving fisheries of the shelf.[101] This represented a compromise between the two departments that gave new scope to President Roosevelt and Ickes's Interior Department to claim resources which they sought to control.[102] The two departments thus agreed: the statement on fisheries would be drafted by State, while the one on the submerged lands would come from Interior.

The State Department carefully drafted its statement to claim only a right to enter into agreements with other nations to conserve fishery resources over the shelf beyond three miles. In creating the document, State drew on the negotiations then being conducted between the United States and the governments of Canada and Newfoundland.[103] This limited approach intended that waters of the shelf should retain their crucial, broader legal status as high seas. No assertion was made about the water column or the surface of the sea. The hope was to head off reciprocal claims that might be made by other nations to full sovereignty off their own shores. In deference to concerns from State, Interior too claimed jurisdiction for specific purposes, not sovereignty.

When the drafts were sent to the State Department for approval, Secretary of State Edward Stettinius raised some key conditions regarding the best way to announce them.[104] Given the president's clear preference, Stettinius was willing to accept extending U.S. jurisdiction offshore, but he was not willing to announce this policy without first consulting with the major maritime nations.[105]

Apparently Stettinius took note of arguments from his Office of Economic Affairs (ECA, a State Department agency). ECA insisted that any new claim to the shelf should establish an equality of treatment between U.S. nationals and citizens of other nations. ECA was seeking to implement a more "liberal, universal economic system" to replace the chaos of a barely postwar world, and given that outlook, "regional, much less unilateral, approaches were to be eschewed."[106] Stettinius then approved the two drafts.

Ickes objected strenuously to Stettinius's request that the claims be announced only after consultation with leading maritime nations. They should only be told that a major announcement was impending, he felt, since he feared that consultations could result in delays or modification of their substance.[107] An adviser's memo read, "If we ever go through a multitude of bilateral Continental Shelf treaties, we will all be dead before there are any results."[108] Because Secretary of State Stettinius was engrossed in preparations for the upcoming Yalta Conference, a decision on Ickes's "counteroffer" fell to Acting Secretary of State Grew. Due in part to rapid turnover and high-level confusion in the State Department, Grew authorized Ickes's plan, despite Stettinius's prior objections.[109]

The acting secretary of state and Interior Secretary Ickes sent a memorandum to FDR in January 1945 suggesting the claims should be made as joint presidential proclamations.[110] In March 1945, a gravely ailing President Roosevelt approved this memorandum, thereby signing off on a policy that sharply departed from long-standing principles of international law. By asserting the U.S. claim to oil and a new right to enter into treaties conserving fisheries of the continental shelf, America was about to lay an unprecedented claim to a large portion of the world long considered to be high seas. But Roosevelt had many times made it clear that he felt international law, as expressed by the classic three-mile territorial sea, had not kept pace with the "inventive genius" of mankind.

The sticking point was that to maintain the traditional definition of open seas and the classic right of all nations to fish up to three miles from foreign shores, other nations could not assert their own claims beyond three miles. Vital to American interests was a right to navigate unimpeded through narrow but strategic straits—passages that could be closed off if other nations claimed broader territorial seas. Hence the State Department hoped that its careful wording—"the character as high seas of the waters above the continental shelf, and the right to their free and unimpeded navigation are in no way affected"—would be enough to head off any counter claims.[111]

After the death of FDR, inertia practically ensured that the two statements would be issued. President Truman assented to the two draft proclamations in May 1945, but there was a brief delay caused by Congress. The Senate Foreign Relations and Public Lands Committees were concerned that the proclamation on the shelf could prejudice the states' case in the domestic question regarding submerged lands. Their fears were assuaged when language was added explicitly stating that ownership of tidelands was not affected.[112] The two proclamations were announced on 28 September 1945. Given the major role played by Ickes and Roosevelt, it is ironic that the announcements became known as the Truman Proclamations.[113]

The two 1945 proclamations represented a radical change in U.S. policy.[114] They owed much to the desires of Ickes and Roosevelt to establish U.S. control offshore. For domestic purposes, Roosevelt and Ickes desired sole federal authority, in essence obliterating the idea of state ownership. (The Department of Interior even considered asserting U.S. jurisdiction over distant shores, such as to submerged deposits off the Pacific islands of Borneo, Java, Sumatra, and New Guinea, reflecting the expansionist culture that prevailed at Interior, far different from the more conservative approach of the State Department.)[115] As a matter of international relations, however, the proclamations were risky business. Though carefully drafted, they raised the distinct possibility that nations would reciprocate with claims to more than limited authority, thus constricting key freedoms of navigation, overflight, and transit through vital straits.

Finally, while the proclamations were purportedly not meant to touch the raging controversy over state versus federal control of the three-mile sea, they had some effect on the domestic Tidelands Debate by largely preempting the coastal states from expanding their claims beyond the three-mile limit.[116] Except for the Gulf of Mexico, the waters beyond three miles thereafter would be thought of as under federal control.[117] That mindset still shapes our thinking, but such a division did not have to be. Establishing some degree of national authority offshore did not have to preclude—as it did—a sharing of this authority with the states.

U.S. Offshore Policy After the Truman Proclamations

Three noteworthy events followed these proclamations in the fall of 1945. First, Harold Ickes resigned in February 1946. That event was precipitated earlier in the year when President Truman nominated Edwin Pauley as undersecretary of the navy, causing a public outcry. Pauley was intimately associated with the oil industry, and as undersecretary he would be the government's chief administrator of the naval oil reserves. Much to Truman's embarrassment, Ickes vocally opposed the nomination and testified against him as in collusion with oil interests. He accused Pauley of requesting that federal officials drop their proposal of a test case to claim the tidelands off the California coast—indeed, making the request on the train returning from FDR's funeral. Ickes stated that Pauley promised significant campaign contributions if the test case were dropped. That charge was repeated by Undersecretary Abe Fortas and corroborated in a story published in the *St. Louis Post-Dispatch*.

Ickes was so incensed by Pauley's nomination that he announced his intention to resign. At a dramatic news conference attended by over 300 reporters, Ickes said, "I don't care to stay in an administration where I'm expected to commit perjury for the sake of the [Democratic] party."[118] An infuriated Truman accepted the resignation and demanded Ickes vacate his office within seventy-two hours. In this climate of charge and countercharge, the colorful Ickes ended a remarkable twelve-year tenure at Interior.[119] Pauley removed himself from consideration, thus ending the bitter dispute. Ickes's departure is notable, since he had originally led the assault on state control of submerged lands. By this time, however, he was no longer vital to the crusade for federal ownership; the cause had taken on too much momentum to be quashed by the loss of a single person.

The second event came in August 1946 when Truman vetoed legislation that had easily passed both houses of Congress and would have returned the submerged lands to the states. Had he signed this quitclaim legislation, coastal states would again have had their assumed title within the three-mile limit. The president took this position despite substantial scholarly support and also fairly lopsided public backing for the quitclaim. Congressional hearings on the vetoed bill had generated 476 pages of testimony, only 53 pages of which contained statements backing the federal position.[120] Nonetheless, like FDR, Truman felt that the federal government should be the sole owner.[121]

A third noteworthy event was the U.S. Supreme Court decision in *U.S. v. California* (322 U.S. 19 [1947]). Events precipitating that fateful decision had begun in October 1945 when Truman asked U.S. Attorney General Tom Clark to file a test case against California in the Supreme Court. A recently installed Truman was at first hesitant about the proposed action; he ordered the lawsuit only after persistent pressure from Secretary Ickes (and just months prior to his resignation).[122]

In briefs and at the trial, the federal government argued mainly that it possessed traditional *title* to submerged lands off California.[123] In response, California produced the "most elaborate and complicated pleading on record in the Supreme Court—an answer in three volumes, running to 822 pages, and weighing 3 pounds 9 ounces."[124] More significant than the length of the rebuttal, however, was the nature and substance of its arguments. Since the great bulk of the federal government's complaint was given over to the assertion that it alone possessed true title in the submerged lands, California concentrated almost entirely on the legal question of who possessed proper title to offshore waters.[125] Hence the state set about proving why California rather than the federal government was properly vested with ownership.

Thus both sides engaged in a dispute that centered on something that lawyers know well—the legal principles surrounding ownership and transfer of property rights. On 23 June 1947, a divided Supreme Court handed down its decision in *U.S. v. California*. The majority found in favor of the federal government, but surprisingly based the decision on the argument that it possessed "paramount rights" to the three-mile sea. This outcome was a shock to both sides, since California's answer had only touched on the idea of paramount rights, a tactic that caused the state to adopt a fatally flawed stance.[126] In the words of Ernest Bartley, this re-markable mistake occurred because "these were lawyers arguing, on the legal bases with which they were familiar, a concept of title and all that title implies. It appears that they saw no reason to argue the larger but ephemeral concept of 'paramount rights,' a doctrine of far greater impor-tance to the general theory of federalism than to the more prosaic and le-galistic concept of title."[127]

In hindsight, it is clear that both sides committed the same error in judgment by arguing over traditional issues of ownership while the Court decided the matter on an abstract basis of paramount rights. However, that result did not give the federal government the immediate powers it was seeking. Instead, the majority opinion by Justice Black held that the fed-eral government possessed paramount rights to the area within three miles of the coast, but this ephemeral notion did not automatically convey the statutory power federal officials needed to issue oil leases. Indeed, the de-cision left much confusion as to exactly what the federal government had been granted. Did "paramount rights" offshore mean title? The Court had held that federal interests in this belt were uniquely superior to interests of the coastal states—but what rights did that give?[128] In an attempt to clear up the issue, federal attorneys submitted a proposed final decree in which the words "of proprietorship" would follow "paramount rights."[129]

The final decree did not include "of proprietorship" as suggested. Pre-sumably the Court wished to emphasize the fact the United States had not gained title to submerged lands—although it may have taken this action as an invitation to Congress to step in and finally resolve this thorny issue.[130] The matter of federal authority offshore was to remain troublesome for years. Greater clarity may be found in the two powerful dissenting opin-ions penned by Justices Frankfurter and Reed. Illuminating their views requires a brief foray into the foundations of American constitutional thought.

When the Constitution bound the thirteen states together, it gave fed-eral officials supreme authority over land and sea, but only for narrowly defined powers such as regulating interstate commerce, navigation, and de-fense. Those few powers were explicitly listed because the colonists had been so vexed by the unlimited powers recently wielded by England's

King George and Parliament. The Constitution was designed to entrust more power to the people through elected state and local officials. In the twentieth century, especially under Franklin Roosevelt, the scope of these enumerated federal powers was expanded many times. In response to the Great Depression, Congress passed new laws giving its federal agencies wide-ranging powers to regulate even small-scale local matters. For instance, Congress enacted laws encouraging farmers to plant desirable crops and regulated local businesses. The expansion of federal authority was frequently driven by an enlarged power over commerce.

In *U.S. v. California*, the extent and scope of federal, versus state, powers were at issue. Justice Frankfurter in his dissenting opinion acknowledged that the federal government of course enjoyed constitutionally derived supremacy over the three-mile territorial sea, just as federal interests were supreme in vital U.S. matters like defense and commerce in every state in the Union. But the Court did not have before it "the validity of the exercise of any of these paramount rights." Right of ownership, as asserted in this case, was a different issue from supremacy of enumerated powers.[131] Frankfurter argued with considerable force that the states had a stronger case, but he failed to carry the day. Justice Reed too questioned the majority conclusion that the federal government possessed paramount rights to the territorial sea greater than its constitutional powers over land.[132]

Despite these dissenting views, Justice Black's argument for national control won out. That Supreme Court ruling had immediate impacts on offshore federalism. Suddenly existing leases issued by the state of California were put in grave doubt. The value on the stock exchange of Signal Oil Company plummeted fifteen points, and Hancock Oil stock dropped eight. These companies and many smaller ones had invested some $50 million in tidelands oil fields. Now the Court's decision left their investments uncertain; not only were their holdings possibly useless but also the companies might be liable for the value of oil already extracted.[133] To ensure continued stability throughout the oil industry, federal officials swiftly worked out an interim agreement with California that put funds into escrow while the matter could be concluded to mutual satisfaction.

Federal officials hoped with the ruling they could promptly begin issuing permits under the existing authority of the Federal Mineral Leasing Act of 1920. However, their hopes for making a smooth transition to federal control were abruptly quashed. In August 1947 the Interior Department solicitor, in conjunction with the U.S. attorney general, issued an opinion that the 1920 Federal Mineral Leasing Act did not apply offshore.[134] While the Interior Department seemed to be the proper federal agency to issue permits, the federal government was deemed to lack the statutory authority it needed to lease offshore lands.

When President Truman sought to establish federal authority to issue prospecting permits under the 1920 Mineral Leasing Act, he was informed that a contrary precedent had been established. That act might have legally applied offshore, but the 1947 opinion by Interior's solicitor was only the latest in a series of contrary opinions rendered since 1935 that foreclosed such an option. Ironically, that precedent had begun when Harold Ickes refused to test the applicability of the 1920 act to submerged lands, believing that it did not apply, and that fateful decision was to haunt the administration for years to come. Ickes reversed this position by the 1940s, but to no avail; the 1920 act was by that time considered inapplicable.[135] This simple decision was nearly as crucial as the Court's decision in *U.S. v. California*.

Invalidation of the 1920 act devastated the Truman administration. Defeat seemed to have been snatched from the jaws of victory. Though the government had obtained paramount rights over the marginal sea, it still lacked the statutory authority it absolutely needed to begin leasing tracts.[136] The Interior Department was stymied. Officials knew from many previous attempts at obtaining federal control through legislation just where Congress stood. More than fifty bills were introduced in Congress to preclude federal control of the submerged lands. Worse still, the congressional reaction to the 1947 decision was swift. Many quitclaim bills were introduced in the Eightieth Congress, most of which were modeled on quitclaim legislation vetoed by the president in 1945.[137] As Hollick notes, with more than a little understatement, "In this environment, proposals for federal management legislation to implement the California decision did not fare well."[138]

Despite these roadblocks, the federal government broadened its effort to gain federal control offshore. In 1948, as expected, the government commenced original actions in the U.S. Supreme Court against the states of Louisiana and Texas. Legal issues presented in these two cases (*United States v. Louisiana*, 339 U.S. 699 [1950]; and *U.S. v. Texas*, 339 U.S. 707 [1950]) were in many respects the same as those considered in *U.S. v. California*, although the Court was now deciding the fate of the nation's entire offshore belt. In language and reasoning similar to that of *U.S. v. California*, the Court again held that paramount rights offshore rested with the federal government.

Yet the fight was far from over. Texas was particularly aggrieved by the Court's decisions in the tidelands cases; since unlike California it had existed as a sovereign nation before becoming a state, Texas believed that it had certain unique rights and privileges arising from its prior status, including a broader territorial sea. Florida also claimed a much broader sea on the basis of its unique history. A coalition of both coastal and inland states made numerous attempts to overturn the Court's decision by an act of Congress.[139] However, the Gulf states now recognized that relief could not be found in a Court hostile to state interests. Except for sorely needed congressional codification, the Court had partially accomplished what neither Harold Ickes nor two presidents had been able to do in the political realm. Against this backdrop, the issue of ownership curiously returned to a standoff between the executive branch and Congress as the 1940s came to a close.

The 1940s were years of radical change and turmoil for U.S. ocean governance. On the domestic front, states were effectively precluded from extending jurisdiction beyond three miles because of the Truman Proclamations. Moreover, with the Court decision in *U.S. v. California*, federal interests had expanded shoreward to deny states their traditional three-mile sea. By the end of the 1940s the federal government came closer to its goal of winning control of all resources beneath and above the continental shelf—in the territorial sea and beyond. And yet the federal government was no more sure of its authority within three miles than before the Court's decision. It had apparently prevailed over the states, only to find it necessary to resubmit the entire controversy to judgment within a hostile political arena. The debate was to return again to Congress. The virulent Tidelands Controversy, seemingly decided any number of times before, was about to return for a final resolution.

The 1950s: Stalemate Between Truman and Congress Is Broken

By the Eighty-second Congress, concern over the intransigence displayed in the tidelands controversy was reaching new heights. The shape of ocean governance being debated was not some obscure academic debate over federalism. Foreign events like the Korean conflict, in combination with rapid economic growth at home, was highlighting the need for secure U.S. sources of oil. Growing concern was translating into pressures for legislation to assure more stable development of ocean resources.[140] Because of uncertainty, oil production in the Gulf of Mexico was falling off substantially. Many bills to settle matters by quitclaiming the offshore zone to states were introduced during Senate hearings held in February–June 1952.[141]

The most important piece of legislation to emerge from these hearings was Senate Joint Resolution 20, a quitclaim bill introduced by Senator O'Mahoney of Wyoming. It was later amended to become a leading attempt to return to state control all submerged lands within their historic boundaries. In its original form, S.J.R. 20 allowed title in submerged lands to remain with the federal government, but gave coastal states much control of offshore oil. It also allowed coastal states to keep 37.5 percent of revenues derived from the oil produced within historic waters (for most states this meant within three miles). However, S.J.R. 20 allowed Gulf states like Texas to revert to old claims. In the spring of 1952 this bill passed in the Senate by a vote of 50 to 35; it passed easily in the House by a vote of 247 to 89, showing that the issue crossed partisan lines. States' rights were enjoying broad support, making it clear that Congress would favor some type of quitclaim legislation.[142]

But it was equally clear that Truman would veto any bill returning submerged lands to the states. He dispelled any doubts when he denounced the

O'Mahoney bill as "robbery in broad daylight—and on a colossal scale."[143] To this remark Sen. Lyndon B. Johnson of Texas retorted, "There is robbery involved in this issue, but who is robbing whom?"[144] As expected, the O'Mahoney bill passed in Congress and Truman vetoed it on 29 May 1952. In his veto message, the president maintained that the federal government alone was capable of orderly development of the coastal sea.[145]

As the leader of the Democratic Party, President Truman had stood foursquare against returning ownership of the submerged lands to states. And with the 1952 presidential election nearing, his party's candidate, Adlai Stevenson, was similarly opposed to state ownership. On the other hand, the Republican candidate, Dwight D. Eisenhower, had given unequivocal support. Ike stated that if elected he would sign a quitclaim bill.[146] While this issue was by no means crucial to the election, Eisenhower's stand probably gave his candidacy a palpable boost in the important state of Texas.[147]

Eisenhower's victory was the breakthrough states' rights proponents needed. Before leaving office, Truman had issued an executive order making the continental shelf a petroleum reserve for the navy, removing it from Interior Department jurisdiction. This last-minute action has been criticized as violating fair play, and it was doubtless meant to harass quitclaim supporters and the incoming president. It had little impact. Soon after Eisenhower's inauguration, numerous bills were introduced in Congress to overturn the order and return control of submerged lands to the states. Almost immediately a flurry of bills were introduced to quitclaim the federal government's rights to the three-mile belt.[148] Significantly, they were modeled closely on those introduced in past sessions—mostly out of fears that the last bill vetoed by Truman was all the new president would sign. Such fears were unfounded. Eisenhower enthusiastically supported any legislation to return submerged lands to the states.[149] Hence an opportunity to create something more sophisticated than a strict partition three miles offshore was politically feasible. And so states' rights proponents need not have constrained themselves to a state-federal division based on a three-mile limit. By playing it safe, however, proponents limited the options to governance structures based on adversarial thinking. Little thought was given to creating an integrated and cooperative regime for conserving marine resources within the newly broadened limit.

The Submerged Lands Act and Outer Continental Shelf Lands Act

Whereas Eisenhower strongly favored returning ownership and control to the states, his cabinet officers and their departments were divided on the issue. Eisenhower allowed each department to reach its own conclusion.[150] During congressional hearings held in February and March 1953, the lines were visibly drawn as the various views became clear. State and Justice maintained much the same negative position as during the Truman administration regarding the return of submerged lands to the coastal states. However, seeing that some sort of legislation was inevitable, the two departments offered some new recommendations, trying to make the final language least offensive to their respective positions.

For its part, the State Department was most concerned about two issues. First it was alarmed by the potentially broad state claims to be made in the Gulf of Mexico by Florida and Texas whereby state control might extend offshore to a distance of nine nautical miles. The State Department feared that allowing coastal states control in the Gulf beyond the three-mile national limit would result in international confusion over U.S. jurisdiction and invite retaliation. But these warnings were paid little heed. The quitclaim legislation finally approved by Congress and signed by the president allowed the coastal states to proclaim broader seaward boundaries if based on legitimate historic claims.[151]

A second point that alarmed State was proposed statutory language that the United States was claiming "sovereignty" over the continental shelf. It felt that such language was more expansive than necessary and preferred claiming "jurisdiction and control" beyond the three-mile limit (although its legal advisor was unable under questioning to adequately distinguish between jurisdiction and control, and sovereignty).[152] By claiming something less than sovereignty, State hoped to limit potential claims by other nations to less than sovereignty off their own coasts. Congress acceded; language was changed, though the two terms appear interchangeable. (The State Department's fears became a reality in coming years.)[153] In all, a conservative State Department enjoyed limited success in presenting its concerns.[154]

The Department of Justice also opposed quitclaim legislation, but in hearings offered some changes in an attempt to arrive at the least distasteful legislation. Testimony by Attorney General Brownell favored some shared control in the three-mile zone.[155] That compromise view was in fact reflected in pending legislation, but it was not considered a serious option, since both the Congress and the president desired that title in the submerged lands should be returned to the states and wished the matter settled. Ironically, if President Truman had suggested that compromise only a year earlier, it would likely have succeeded. However, Eisenhower supported states' rights. He later recalled, "I respected the right of [State and Justice] in their testimony favoring submerged-lands legislation to express their independent opinion on the technical distinction between outright ownership and mineral rights. [But] I had made clear my own determination to try to restore ownership to the states."[156]

The changeover to a Republican administration did bring a remarkable shift among some of the other departments. In stark contrast to their stance during the Roosevelt-Truman years, the Departments of Navy and the Interior adopted entirely new outlooks. In congressional hearings, the secretaries of defense and the navy indicated they would be neutral on the quitclaim issue—the navy even withheld its support for a petroleum reserve. The incoming secretary of interior went even farther and totally rejected his predecessors' policies. Unlike Secretary Ickes, Interior Secretary McKay made it clear during hearings he would be happy to see restored to states "the coastal offshore lands to the limits of the line marked by the historical boundaries of each of the respective states." He expressed no concern that boundaries of the Gulf Coast states would again extend beyond three miles.[157]

Congressional hearings went on through February and March 1953. On 1 April 1953, the House by a 285–108 vote approved H.R. 4198, giving states title over submerged lands within historic boundaries. A Senate version (S.J.R. 13) was stalled by opposition, but that was overcome when the president on April 24 urged "prompt passage" of the bill.[158] It passed the Senate by a voice vote, and on May 22 became law. Thus the Submerged Lands Act of 1953 (SLA) was created, which returned ownership of the coastal sea within three miles to the states. An exception was the broader zones given to Texas and Florida in the Gulf of Mexico. Thus although federal officials retained their constitutional powers over interstate commerce, navigation, and defense within three miles,[159] the three-mile coastal belt at last returned to state ownership.[160]

The Senate in its deliberations separated this legislative language from another section of the bill that granted ownership of the continental shelf beyond three miles to the federal government. Following House-Senate joint hearings, this language was reconstituted as a second piece of legislation that passed Congress and was signed by the president. And thus on 7 August 1953 the companion Outer Continental Shelf Lands Act (OCSLA) came into being. It codified a U.S. claim to outer continental shelf oil asserted in 1945 by the Truman Proclamations and gave the federal government exclusive new authority to develop natural resources found on the shelf. Hence these two acts—SLA and OCSLA—cemented a strict division of state from federal authority offshore.

Conclusion

The two fundamental statutes that emerged out of the Tidelands Controversy were a result of powerful political machinations back at a time when offshore oil was king. At that time sparse attention was given to wise governance of the environment. Nor was much concern given to preventing ecological harms that stem, for instance, from overfishing, destruction of marine habitat, or offshore oil development. This is no surprise, for the environmental protection movement and its attendant ecological consciousness had not yet arrived. However, the shape of ocean governance that was fundamentally determined by SLA and OCSLA now determines the efficacy of much ocean resources management.

Notably, this division of state-federal authority, like the three-mile limit itself, was mostly the result of political compromises and the personal proclivities of a few key actors. Factors such as the persistence shown by Ickes, the mood in Congress following *U.S. v. California*, and the election of Eisenhower were most relevant to laws governing the coastal sea. Unfortunately such eclectic political factors no longer facilitate the most effective protection of the marine environment—if they ever did.

The origins of the three-mile limit and the subsequent Tidelands Controversy defined the current shape of U.S. ocean governance, but they offer little wisdom that should be carried into the new millennium. Half a century has elapsed since passage of the SLA and its companion, the OCSLA. During that time humanity's technological ability to exploit the seas has increased greatly and in far-reaching ways. Scientific understanding of marine ecosystems has also expanded. Yet the modern regime governing our uses of the sea has not kept pace with these changes. There is much that can be done to build an improved, second-generation governance that reflects the nature of marine processes.

3

Is This Holistic Ecology,
or Just Muddling Through?

There need not be a concern with protecting [fish] against
being driven to such low levels that they can never recover
[because] a fish population is an open-ended biological system which replenishes itself from the effects of losses.

Scientific report for UN Convention on Law of the Sea, 1958

As recently as a half century ago, the sea still seemed to
be in excellent health physically, chemically, and biologically. . . . [But] since the 1970s, commercial fisheries have
pushed fish stocks to collapse.

Kieran Mulvaney, "A Sea of Troubles," January 1998

We pass the word around; we ponder how the case is put
by different people; we read the poetry; we meditate over
the literature; we play the music; we change our minds;
we reach an understanding. Society evolves this way.

Lewis Thomas, The Medusa and the Snail

OCEAN POLICY MAKING has never been a static enterprise. Rather, the
goals pursued there reflect evolving human values, so it is notable that the
dawn of the twenty-first century is witnessing a "greening" of public attitudes. Conservation of natural resources and preserving biological diver-

sity are given new importance, and the implications of this change are staggering. Of course, the environmental movement has been gaining ground for decades. A threshold question now should be: to what extent is sound environmental protection already incorporated within current policies? There are already a few statutes in the United States that strive to prevent harm to the seas in the first place. Laudably, they have begun to implement science-based management to safeguard marine ecological integrity.

Yet many ocean and coastal policies still reflect a fundamental ignorance of ecology. Such ignorance is seen, for instance, in the patchwork of political lines atop the sea that break up governance into discrete parts. To continue in that way while ignoring the broader interconnectedness of marine processes is to miss the mark.[1] Instead of politically based laws that show little regard for the natural laws of marine ecology, it would be wiser to draft legislation with an eye to the actual functions and structures of ecosystems. As marine biologist Carleton Ray observes, a key error is that "marine management is rarely undertaken from an ecosystemic point of view."[2]

The existing policy framework would be adequate if it were limited to such applications as determining the neutrality of belligerent warships. But when it is exercised for intrusive modern purposes such as managing resources of the marine environment, it becomes much harder to justify. Given the rapid evolution in values worldwide and attendant rise of ecological consciousness, it is time to set a new course that better joins laws governing the sea—with our growing knowledge of the nature of the sea. Advances in scientific understanding of marine ecosystems are illuminating the impact of human beings on the sea and are helpfully pointing toward new policy directions.[3] To chart this course, however, we must first fix our present bearings by reviewing recent events.

Demise of the Three-Mile Limit

The traditional three-mile coastal sea still plays a part in America's domestic ocean policy by dividing state and federal authority. In an international context, however, this limit has lost its significance. Ironically, it was the United States, long champion of this principle, that dealt the crippling blow. Chapter 2 describes how drafters of the Truman Proclamations had hoped that the two pronouncements would not give other nations a rationale to extend their own sovereignty offshore. These efforts were doomed from the start.

As late as World War II, the seas were still being used in largely unrestricted ways such as for fishing, warfare, trade, and dumping refuse, just as in centuries past. But after the war nations increasingly began to feel the need to protect their fishing grounds from encroachment by foreigners, citing this as a rationale for extending their jurisdiction seaward. How far control should be extended was a contentious matter. Nations were in conflict, both with each other and internally. Distant-water fishing nations like the United States, Japan, and Britain, with their large fishing fleets, generally favored limited territorial seas so as to maximize the area in which they could capture fish.[4] Especially vocal within these nations were offshore fishermen who went after marine species that flourished far from their own shores, but near the shores of other nations. For example, the U.S. tuna fleet, based in western ports such as San Diego or Los Angeles, traveled thousands of miles to the tropical Pacific waters off the coasts of South and Central America where tuna abounded.

But the distant-water fishing nations were hardly united in seeking narrow seas. Complicating the issue were numerous U.S., British, and Japanese fishermen who fished near their own shores. Whether seeking benthic species (which live on or near the ocean floor), or pelagic species (which live in the water column), these fishermen felt the sting of competition from foreign vessels fishing near their shores. Therefore fishermen themselves were divided by type of fishery. Even distant-water fishing nations had sizable populations of nearshore fishermen—and these groups were further divided by the major schism between sport and commercial groups.

After the war, fishermen from many nations witnessed more and more foreign vessels landing huge catches near their coasts, in quantities which they feared their stocks could not sustain. Like Alaskans who had petitioned the Roosevelt administration in the 1930s to extend U.S. jurisdiction over salmon fishing, and in a scene repeated in country after country, fishing interests pushed their governments for a limit broader than three miles to keep foreign boats off their coasts.

For poorer nations without large distant-water fleets, this was a simple matter to address. They simply wanted their exclusive fishing zone pushed seaward to ward off outsiders. Nations boasting rich and important fisheries in nearby coastal seas like Ecuador, Iceland, and Korea thus sought to move beyond a three-mile sea to exclude distant-water fishing fleets from the United States, Britain, and Japan, respectively.[5] After the Truman Proclamations (and even though the proclamation on fish claimed a right only to enter into conservation treaties), a host of developing nations began claiming their own exclusive zones that were much broader than three miles. These expansive new claims began to appear in the early 1950s and were particularly popular among Latin American nations.

At the same time, larger East-West (Soviet-U.S.) tensions and widening divisions between North and South (the United States and the USSR versus Third World nations) combined to make unprecedented fisheries zones feasible. Most famous of these early claims was a joint declaration made in 1952 by Chile, Ecuador, and Peru to an exclusive 200-mile fishery zone. They argued with considerable logic that the mere coincidence of a wide continental shelf off parts of the U.S. coast allowed the United States to extend its control to 200 miles, as in the Gulf of Mexico. Chile, Ecuador, and Peru felt that the geological happenstance of a much narrower continental shelf in the Pacific should not prevent them from having wide seaward zones of their own. They also had difficulty accepting the United States' view that the Truman Proclamation was not tantamount to jurisdiction over fish.

Chile, Ecuador, and Peru instead proposed a novel "bioma" theory that —as a harbinger of things to come—saw coastal seas as part of a larger land-sea ecosystem based on a dynamic equilibrium in which ecologically harmful activities like overfishing should be prohibited.[6] Like Jefferson's idea that the extent of U.S. control should be the Gulf Stream, this was a predecessor to the idea of marine ecosystems management. Korea, whose fishermen relied on fishing by hand that did little damage to stocks or habitat, also acted; alarmed by the many Japanese bottom trawlers that destroyed benthic habitat and sea grasses off its shores, Korea extended its claim seaward. As expected, the U.S. tuna fleet did not recognize the claims by Chile, Ecuador, Peru, and others to seas beyond three miles, so they continued to operate within waters claimed by these nations. Economically speaking, tuna fishing in tropical Pacific waters was enormously profitable. Yet from an ecological perspective, the indiscriminate hauls by powerful U.S. boats were causing terrific damage.[7]

In frustration, Chile, Ecuador, and Peru began arresting foreign vessels within 200 miles of their shores. Ecuador started by arresting U.S. tuna boats, and other Latin American nations followed suit. Rather than see this clash escalate into an armed conflict and one within the United States' "own" Western Hemisphere, and also eager to compensate fishermen, the U.S. Congress in 1954 passed the Fishermen's Protective Act. This measure reimbursed U.S. fishermen for their boats seized on what was deemed the high seas under international law (beyond three miles).

At the same time, issues of national defense were also shaping policy regarding ocean jurisdiction. However, defense matters proved mainly a contest between the United States and its allies on the one hand, and the USSR and its allies on the other. At first there was a clear divergence between the two sides. After World War II, the tattered Soviet Union had a maritime outlook far different from that of the United States. As a young and historically land-based continental power, the Soviet Union saw no advantage in a three-mile territorial sea. Moreover, much of the perceived U.S. military threat was based on the U.S. fleet mobility and a powerful blue-water navy that could roam unchallenged.

The USSR thus felt that simply by claiming a much broader territorial sea, it could extend its own security while limiting U.S. military might. The Soviets knew that a broader territorial zone would hamper spying from Western ships offshore and from aircraft overhead that was proving irksome. And by spreading a broader limit among fellow Warsaw Pact nations it could contain the mobility of the U.S. and NATO fleets. As a result, the Soviets, along with the communist bloc, strongly advocated a new twelve-mile territorial sea. This twelve-mile limit had first been claimed by the Soviet Union decades before, but with the advent of the cold war it backed the concept with newfound zeal.[8]

The Soviet Union also viewed the crucial concept of "innocent passage" quite differently from its traditional meaning. Normally each nation has the right of innocent passage set out in international law and the Hague Convention of 1907. The agreement states that warships must be allowed free passage through territorial seas, as long as that passage does not threaten the peace or security of the coastal nation.[9] The USSR, however, wanted to require that warships first give notification before crossing territorial waters so that the Soviet government could choose whether or not to grant passage. That violated the historic freedoms that Western navies had long relied on. More troubling, the Soviet Union and its allies sought to make passage through international straits, known as "straits passage," subject to similar rules. To a United States that relied on the mobility of its blue-water fleet as a chief means of projecting power, maintaining both innocent and straits passage was beyond negotiation.

Therefore the United States reacted negatively to the Soviet proposals for a twelve-mile sea, just as it did to possible restrictions on both innocent passage and straits passage. The United States and its allies relied on open passage, whether innocent or not, as the fundamental means to navigate from one ocean area to another. Without freedom of navigation, Western navies would be severely crippled.

In fact, a test of whether the Eastern bloc could restrict innocent passage was the first contentious case to be brought before the new International Court of Justice (ICJ) in 1949. Albania had mined the Corfu Strait, an act generally regarded as illegal and contrary to the right of innocent passage. That act damaged transiting Royal Navy warships and caused the death of British sailors. Thus a case was brought before the ICJ, in which Great Britain contended that Albania had violated international law. Albania responded that no such right of passage existed in this channel, and that anyway the strait was of secondary importance for navigation. The International Court ruled in favor of Great Britain, but this result was handed down in a hostile cold war setting and Albania refused to pay the fine.[10]

After this time, a number of incidents further buttressed the view that the Soviet Union and its allies refused all innocent passage within twelve miles. For example, in 1952 the Soviets shot down two Swedish planes that it claimed had violated sovereign territory (which includes air space) extending to twelve miles. In 1955 the Soviet navy seized four Swedish fishing boats claiming to seek shelter in Russian waters during a storm; the men were all fined and imprisoned on spying charges, and their boats were confiscated.[11]

A Trio of Conventions on the Law of the Sea

By the 1950s offshore claims were growing increasingly complex and it became clear that the laws would have to be harmonized by multinational agreement. Preparations began for a first United Nations Conference on the Law of the Sea (UNCLOS). After substantial groundwork, seven hundred delegates from eighty-six countries met in Geneva in 1958 for this first global effort to codify a standard law of the sea.[12] Their daunting task was to distill from an array of views a unified policy, a task made more complicated by both East-West and North-South tensions.

The United States sought from the start to build consensus around a three-mile territorial sea—but it was prepared to concede a territorial limit as broad as six miles. The United States also sought to guarantee that traditional innocent passage should be recognized for warships. The Soviet Union on the other hand felt that warships by their very nature and purpose could not engage in innocent passage. It stood firm on demanding notification prior to passage, as well as a much broader twelve-mile limit for the territorial sea.

Not surprisingly, the United States failed to drum up significant support for a three-mile sea. In response, it offered as a compromise a six-mile territorial sea, combined with a nine-mile contiguous zone in which a coastal nation could assert exclusive fishing rights. That position was alluring to many, but it lost out during conference negotiations (although by only a small margin).[13] The Soviet Union played its hand. It was now a nuclear superpower, the undisputed leader of a bloc of communist nations and aspirant to the role of moral compass for a new group of nonaligned nations. A confident Soviet Union thus stood firm.

The USSR's commitment to the broader twelve-mile territorial sea, as expected, was supported by the Eastern bloc. But it also won support from developing nations of the South. These newly independent nations were now striking out on their own and taking different paths from those of their former colonial masters.[14] The divergent territorial claims advanced in 1958 were evident in the following sampling: Australia, three miles; Finland, four miles; Cambodia, five miles; India, six miles; Mexico, nine miles; Albania (never one to follow the herd), ten miles; Ethiopia, twelve miles; Chile, thirty miles; El Salvador, two hundred miles; Korea, the continental shelf; West Germany, whatever distance accorded with international law.[15] Many liked the notion of twelve miles simply because the Americans strongly opposed the idea. Others felt that expanded control beyond three miles gave greater protection to their fisheries.

Like the international community, the U.S. delegation was characterized by a complex mixture of goals. Distant-water fishing interests clashed with coastal interests, while the navy competed with the Interior Department. But the aims of the Soviet Union were also buffeted by a complex mix of concerns. The puny Soviet navy was now exploding in size and capability to a competent blue-water force that projected power far at sea. Recognizing this fact and given the rapid growth of the Soviet distant-water fishing fleet, the USSR preferred that offshore claims by other nations should not become too wide—in any event no more than twelve miles. On this point Soviet aims increasingly accorded with those of the U.S. Navy and distant-water fishing interests.

However, these twin goals conflicted with the goals of the great number of fishermen around the world who fished in their own coastal waters and wanted still broader offshore limits. Events at the UNCLOS discussions highlighted this North-South rift. Developing nations from the South, anxious to protect nearby fisheries from powerful distant-water fishing nations, felt that the best way to protect marine resources was to establish claims even broader than twelve miles. The South saw little need for narrower limits mainly designed to provide mobility for blue-water navies, or for distant-water fishing fleets, which none of them had.[16]

The end result was the 1958 UNCLOS I package, which produced four separate conventions (or treaties). These were the Territorial Seas Treaty, the Fisheries Treaty, the Continental Shelf Treaty, and the High Seas Treaty. In some places these agreements broke new ground. An ongoing evolution in marine policy reflects the dominant values of the time, and a main interest in 1958 was defining the territorial sea and preserving the mobility of naval and fisheries fleets. While innocent passage rights were retained by a slim majority, consensus on the territorial sea eluded negotiators, and because of that fact, UNCLOS I was deemed a failure.

There was limited progress on some subjects, although they were generally overshadowed by the territorial sea issue. The Fisheries Convention adopted at UNCLOS I did allow nations in line with the Truman Proclamations to enter into new multilateral agreements to conserve fisheries. It also permitted limited conservationist actions. But this convention did not establish any timetables for actual conservatory measures. Nor from an eco-logical perspective did it set any hard targets for sustainable levels of fishing. Given the attitudes of the day both scientific and lay, which often envisioned fish as a limitless resource incapable of depletion, it is easy to understand why UNCLOS I produced so little action.

The lack of decisive action may have been explainable but hardly help-ful. A vital issue, yet widely overlooked, was a profound need to improve the state of marine science. The crude state of scientific understanding is evident in a report given at UNCLOS I entitled "Scientific Investigation of Tropical Tuna Resources," which rejected warnings of overfishing: "There need not be a concern with protecting [the fish] against being driven to such low levels that they can never recover." Such a view "rests in part on the fact that a fish population is an open-ended biological system which replenishes itself from the effects of losses."[17] This view was badly wrong; for while biological extinction of marine species is rather unlikely, many stocks were already being driven to such low levels that they were well on the way to becoming "commercially extinct." Yet reports repeatedly and erroneously denied that sharp declines in catch could be a sign of over-fishing.[18]

Given the failure of UNCLOS I to reach consensus on the territorial sea issue, a second, briefer Convention on the Law of the Sea was held in 1960, but it too failed to reach agreement. UNCLOS II did make clear that this twelve-mile limit, whether as a sovereign territorial sea or for fish-eries purposes only, was indisputably a leading concept. Even among the advanced European nations it was becoming acceptable to establish fishery claims beyond the three-mile limit. Thus Norway, which heavily depends on fish protein, abandoned its long-standing fisheries zone of one Scandi-navian league and made the unilateral claim to a twelve-mile fisheries zone in 1961. Denmark followed suit for its own island possessions in 1963.[19] In the next year, Austria, Belgium, Denmark, France, Federal Republic of Germany, Ireland, Italy, Luxembourg, the Netherlands, Portugal, Spain, Sweden, Switzerland, and the United Kingdom adopted variants on the twelve-mile zone for fisheries protection.[20]

Owing to a chorus of New England and Washington State fishing interests who joined Alaskans in pushing for extended jurisdiction, the United States soon acted in like fashion. Congress in 1964 passed fisheries legislation acceptable under UNCLOS; it banned foreign boats from taking living resources out to a depth of 200 meters.[21] The law was aimed at Japanese, Russian, and Cuban trawlers working close to U.S. shores.

Then in 1966 even the United States joined the growing chorus by enacting its own twelve-mile limit for the protection of fisheries. In the battle leading up to its passage, the bill had been opposed by two different groups for entirely different reasons. California's congressional delegation, which represented the tuna fleet, still wanted to keep the U.S. claim narrow at three miles so that the United States could argue with moral force for a narrower sea off the coast of Latin America. Also opposed to the bill were the Alaskan, New England, and Washington State delegations who felt twelve miles was too narrow—and two hundred miles was more appropriate![22] Once passed, this U.S. statute acknowledged the authority of all nations to ban foreign boats within twelve miles. However, it did not set out any requirements that fisheries within newly claimed U.S. seas should actually be conserved.

By the late 1960s the Soviet Union had clearly overcome its prior handicap of an inferior navy and small fishing fleet, and so sought its place beside the leading maritime powers. The USSR saw that trends toward growing territorial seas of up to 200 miles were now hurting its own interests. For instance, a Soviet hydrographic survey ship operating far from shore was arrested by Indonesia in the 1960s for violating "internal" waters; although taken to an Indonesian port, the ship managed to get under way and escape with local authorities in hot pursuit.[23] Argentina also claimed a 200-mile territorial sea. After Argentine aircraft spotted five Soviet fishing trawlers "illegally" fishing 120 miles offshore, nearby Argentine warships captured two of the trawlers. As they were being escorted to shore, one broke free. War planes fired on the boat, but it escaped.[24]

With their mutual interests as well as growing troubles in mind, the USSR approached the United States in the late 1960s with an aim of convening a third UN Convention on the Law of the Sea (UNCLOS III). A hope was that together they could enter into negotiations for halting this creeping expansion of jurisdiction.[25]

The tacit bargain was the Soviets could have their broader twelve-mile territorial sea, if the United States got *free* passage rather than mere *innocent* passage, granting Western warships and submarines the right to traverse international straits unmolested.[26]

As expected, the developing nations of the South endorsed the idea of UNCLOS III for they felt that it would lend authority to their demands for broader jurisdiction. But they bitterly denounced the joint United States–Soviet proposal that the territorial sea be no more than twelve miles.[27] Ambassador Arvid Pardo from Malta set the pace by proposing a new public order for oceans, with the seabed becoming a "common heritage of mankind." He envisioned neither *mare liberum* (open seas) nor *mare clausum* (closed seas); instead, resources of the high seas would be considered as a novel *mare nostrum* (our seas), with all the profits distributed to the world.[28]

This unique idea of the seas as a common heritage of mankind found wide support among the developing nations as UNCLOS III talks took shape, and its communitarian goals were later reflected in the initial UNCLOS III minerals regime. But the common heritage idea was denounced by the rich industrialized nations who already had the technical capability to exploit the seabed. These nations anticipated, quite wrongly, that manganese nodules were soon to be extracted in immense quantities. (Since then, the prospect of mining manganese nodules from the seafloor has been repeatedly pushed back; as long as strategic minerals like cobalt and manganese can be economically mined on land in places like the Congo, and these metals are accessible on the free market, then deep seafloor nodule mining is unlikely for the foreseeable future.)[29]

The start of UNCLOS III negotiations revealed that two main groups of antagonists were the large maritime nations of the North (the United States, USSR, France, and Great Britain) versus a "Group of 77" from the South (developing nations of Latin America, Asia, and Africa). But as talks wore on into the mid-1970s, it was also clear that several more subinterests had grown up around new economic and geographic considerations, creating roughly eight subgroupings. The first group was loosely made up of Chilean, Ecuadorian, and Peruvian territorialists who continued to prefer a 200-mile territorial sea. A second group was comprised of broad-margin states who favored allowing jurisdiction over the shelf even beyond 200 miles. These nations included Australia, Brazil, Canada, India, Norway, and New Zealand.[30]

Third were the patrimonialists who desired 200-mile economic or resource zones (so-called patrimonial seas, a precursor to the Exclusive Economic Zone), where coastal nations would have authority, but only over marine resources. Leading patrimonialists were Mexico, Colombia, and Venezuela. Fourth were the archipelagic nations that wished to bring the waters between and around their islands under their exclusive jurisdiction. These nations argued that the coastal seas between their islands had been long regarded locally as sovereign territory. This group included Fiji, Indonesia, and the Philippines. Fifth were the traditional maritime states who sought to limit any claims beyond a twelve-mile limit in order to preserve both their naval fleet mobility and distant-water fishing interests. The main representatives here were the United States, the USSR, Japan, Great Britain, and France.

The sixth view—the position of the landlocked and geographically disadvantaged states—was a novel concern in ocean policy, one that grew out of a regard for international equity and rights of all nations. Seventh was the Group of 77, made of developing nations, which supported (among other things) a new global regime to share the resources of the seabed. Their view mirrored the South's antagonism toward the North and especially disenchantment with capitalist states on most matters. Eighth and last were the technologically advanced mining states who desired a regime for the seabed based on the principle "First in time, first in right." Thus only nations technically capable of retrieving deep-sea minerals could gain legal title; this group was made entirely of northern nations.[31]

The United States had precipitated this onslaught of varied claims to the sea when it announced the Truman Proclamations in 1945. Now hoist by its own petard, the United States found that there was no turning back the clock on expanding maritime pretensions. As an internal matter, during the 1970s the U.S. position evolved rapidly as the United States struggled to both orchestrate and embrace an ocean order radically different from the traditional three-mile sea of the past. A fundamental change came in 1976, with passage of the U.S. Fisheries Conservation and Management

Act (now called the Magnuson-Stevens Act).[32] This law greatly expanded American jurisdiction over fish by moving U.S. management authority from twelve miles to two hundred miles. It was also very popular politics; the outcry over foreign fishing had by the 1970s grown so strident that it forced a reluctant President Ford to sign the bill into law, despite firm opposition from the State and Defense Departments.[33] The act signaled the eroding political power of the distant-water fishing fleets and the growing voice of coastal fishing interests.

By the early 1980s and after more than ten years of debate and compromise, the Third UN Convention on the Law of the Sea was at last completed in 1982 and opened for signature. The treaty can be interpreted in a number of ways. Seen in a positive light, UNCLOS III usefully codified much customary practice as the law of the sea. It was a high-water mark in international negotiations; over 150 nations had taken part in negotiating a treaty of unprecedented scope on matters of navigation and overflight, fishing, conservation of marine resources, development of offshore minerals, maritime boundaries, piracy, and much more. The lengthy UNCLOS III talks also served as a diplomatic training ground for many nascent countries that had not achieved independence until after 1970. It reflected the voting rules of a United Nations that empowered smaller nations and the rising aspirations of a still-developing South.[34]

However, after the treaty drafting was completed in 1982 and with a dissenting United States at the helm, the industrial nations strongly objected to the UNCLOS III provisions for global sharing of deep sea-bed minerals. Their objections caused an abrupt slowing in the worldwide acceptance of the convention as a practical matter. Not all provisions of UNCLOS III were objectionable to the United States. In March 1983, President Reagan issued Proclamation 5030, declaring a 200-mile Exclusive Economic Zone (EEZ) for the United States, in line with central provisions of UNCLOS III.[35] By the stroke of a pen and in an act that cost the United States nothing, America had in essence more than doubled in size. Debate continues over the exact size of this U.S. EEZ, but it is probably about 4 million square miles. With its EEZ, the U.S. territory around Hawaii alone is about 1 million square miles, or an area larger than Mexico. Historically, this action is comparable to the Louisiana Purchase of

1803. Yet because the seas draw so little attention, this proclamation was hardly reported in the news.[36]

By declaring this EEZ, the United States was able to cement its rights vis-à-vis other nations to exploit mineral and other resources within 200 miles of its coastline. And in making this claim, the United States acknowledged that recognition of the EEZ was fast evolving into customary international law.[37] However, critics charged that the United States was upholding only those provisions of UNCLOS III it preferred, while rejecting those it found distasteful. This action was seen as contrary to the spirit of UNCLOS, which specifically prohibited making such reservations against portions of the text. Although all nations that signed the treaty had certainly been opposed to portions of it, they agreed to the entire package in order to gain the total benefits it provided.

By the early 1990s, changing sentiments and the lack of economic viability of deep sea-bed mining led to an interest in revisiting the treaty's offending passages on deep sea-bed mining. Talks were undertaken from 1990 to 1994 on modifying the deep sea-bed regime to gain the acceptance of the industrialized nations, and especially the United States. Meanwhile, the landmark sixtieth ratification of UNCLOS III was deposited in 1993, which by the terms of the treaty triggered its coming into effect one year later, in November 1994. That hastened efforts to rewrite the agreement's sea-bed mining provisions.[38] In time, a settlement was reached to modify the offending sections on sea-bed mining. With this breakthrough, the United States took a step toward at last signing the UNCLOS III regime.

The United States Adopts a Twelve-Mile Territorial Sea

For all intents and purposes, the three-mile sea has passed from international use.[39] As recently as 1945, forty-six nations, or 77 percent of the world's coastal or island nations, were claiming a territorial sea of three miles. By 1965 the number had dropped to thirty-two (or 38 percent of coastal nations). In 1979 that number dropped further to twenty-three (or 18 percent).[40] And by the late 1990s the three-mile measure of territorial seas had essentially disappeared. Conversely, as the three-mile sea waned, more and more nations declared jurisdiction over twelve miles. Once again, the numbers speak for themselves. In 1945 only the USSR and one other nation had a twelve-mile territorial sea (3 percent of the total). In 1965, twenty-six nations claimed a twelve-mile sea (31 percent); in 1979 the number jumped to seventy-six (or 58 percent); by 1989, over one hundred nations claimed a territorial sea of twelve miles (75 percent).[41]

Although it was clear to the U.S. Navy that a twelve-mile limit was becoming the norm for the territorial sea, the United States continued into the mid-1980s to resist the adoption of such a limit. Part of the reluctance stemmed from Defense Department concerns over rights of transit passage through straits, overflight, and innocent passage across territorial waters. The navy had long ago recognized that a twelve-mile territorial sea, without rights of innocent passage and straits passage, could severely constrict the mobility of the U.S. fleet and overflight capability, since over one hundred strategically essential ocean straits are less than twenty-four miles in width. Nations bordering these vital straits might hamper navigation such as by requiring advance notification or by covertly putting in dangerous navigational "aids." Submarines derive their value from stealth, for this allows them offensive advantage; moreover, once found, a submarine can be easily destroyed. Thus it was essential that submarines should be allowed to pass through straits submerged, as opposed to coming to the surface as required by innocent passage.

However, by maintaining a three-mile territorial sea, the United States was also unwittingly providing the Soviet Union with an important tactical advantage. While U.S. spy ships were forced to remain outside the Soviet Union's proclaimed twelve-mile territorial sea, Soviet spy ships could venture as close as three miles from American shores (although both sides clandestinely violated such rules, if the need arose). Eventually this inequity caused the United States, one of the last remaining defenders of three miles, to switch over to the broader twelve-mile sea. With rights of transit passage through straits and innocent passage through territorial waters becoming customary international law, there was no longer any reason to resist the creeping jurisdiction that a twelve-mile sea represented. In the words of an insider intimately involved with this decision,

> The one issue that drove [the extension] was national security. Had the Navy, the Pentagon, not wanted the extension of the territorial sea, I don't think the U.S. would do it within the next decade. The desire to move Soviet elec-

tronic listening ships out to beyond twelve miles really drove the whole thing. In the four years or five years following Gorbachev's rise to power in the Soviet Union, the number of Soviet electronic spy ships off our coasts increased 400 percent. . . . To really be blunt about it, [the secretary of the navy] was almost theologically opposed to extending the territorial sea. [He] was very much of a mood that the United States is an island country and depends on shipping for its international commerce and we need all—the maximum amount of maritime mobility we can get. On that basis, it was thus something that had to wait until he left, and then almost as soon as he left, the CINCPAC [commander-in-chief, Pacific] sent a note in to the Pentagon saying we would like to revisit this issue, and from our perspective it makes sense for the U.S. to go to twelve miles; . . . well, the CINC in Honolulu, in Pearl Harbor, can look out of his window and see the Soviet AGIs [intelligence-gathering spy ships] bouncing microwave beams off his window in the morning, so to him its a very real thing. He got back here in Washington . . . mid-1987, but it was about April 1988 by the time [the secretary of defense] wrote [the secretary of state] asking for the process to be geared up.[42]

On 27 December 1988, in one of his last acts in office, President Reagan issued a proclamation extending the U.S. territorial sea to twelve miles.[43] Internal machinations leading up to the proclamation paint a fascinating picture of government departments jockeying for positions of relative strength. In some ways, internal discussions surrounding the territorial sea extension were similar to earlier battles between the Departments of State and Interior more than four decades earlier.

Confidential memoranda show that by 1988, federal officials recognized that three miles was no longer an appropriate breadth for the U.S. territorial sea. The replacement was obvious; the twelve-mile limit was regarded as having matured nearly into customary international law.[44] That development, together with the presence of active Soviet intelligence gatherers hovering three miles offshore, had left little reason to adhere to a three-mile limit. Thus in May 1988 a memorandum was sent to the defense secretary stating in part, "The Joint Chiefs of Staff have recommended . . . you write the Secretary of State, requesting that he initiate interagency consideration of extension of the U.S. territorial sea and contiguous zone. I strongly support that proposal and recommend that you sign the attached letter to Secretary Shultz."[45] Three days later, Secretary of Defense Frank

Carlucci wrote Secretary of State George Shultz supporting a twelve-mile extension and requesting that an interagency group study the proposal.[46] A meeting was held in May 1988, chaired by a representative from the State Department. The proposed extension was supported, though some expressed serious concern over its potential domestic impact.

That meeting showed that Reagan administration officials were not of one mind regarding the desirability of the proposed extension. While officials at Defense were opposed to the narrow three-mile sea, representatives of other federal agencies expressed considerable anxiety over the domestic implications of an extension. The Interior Department, as the federal entity overseeing oil and gas in federal waters offshore, was particularly troubled. Interior officials did not wish to upset the allocation that had sharply divided state waters (0–3 miles), from federal outer continental shelf waters (3–200 miles). Interior's fear was that extending the U.S. territorial sea to twelve miles, even if for security reasons, might extend coastal states' authority over oil as well.

Especially relevant was the Coastal Zone Management Act of 1972 (CZMA), which gave coastal states limited authority beyond three miles.[47] The CZMA gives states unique authority to request that federal activities directly affecting the "coastal zone" should be consistent with state policies. Because the extent of this coastal zone under CZMA did not explicitly end three miles seaward, but instead was vaguely tied to the U.S. territorial sea, states could potentially view the proposed extension of U.S. sovereignty as enlarging their authority. Thus if the territorial sea was extended to twelve miles, Interior feared that this could also give the states new authority over federal ocean activities.[48]

Interior Department officials were not about to surrender their exclusive authority over the outer continental shelf beginning three miles offshore. The three-mile limit had been established under circumstances that were no longer relevant, but this fact was either forgotten by federal officials or, most likely, deemed irrelevant. For unrelated reasons, federal officials were briefly forced to put the matter on hold. The State Department wanted a proclamation ready for the president's signature by August 1988, but was forced to wait for a legal opinion from the Justice Department confirming that the president had constitutional authority to extend the territorial sea without an act of Congress. During this waiting period, Secretary of Defense Carlucci wrote Secretary of Interior Hodel repeating his position: he wanted to avoid any adverse effects on U.S. offshore federalism and recognized that Interior did have valid concerns over the possible domestic impact of the law.[49] Carlucci repeated the consensus view that a proclamation could extend the territorial sea and that "legislation affirming the status-quo of existing domestic laws would be beneficial but not required."[50]

Several months later, the Justice Department confirmed that the president indeed could act alone. Thus despite the ungainliness of moving ahead without Congress, the Reagan Proclamation was issued in December 1988. It responded to the concerns of the Interior Department in that it claimed to apply for international purposes only. By this tactic, the federal government was able to proclaim its twelve-mile sea vis-à-vis foreign nations while retaining a traditional three-mile division regarding the states. In effect, the federal government was attempting to have its cake and eat it too. This was however a rather awkward solution, since it severed a long-standing link that matched the international U.S. territorial sea with the division between state and federal jurisdiction. It also effectively ended the rationale for confining states to a three-mile sea. (See figure 7.)

With U.S. sovereignty extending twelve miles, it is now possible to consider extending state authority for more cooperative, ecological purposes. Despite the concerns of some federal officials, expanding U.S. control has opened issues for debate. One major question concerns the legal nature of this new three-to-twelve-mile "federal" ocean zone—what precisely is it, if traditional American domestic laws do not apply there?[51] For instance, a key possibility raised by this extension is that it is now conceivable to construct a new, more ecologically oriented ocean governance (to be discussed in following chapters). But before developing this second-generation approach, we should address some of the problems created by present ocean governance. So far, the laws undergirding that governance have not sought to learn from the "laws" of ecosystem processes. In short, we can do better by listening to the sea.

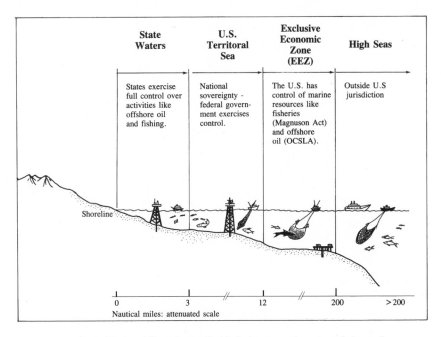

State Waters	U.S. Territorial Sea	Exclusive Economic Zone (EEZ)	High Seas
States exercise full control over activities like offshore oil and fishing.	National sovereignty - federal government exercises control.	The U.S. has control of marine resources like fisheries (Magnuson Act) and offshore oil (OCSLA).	Outside U.S jurisdiction

Shoreline

Nautical miles: attenuated scale
0   3   12   200   > 200

Figure 7. Jurisdictional lines have divided the ocean in spite of the truly holistic and interconnected nature of marine ecosystems. *Artist: Jill Townsend*

Recent Failures of Fisheries Management

The 1982 UNCLOS III goes much further in its aspirational language on conserving marine life than the previous two conventions. By providing mechanisms for coastal nations to claim large areas of the sea, it allows for conservation measures. For instance, coastal nations can manage large areas of adjacent coastal waters by claiming a 200-mile EEZ. And in inspirational (though not mandatory) tones, UNCLOS III calls on nations to manage their fisheries better than in the past within these zones.[52] With these laudable goals in mind, we must ask: have aims of improved environmental protection met with success? Has UNCLOS III gone far enough or demanded enough to bring about ocean governance that is as good as should now be expected?

There have been some notable successes since the adoption of UNCLOS III. But where fishing pressures are greatest—thus where stricter governance is most needed—there are often failures of alarming proportions. Yet the rudimentary state of policy provides opportunities to build improved governance of the sea.

A prime example is the Grand Banks off Canada's Atlantic provinces, once the world's richest fishery. Only thirty years ago, children of New-foundland caught cod simply by dipping baskets into the sea. Now re-search vessels have difficulty finding even a single school of cod. The saga of the collapse of Grand Banks fish stocks occurred over a span of mere decades and illustrates the difficulties confronting even the state-of-the-art fisheries management assumed by UNCLOS III. Imagine the protein and profits that this resource could provide, and one may ask, "How could an advanced nation with an army of scientists allow one of the richest fish-eries in the world to be destroyed?"[53] Reflecting the complexities of the sea, there is no simple answer.

The crash of Grand Banks stocks has been blamed on various factors: (1) government agencies that set higher catch limits than scientists advised; (2) lack of incentives to limit the size of the catch—as fishermen argue, "If we don't catch them, other boats will"; (3) overcapitalization of the fleet whereby too many boats chase too few fish; and (4) a small number of fishermen who illicitly exceed their quotas, causing inordinate damage.[54] There is no consensus as to the key cause, and each party blames the other. Moreover, some fishermen hope (without scientific basis) that the deple-tion of stocks is just a natural fluctuation in supply that time will reverse.

But another factor, too rarely discussed, may be also at work. Scientific models can themselves encourage overfishing. This is a controversial charge, especially among fisheries scientists. If true, it is troubling, since greater application of scientific knowledge is often asserted as a key to protecting marine biodiversity. Nonetheless, predictions based on theoretical models are frequently very different from real outcomes. For instance, models had predicted that the Grand Banks should now boast much healthier stocks than they do. The possibility that the models may have some hidden faults merits discussion because the consequences are weighty. "It is a commonly held fallacy among fisheries biologists that only the fishers, or the politi-cians, are at fault when overfishing occurs," notes an observer from the International Centre for Aquatic Resources Management, but it is also pos-sible that "models routinely used by biologists induce overfishing."[55]

To be sure, fisheries biologists are well aware of the uncertain nature of their predictions. Yet their task is to estimate recruitment (the number of juvenile fish surviving to catchable states), information that is essential for fishery management. It is widely understood that scientists' models may produce wildly inaccurate data on the present size of adult stocks and may err in predicting recruitment success (necessary for aiding managers in set-ting total allowable catch).[56] The first problem arises because it is difficult to estimate the number of fish; oceans are opaque and fish move over large areas. The second problem is forecasting; fish reproduction rates are chaotic and unpredictable, making recruitment not directly measurable. This cru-cial figure must instead be inferred from patchy data on observed age pro-files of a stock, a statistic that is itself the product of many variables.

This uncertainty has so far meant that model builders are forced to make many assumptions. For example, they may be required to assume that fairly accurate age profiles are known and mortality is constant. However, as Sidney Holt (who helped create a widely applied Beverton-Holt model for modeling stock sizes for age profiles) warns, "If those assumptions are wrong, your estimate can be wildly off."[57] Critics now argue that errors inherent within these models' assumptions may tend toward overestimat-ing biomass. That would mean that the initial estimates of stock size and recruitment success rates submitted by scientists to managers are too high. As a result, scientifically derived total allowable catch suggestions, which are themselves subject to political pressures, may start off too large, lead-ing to overfishing.

A second element exacerbates this problem. To handle so many vari-ables, and given the varied reproductive strategies of fish, models often as-sume that recruitment success is independent of stock size. As an example, the number of cod adults is held to be irrelevant to the number of cod off-spring because a single female cod can produce 8 million eggs. The models assume that because only a tiny fraction of eggs survive, even a "tiny differ-ence in that survival rate makes huge differences to the resulting number of fish, far more difference than comparatively small variations in the number of parents." Models have focused primarily on the possibility of a robust recruitment of new fish rather than on conserving the total number of adults. Yet there are now indications that it is wrong to ignore stock size, and scientists may have significantly overestimated the sustainable catch available from depleted stocks. That error may have created a feedback loop whereby a stock eventually collapses under the yearly onslaught of excessive fishing.[58]

Indeed, the present situation illuminates the mistakes that have been made in governing the Grand Banks. Fisheries scientists began managing this area decades ago, yet despite their efforts the cod, rather than rising or even holding steady, fell from 810,000 metric tons (mt) in 1967, to just 150,000 mt by 1977. Blaming foreign ships fishing just twelve miles offshore, Canada claimed a 200-mile EEZ. Canadian scientists then predicted that the catch would increase sharply to 400,000 mt by 1990. In anticipation, the government assisted the hard-hit fishermen of the Atlantic provinces by offering special loans for purchasing new boats and building large processing plants.[59]

Canada's Department of Fisheries and Oceans (DFO) was confounded when the supply of cod did not rebound to healthy levels, as their models had confidently predicted. Much of the problem resulted from the lack of good data on stocks. The underfunded DFO could make only one cruise that randomly collected trawl samples to estimate recruitment from age profiles of their catch. To compensate for such sparse data, they compared their catch rates with those of a commercial fleet making hundreds of cruises. If commercial catch per unit effort was up, they believed stocks were growing; conversely, they felt that stocks were decreasing if it was down.

Back in 1989 DFO estimates and commercial figures had begun to diverge. Scientists' data indicated the presence of only half as many fish as the commercial catch suggested. The difference was due to the fact that fishermen were using highly accurate sonar to find fish that congregated in warm patches of water, while the scientists (appropriately enough) were cruising along random headings and catching only a few fish, thus getting an accurate picture of depleted stocks. Yet fisheries biologists were understandably reluctant to trust their contrary data from just one trip over the assertions of experienced fishermen who claimed that cod fishing was never better. Meanwhile, unknown to all, the cod were naturally increasing congregation within ever smaller schools as their numbers became depleted. The result was remarkable success for fishermen, since those schools could be located mechanically, encouraging a mistaken view among the fishermen that there were still plenty of cod in the sea.[60]

Nonetheless, the DFO did at last revise its total allowable catch quotas downward, earning it the enmity of angry fishermen who believed that scientists just did not "go where the fish are."[61] Yet the scientists' estimates were more accurate than they realized, in fact too high. Moreover, their models did not account for a modernized fleet fostered by the government with loans in the 1980s. This fleet now had a higher commercial catch per unit effort, further skewing figures toward overestimating biomass and thus overfishing.

In 1990, with cod stocks obviously plummeting, Canada's Department of Fisheries and Oceans advised the total allowable catch be set at only 125,000 mt, which the fishing industry regarded as unacceptably low. That figure was raised to 235,000 mt, owing to the high human costs, such as unemployment, it would bring. Yet that well-intentioned act turned out to be very wrong. By 1992 the undeniable fact was that cod had crashed, forcing the Department of Fisheries and Oceans to recommend a total ban on cod fishing, causing a sizable loss of jobs. But all agreed that such extreme measures were necessary, and in 1993 the ban was extended indefinitely.[62]

In U.S. waters off New England just to the south, quite different policies were formulated, as if fisheries in that area were in a separate part of the world. The World Court had partitioned the seas. MacKenzie writes, "Approaches of the two countries have been completely separated from one another. Fishing and management have continued as if populations of haddock and cod observe the political boundary as drawn by the World Court."[63] But a collapse has also come to U.S. waters, as the number of groundfish (for example, cod, haddock, flounder) plummeted. An alarm was sounded in the 1960s, when Americans were disturbed by foreign distant-water fishing nations in the Gulf of Maine—but outside the twelve-mile limit. With the passage of the U.S. Fisheries Conservation and Management Act in 1976 (discussed earlier), those foreign ships were largely excluded from Gulf waters.

Did U.S. ocean governance in the new EEZ live up to aspirations of UNCLOS III and the Magnuson Act to better conserve fisheries? The answer is no. What happened in the United States was in some ways similar to the fate of Canada. With foreign vessels banned, New England's fleet at first exploded in size, driven by low-interest government loans and unrealistically high expectations. As an aid to the fishing industry and despite its problems with depleted fisheries, the United States in the 1980s created a National Seafood Promotion Council, whose goal was to increase per capita seafood consumption from fifteen to twenty pounds per year. Like other efforts (such as vessel subsidies), this was a simplistic attempt to wring ever more profit from the sea rather than focusing on conserving renewable resources and essential ocean habitat.[64] Draggers (fishermen who take groundfish by trawling heavy nets across the seafloor) suddenly had subsidized loans for gear and boats. The dragger fleet in the Gulf of Maine nearly doubled in size to over 1,000 boats.[65]

Swiftly, U.S. groundfish landings spiked from 219 million pounds in 1976 to over 380 million pounds in 1982. Then in the early 1980s New England's fishery management council—already hostile to regulation—dropped quotas entirely, thus eliminating any ceiling on the total allowable catch. In 1983 this council adopted as official policy that fisheries should be managed with a "minimum of regulatory intervention."[66] Amazingly, during a time when stocks were plummeting, the culture at this fishery management council was that only nonintrusive conservationist measures would be acceptable. Inevitably, during the late 1980s and into the 1990s, the catches for a wide array of fish crashed. Fishermen who could recall a typical catch of 3,000–4,000 pounds of flounder a day in the 1950s found that by 1997 they were lucky to catch 500 pounds—barely covering costs.[67] In the late 1990s, increasingly severe restrictions were hastily imposed by a reluctant council that was now faced with sharply worsening catches. Fishing communities like New Bedford, Massachusetts, were simply devastated.

By the late 1990s, the Georges Bank cod spawning stock biomass had slowly inched back up to 39,000 mt—something still less than the threshold of 70,000 mt that was believed necessary to sustain catches. Gulf of Maine cod was even worse hit. Estimates in 1997 declared that only 10,000 mt of spawning stock remained. However, a lack of good data still prevents fishery biologists from estimating the levels of cod needed to return to a healthy fishery.[68] Meanwhile, pressures are increasing on previously overlooked "trash fish" like the spiny dogfish, which are now in turn being overfished. For an advanced nation like the United States, the lack of good management is alarming and short-sighted. But there is some hope. Georges Bank yellowtail flounder and a few other fish have regenerated moderately. Despite being blasted by local fishermen, the New England council had the courage to slash catch limits for cod by 63 percent in 1998. The next test will be whether managers can resist intense political pressures to again permit overfishing, should signs of improving stocks emerge.[69]

Useful lessons can be learned from failures in the once rich Grand Banks and the Gulf of Maine. Institutions that make ocean policy have failed to take a sufficiently cautionary, long-term, big-picture view of marine ecosystems, seriously damaging what should be a rich renewable resource.[70] In part this is because declines in ocean species are far from obvious to our own species, which is unfamiliar with complex marine environments. We do not yet comprehend the need to protect habitat. Many species of commercially caught ocean fish of the eastern United States typically depend on coastal wetlands, or estuaries, as nursery grounds. Estuaries in the eastern United States are thus special, providing ample light and planktonic food that is small enough to be ingested, a constant resuspension and mixture of sediments by winds, riverine and tidal flows, and complex three-dimensional settings that allow small fish to avoid predation. Without these estuaries, the stocks of many ocean fish would inevitably begin to decline.[71]

Yet like other fishery management agencies the world over, the U.S. National Marine Fisheries Service (NMFS) has traditionally lacked the authority to protect nurseries. The agency is charged with conserving marine fisheries, yet it can only offer advice on whether other federal agencies should issue new permits to fill or dredge wetlands.[72] For example, in the Pacific Northwest, the NMFS has lacked authority over how large dams on the Columbia River are operated—such as when or if water is released to assist migration of salmon smolts. This is despite the fact these dams may kill over 90 percent of the salmon smolts migrating to the sea annually. Surprisingly, the authority to protect habitat essential to a vital portion of a valuable fish's life cycle had long been lacking.

Habitat destruction that can harm fish is caused by a number of factors, including logging that degrades the quality of river water and destroys salmon-spawning habitat.[73] Curiously, the NMFS was charged with promoting healthy fisheries, but it was given no authority when it comes to protecting habitat that is essential to fish reproduction. Such a separation of land from sea is foolhardy. Given the highly interconnected character of all natural life, it is essential to govern ocean resources in an integrated, ecologically coherent fashion.

It is therefore significant that Congress has taken action. Twenty years after passage of the FCMA (1976), this statute was strengthened by amendments creating a Sustainable Fisheries Act in 1996. With those changes, this major law for fisheries management was renamed the Magnuson-Stevens Act, and innovative provisions were added that, among other things, recognize the need to conserve essential fish habitat.

The new Magnuson-Stevens Act is a step toward more integrated ocean governance. For instance, it directs that habitat essential for managed species should be identified and measures should be taken to conserve such habitat. Therefore in 1998 the National Marine Fisheries Service began to require that regional fishery management plans describe and account for the role of essential habitat. Certainly, such changes are a step in the right direction; but whether this is yet another case of fisheries conservation efforts amounting to too little, too late, remains to be seen. Moreover, because of pressure from special interest groups, political calls are rising in the U.S. Senate for the NMFS to be more "flexible" and to "go slower"— that is, to be less effective in implementing the recently passed Sustainable Fisheries Act.

Tying Holistic Ecology to Ocean Governance

The need to better link ocean governance with the actual nature of marine ecological processes is underscored by the crude fisheries management presumed under UNCLOS III. Under that agreement, fisheries management worldwide is often conducted using a single-species sustainable yield curve to predict the total allowable catch for a targeted stock. This simplistic bell-shaped yield curve is designed to link the biomass of a species to levels of fishing effort. In theory, as long as a fishery's take remains on the ascending side of this curve, increasing efforts will safely and sustainably produce a larger take. But once the quantities of fish caught are plotted on the downward slope of the curve, greater fishing efforts theoretically mean decreasing catch and should be curtailed. Managers strive for maximum sustainable yield, statistically plotted at the apex of this curve.[74]

The belief that maximum sustainable yield can be consistently and accurately predicted is a basis for much of UNCLOS III policy on managing fisheries (such as Article 61), as well as the United States' Magnuson-Stevens Act, both of which anticipate harvesting fish stocks near the maximum sustainable yield. (The Magnuson-Stevens Act actually uses OSY, optimum sustainable yield, an approach that modifies standard maximum sustainable yield by factoring in economic, social, and environmental considerations.) Moreover, if a nation lacks the fleet capacity to harvest fish at maximum sustainable yield, according to UNCLOS III they should allow other nations to catch the "surplus" fish. The emphasis is thus on seeing fish as a global resource to be exploited to the fullest extent possible.

Yet as shown with collapses on Grand Banks and Georges Bank, a thorny problem is that maximum sustainable yield is devilishly hard to predict accurately. When New Zealand began a commercial fishery for orange roughy, it asked its fisheries biologists to forecast maximum sustainable yield for this sparsely studied species. Extrapolating from other species, scientists recommended a total allowable catch of 47,000 mt. But later studies showed this figure to be grossly exaggerated: it was six times too large. The total allowable catch was swiftly dropped to 7,500 mt, but the ecological damage from this folly had been done.[75] An individual specimen of orange roughy can live over a hundred years, but the fish were being harvested at much faster rates than were renewable.

Mistakes such as these highlight three areas where ocean governance has substantial room for improvement. These represent exciting opportunities for progress. First, politically drawn lines dividing land from sea and crisscrossing the oceans such as at three miles, twelve miles, or two hundred miles offshore, do not reflect ecological reality. In the words of Elliott Norse,

> The overwhelming fact of marine conservation is that the sea does not respect the imaginary lines that we put on maps. Rather it is replete with real lines; island arcs, barrier reefs, currents, boundaries of water masses, migration

routes, larval trajectories, the edges of species distributions. Some are reasonably fixed; others are fluid. Thus to more wisely maintain the sea's wealth, we must learn what the true lines are and respect them at least as much as we do legal boundaries that predominate on land.[76]

Doing so would constitute a large leap forward for ocean governance.

Second, the bureaucratic agencies whose portfolios include managing the sea are often too narrow in their outlook. A glance at the organizational charts delineating agency responsibilities such as for the U.S. Interior Department or the State Department reveal a confusion of cross-purposes. Crude problems still loom large today because modern governance is still rudimentary. Even though marine environments continue to deteriorate, Norse writes,

> governments' traditional response—to the extent that they have responded —has been to treat each economic or social sector's activities separately. Thus, there might be one law and set of regulations that deal with commercial fishing, another for pollution from factories, and still another for conversion of mangrove forests to build tourist hotels, all administered by different agencies. This sector-by-sector approach produces piecemeal decisions that are often at cross-purposes, as each agency applies its particular tools to the problem or protects its constituency by allowing it to externalize the costs of its activities.[77]

Third, some nations are exploiting or abusing the seas under their exclusive control without appropriate environmental safeguards. Thus the idea of bringing areas of the sea under national control is no panacea. One would think that the expansion of ocean areas brought under exclusive control in the later twentieth century should sensibly carry a closely linked duty of stewardship. So far, this has not been the case. New efforts are needed to capture the ecological and economic benefits that will follow from an improved ocean governance. This second-generation environmental approach should:

* be cross-sectoral, embracing all categories of marine ecosystems and species, all types of human use, and all sources of threats.
* govern actions on land as well as in the sea since much damaging impact on marine ecosystems originates on land.

- be capable of decentralization or cooperation across political divisions.
- have the flexibility to address changing priorities given new knowledge and varying circumstances.[78]

The question is no longer whether nations should have more control over broad zones of sea—that has been accomplished. Rather, it is how should nations begin to act to best conserve the marine resources and integrity of marine environments that have come under their control. We must begin by fashioning the basic framework of marine law and policy that better reflects the nature of the entire ecosystem. No matter how great the need, thorny political obstacles stand in the way.

Governance as Bounded Rationality and Incremental Decision Making

The difficulty of joining the laws of nature with the human laws that control the exploitation of marine resources was first evident in the late eighteenth century, which saw the origins of the three-mile limit. As discussed in chapter 1, both England and France were engaged in capturing each other's ships as prize off American shores and needed to know how far the area of neutrality extended into the sea. Yet President Washington was hindered in his efforts to select an appropriate U.S. neutrality claim, since the practices of European nations varied widely.[79]

France, however, continued to press its requests for a claim to neutral seas, so the young United States was forced to act. Diplomatic correspondence delivered in November 1793 thus tentatively claimed a narrow three-mile coastal belt for purposes of neutrality. Yet the U.S. leaders who invented the three-mile limit felt little affection for their creation. In fact, they explicitly stated that this narrow claim was temporary. Unexpectedly, the three-mile measure was seized on by the British, who recognized its advantage for allowing greater freedom of navigation; eventually it grew fixed and became a global standard.[80] And so unintentionally the three-mile limit became the basis of the division between state and federal authority that characterizes U.S. offshore federalism today.[81]

The decision to assert a three-mile claim is a fine example of what public policy and administration studies theorists describe as bounded rationality decision making.[82] The bounded rationality model, as proposed by Herbert Simon and James March, rejects the traditional assumption that policy decisions are normally reached through a rational process. They questioned the "rational-comprehensive" model of decision making, which assumed that a public decision maker had the luxury of a well-defined problem, with a full array of alternatives to consider, full baseline information and knowledge about citizens' values and preferences, and adequate time, skill, and resources with which to apply this data to solving a problem.[83]

The alternative March-Simon bounded rationality model makes no such assumptions about real-life decision making. Put in the context of ocean policy, President Washington was forced in 1793 to assert a stopgap U.S. claim in a pressing situation. Because harried American leaders expected their three-mile sea would be only temporary, they did not fully explore the consequences of their suggestion, nor could they have obtained full information about the consequences of pursuing various alternatives.

In fact, a decade later, Jefferson made it abundantly clear that the nation's first president had intended to assert a much broader neutrality claim but that he was pressed into deciding on this stopgap measure at the insistence of the French minister. This is how decisions are often made. Actual decision makers live in a messy real world in which they usually face ambiguous and poorly defined problems; incomplete information about alternatives, the baseline, the background of the problem, and the consequences of supposed alternatives; and are hampered by limited time, skills, and resources.[84]

Such was the tough decision-making environment faced by Washington and Jefferson. Washington seized upon a solution that fulfilled his immediate needs, regardlesss of its value in a broad or ecological sense.[85] To reiterate, this three-mile figure was never based on any consideration of the marine environment; it was merely a distance too narrow to engender political opposition.[86] Here policy theory provides some interesting observations. Regarding the choices made under conditions of bounded rationality, Charles Perrow notes,

> Given the limits on rationality, what does the individual in fact do when confronted with a choice situation? . . . Sometimes he must engage in prob-

lem solving. When he does so, he conducts a limited search for alternatives among familiar and well-worn paths, selecting the first satisfactory one that comes along. He does not examine all possible alternatives nor does he keep searching for the optimum one. He "satifices" instead of "optimizes." That is, he selects the first satisfactory solution rather than search for the optimum.[87]

The first satisfactory solution was not an optimum choice for the long run. The decision making here suggests what Charles Lindblom calls "muddling through," the incremental process whereby decision makers create new policies that are not much distinct from previous ones.[88]

Under Lindblom's incrementalism, the test for a good policy is simply to ascertain whether the chosen policy is generally agreed upon. (Three miles surely would have had opposition, had anyone realized at the time that this limit would eventually become a uniform rule for general purposes.) Viewed this way, the concept was good policy only because it had no opponents.[89] It was a short-term compromise, irrelevant to modern policy or good ecosystems management. Simply put, the practical politics that once led to this three-mile decision have no ecological relevance today.

State Governance of Marine Environments

Despite the argument for expanding states' rights seaward, it is critical to note that like federal officials, the states have not built an admirable record of conserving the coastal areas entrusted to them. Therefore, simply giving the states exclusive control of marine resources is not a solution. Instead, the argument for shared state-federal governance is based on a belief that cooperative management is preferable to exclusive division of federal from state control three miles from shore. Neither federal officials nor state agencies have done enough to tailor laws to ecological considerations; together, however, they might move in this direction.

States acting alone have done a remarkably poor job of managing marine resources, as shown by the important example of California. Its remarkably rich three-mile belt of coastal waters that stretches for roughly 1,100 miles is managed by the Department of Fish and Game, a subdivision of the California Resources Agency. With reason, the department is often criticized for the sharp declines in resources under its control such as rockfish, white sea bass, and abalone. These declines are partly the result of perennial underfunding that has only gotten worse. The department budget fell by some 60 percent from 1990 through 1996 to a remarkably low $3 million, which amounts to just $.11 per state resident.[90] Such a small budget reflects the low priority given to ocean management by the state. For example, the Department of Fish and Game was forced to sell three major ocean patrol vessels because operating costs were too high in relation to its puny budget. This despite the fact that enforcement is critical to preserving marine resources that are worth many times what this budget suggests. Federal agencies have not taken up the slack in patrolling ocean waters; one federal fisheries agent is responsible for all federal waters from Monterey to the Mexican border, an area of about 80,000 square miles. Only seven federal agents police the 197-mile-wide sea under federal jurisdiction.[91]

California's secretary of resources, Douglas P. Wheeler, acknowledges that the Department of Fish and Game neglects California waters. But it would be hard to contend otherwise. Under the nose of the department, estimated numbers of bocaccio (a popular and tasty rockfish) in the California ocean dropped about 80 percent between the 1970s and the 1990s. This is only one of many abuses. At the sparsely inhabited northern end of California's coast, abalone poaching is rampant. About 200,000 California abalone (big mollusks that can be pried from rocks in shallow waters) are now illegally poached each year, in large part because abalone fetch $20–$30 each, or $60–$80 per pound on the retail market. Every day up to $100,000 worth of abalone is illegally taken from that section of coast. Abalone are easily caught and their meat is delicious, which makes their fate unpleasant to ponder.[92]

The Department of Fish and Game is charged with managing the five commercial abalone species: white, red, green, black, and pink. Yet for decades that agency has curiously stood idly by while stocks of white abalone were decimated. As recently as the 1970s, between 80,000 and 140,000 white abalone were harvested each year. Despite obvious subsequent yearly declines in numbers—only twelve whites, or thirty-eight pounds, were commercially harvested in all of 1995—the Department of Fish and Game did not move to halt the white abalone fishery until 1996. Only eleven white abalone were found in a biological survey done by submarine at the Santa Barbara Channel Islands. In addition, black and green abalone were also hit by overfishing, as well as diseases like withering foot syndrome, possibly caused by pollution. Red abalone too were taken in significant numbers, declining by 67 percent from 1975 to 1995, before that fishery was finally halted. Abalone of all kinds covered California's rocky shores as recently as the 1950s; now their absence indicates an ecosystem in distress.[93] Ponder the profits and jobs this renewable resource could have provided, if adequately managed, and the scale of the decline becomes apparent.

All along the California coast, other ecological insults abound. In the fishing port of Bodega Bay, an investigation of the commercial fisheries found that over half a million pounds of assorted landings went unreported. Not reporting catch is a way of avoiding limits as well as shirking taxes, but it also severely skews catch data toward underestimating the total biomass removed from the sea. Harmful activity can occur in many forms. Whether it is outright poaching, taking a species beyond legal limits, failing to report a catch at the dock, improperly reporting on pink tickets that track total landings, reporting a high-value catch as a low-value one, or selling sport-caught animals on the commercial market, myriad activities add up to illegal removal of perhaps 43 to 64 million pounds of marine life per year. Recently one elaborate poaching ring was uncovered that had taken 20 tons of abalone, worth over $2.4 million, from the Sonoma County coast.[94] Of course, most fishermen and seafood processors are law-abiding and careful, but the illicit take is sizable.

Stopping such criminal activity has proven more difficult than it need be, in part because state and federal marine resource agencies have not cooperated. California has a useful computerized list of fish catch that it calls CMASTER, but this handy tool is not made easily available to federal law enforcement officials. According to one federal agent, simply gaining access to CMASTER is difficult: "We have to go through our general counsel, who will then go Fish and Game's general counsel, who will send the request to the marine statistics branch in Long Beach, who then sends it back to Fish and Game's counsel, who will send it back to our legal counsel, who will then get it back to us."[95] There is clearly much room for better cooperation.

In the heavily urbanized San Francisco Bay area, the state again fails to protect marine resources. A chronic abuse is the daily removal of and disturbances to marine creatures from nearby tidal pools. On a much bigger scale is the alarming fact that 92 percent of salt marshes and wetlands of the San Francisco Bay have now been destroyed. Ecological functions once performed by the marshes and wetlands such as filtering runoff or serving as critical nursery grounds for fishes like the halibut are lost. Moreover, chemical contaminants in California's wetlands may play a role in causing transitional cell carcinoma that has shown up in marine mammals. Cancer was found in an unusually high proportion of sea lions stranded on state beaches since 1979: 66 of 370 specimens. A cancer rate of nearly one in five specimens is reason for concern.[96]

In the heavily urbanized megalopolis that is southern California, even the normal daily flow of waste pollutes coastal waters. Southern California's population of 15 million contributes daily runoff to what is an ultimate downhill trash bin—the sea. Runoff comes from countless sources such as parking lots and streets, as well as farms, which contribute pollutants from pesticides, herbicides, and nitrogen-laden fertilizers. Each day Santa Monica Bay receives sewer waste piped throughout 5,000 miles of storm drains in the 414-square-mile Los Angeles watershed. On a dry day, roughly 200 drain outlets spew 10–25 million gallons of untreated "water" into Santa Monica Bay. On a rainy day, this release spikes to 10 billion gallons.[97]

Studies reveal that roughly 160 toxic chemicals are being released into Santa Monica Bay, such as polycyclic aromatic hydrocarbons (PAHs) linked to car exhaust from burning gasoline, old tires, and used motor oil, and volatile organic compounds (VOCs) associated with chemicals used for dry cleaning and household purposes. Now dolphins off the coast of southern California are found to have the most DDT ever measured in any marine mammal in the world. Similarly, all fish sampled in San Francisco Bay were found to have high levels of polychlorinated biphenyls (PCBs), a potent carcinogen that was once commonly used in industry. Many fishes also had measurably high contamination from mercury, dieldrin, chlordane, DDT, and dioxin.[98]

Until recently the state, as well as the federal government, had almost entirely overlooked the ecological problems caused by runoff. Yet this has been a death by a thousand cuts, with the ecology of coastal seas continuously assaulted day to day by "normally" polluting activities that are seldom given a thought. As noted by Jane Lubchenco, a marine biologist and president of the American Association for the Advancement of Science, "Excessive amounts of pollutants such as nitrogen from agriculture, sewage and lawn chemicals are, in fact, flipping natural systems over to a new state, totally changing marine ecosystems."[99] The fact that ecosystems may be switching over to new states owing to human activities, and in faster ways than are comfortable for complex social and political systems, should give us pause. Preventing harm may be the wisest strategy.

California has yet to establish cost-effective and forward-looking ways to prevent pollution. Quite the contrary: the state Department of Fish and Game is heavily criticized for failing to carry out even a traditional mission of managing areas under its jurisdiction.[100] But with ecological shifts occurring and other changes just beginning to be seen, like a drastic 80 percent decline in zooplankton off southern California (perhaps due to rising water temperatures, or possibly global climate change), it is time for a new course.[101] In sum, the states acting alone have not yet shown the will to initiate conservationist measures. The late 1990s have seen renewed public attention to the ocean in California, yet most of the new laws actually enacted concern highly specific issues that arise only at the margins of the problem. It is time to examine the big picture. Addressing declines in ecological health requires a concerted effort that unites federal, state, and local forces. Rather than muddling through, governance must be based on science. Even more than this, it must be based on the emerging principle of biological diversity.

Biological Diversity

The term *biological diversity*, or *biodiversity* for short, first appeared in its current form about 1980. Since that time, the concept has swiftly grown into a popular way of describing the diversity of life at several hierarchical levels of biological organization.[102] The term is now increasingly part of the environmental lexicon; however, many incorrectly assume that the idea of biodiversity exclusively means the diversity of species. In fact, it refers to three hierarchical levels: genetic diversity, species diversity, and ecosystem diversity. Genetic diversity, found at the most fundamental level, and ecosystem diversity at the broadest level of this hierarchy, are both very important, yet a midlevel *species diversity* is at present best understood.

As on land, the greatest degree of midlevel species diversity exists among smaller marine species like tiny diatoms or snails, rather than at the size of the larger species (such as sharks, whales, and mangrove trees). Until only a few decades ago, it was widely (and incorrectly) believed that the seas, especially in deep waters, boasted far fewer species than are found on land. An implication of that view was that the marine environment did not merit robust conservation efforts. So our attention has focused on conserving terrestrial biodiversity, such as in the rain forests. But more recent scientific insights show that at a basic taxonomic level comparing phylum to phylum to phylum, the marine realm in fact contains a richer diversity than on land. Steven Jay Gould and others call this other type of differentiation *disparity*, highlighting the fact that it is based on a divergence of body parts and of functions that adopt vitally contrasting approaches to life in the sea.[103]

Examine life on land, versus life in the sea, and one sees manifest differences with respect to biodiversity. On land, the great variety of species resulted from what is a splintering of species within just one phylum, Arthropoda. (*Phylum* refers to a basic, major grouping in animal taxonomy, below *kingdom*). On land, the many millions of species within the arthropod class Insecta are more numerous than all other terrestrial species.[104] However, insects have not done well in the marine context, so that major class is relatively absent there.

On the other hand, whole classes of (what are to us) unusual animal taxa occur exclusively in the marine sphere. Norse writes, "Thus, the sea hosts almost the entire extant variety of basic animal body plans, whereas land and freshwater animals comprise myriad variations on the theme of insectdom and just a smattering of other body parts."[105] Life in its greatest variety is biased toward marine environments. Of some thirty-three animal phyla on earth, all but one can be found in the sea. Meanwhile, of these, a full fifteen phyla including pervasive creatures like echinoderms occur only in the sea. The common sea star, for instance, belongs to the phylum echinodermata, which encompasses three different classes of animals, comprising roughly 3,600 species. Five more phyla are nearly 95 percent marine.[106]

Marine biodiversity is increasingly threatened by human activities, yet modern ocean and coastal governance fails to protect a precious ecological balance that has taken eons to build. Consider the functional extinction of the once vast valuable oyster reefs in Chesapeake Bay. A native oyster, *Crassostrea virginica*, supported an immense fishery. Yet it has been decimated over the last century by pollution, overfishing, dredging, siltation, and two diseases, "MSX" and "Dermo." Bay oysters were previously so profuse and essential that they were able to filter much of the bay's brackish water once a week; now a small remnant population requires an entire year to perform this same necessary ecological service.[107] Many believe that with the loss of oyster reefs as a keystone element of the ecosystem, the whole bay is now in an altered state.[108]

For the amazing and complex ways in which marine biodiversity can be lost, picture the impact of whaling. Whales are popularly seen as awesome creatures, and their decline due to whaling seems a loss of almost spiritual dimensions. But it was assumed that the ecological impacts were limited to whales alone. Now coming to light, however, are the myriad organisms of the deep oceans that depend on them. For the many sea creatures that rely upon organic materials raining down from the surface, the whales are especially important. Carcasses of whales dying in a natural setting will sink relatively swiftly, with much of their tissue left intact for consumption below. In many cases, creatures found exploiting lipid-rich skeletons are the same chemosynthetic-based community found at hydrothermal vents. Hence rather than being restricted, as was thought, only to hot seafloor vents, sulfur-reducing chemoautotrophic bacteria that support undersea communities are also nourished by whale carcasses. A National Research Council study concludes, "Whale skeletons scattered like islands in the deep sea may thus provide some of the critical stepping stones for organisms between hydrothermal-vent communities, themselves temporary and insular habitats."[109]

Seen this way, the fact that whale hunters after the start of the twentieth century retained the whole animal means that whaling has acutely decreased available supplies of nutrients. Loss of whale carcasses near the surface may mean at the seafloor "a severe spatial interruption, if not elimination, of dispersal corridors between reducing-habitat communities, with potentially marked alterations to biodiversity in hot-vent and cold-seep regions."[110] Humankind, clearly and in countless hidden ways, is recklessly altering marine biodiversity. But rather than reflecting a holistic concern for ecological processes, our ocean governance has reflected a process of muddling through that assumes the sea can absorb all harms. The way forward is plain: a better system of governance is one that prevents harm before it occurs.

Conclusion

Times change, and social values change with them. Major events that shaped the present ocean regime like President Washington's assertion of the three-mile limit, or Reagan's proclamation of a twelve-mile sea, have brought unexpected factors into play. As a result, mounting concerns today for greater ecological integrity are being poorly addressed by old and outdated marine policies. By simply dividing jurisdiction between states and the federal government, current regimes for ocean management "are intrinsically unstable. [We] are attempting to regulate ocean space as if it were land by drawing arbitrary boundaries through waters that constitute an ecological whole."[111]

It is time to move beyond mere muddling through. A more integrated governance is needed to better address the complex human impact on marine environments. This regime should consider not only short-term goals of maximizing the fish catch, or the amount of oil taken from beneath the sea, but also conservation, ecosystem function, as well as the rights of future generations.

The next chapters outline three important and obtainable goals as paths to improved ocean governance. First, federal agencies should cooperate with coastal states in managing ocean resources. Second, market forces should be harnessed to prevent ecological harm while reducing total energy demand, minimizing pollution, and improving efficiency. Finally, a new ocean governance should account for the interconnected *seascape*, a valuable idea for overcoming the conventional division of governance between the land and the sea.[112] Improved ocean governance demands increased attention to our actions on land.

II

The Present and Future

4

Fine-Tuning the Governance of Offshore Oil

> The reasonable man adapts himself to the world, the un-
> reasonable one persists in trying to adapt the world to
> himself.
>
> *George Bernard Shaw*

AFTER A HORRIFIC oil spill offshore Santa Barbara in 1969 and America's ripening environmental movement that followed, the cost of offshore development was for the first time widely seen as outweighing the benefits. An era dawned in which states no longer supported new offshore oil drilling without question. Since that time, the management of offshore oil has become unwieldy. States and the federal government have generally adopted sharply opposing policies;[1] except for Gulf of Mexico states and Alaska, most coastal states are strongly opposed to new offshore drilling, while federal agencies often seek to expand production.[2] The result is in-effective ocean governance.[3]

This archaic ocean regime fails to meaningfully involve all interested parties. Nor does it provide comprehensive thinking that considers ecology or other ocean users and concerns.[4] Indeed, if the basic policies underlying marine resources management were today reopened for serious debate, the states would hardly accept control over only a narrow three-mile belt, with the federal government controlling an area extending 197 miles out to sea. Because state control was separated from federal control of the outer continental shelf over forty years ago, that decision ought to be reconsidered in light of new realities.[5]

Change will not be easy. This chapter therefore suggests ways of fine-tuning the management of offshore oil and gas over the short term. The main solutions offered are, first, to build a state-federal partnership that can bring broader perspectives to offshore policy making, and second, to promote more efficient sources of energy to reduce the demand for offshore oil.[6] The goal is integrated management, which will require a greater role for the states. California's position is typical: "There should be no further leasing of [outer continental shelf] areas offshore of California." Oregon similarly opposes new offshore leasing; to be acceptable, a proposed lease sale in Oregon must be "part of a balanced national energy program."[7] In short, there is nothing magical about the three-mile limit and no reason why it should not be reexamined.[8]

The Benefits and Costs of Outer Continental Shelf Drilling

From a purely economic perspective, offshore oil and gas production in federal waters has major advantages for the federal government. Thus since 1954 the leasing and production of outer continental shelf oil and gas has brought over $100 billion into the federal treasury. In 1985, output from the outer continental shelf (OCS) amounted to about 13 percent of all U.S. oil production and some 25 percent of its gas supply.[9] "In the 34 year period starting in 1954 and extending to 1987, private oil and gas companies paid into the federal government $53 billion in pre-exploration (bonus) payments for the right to explore and, if fortunate, to extract oil and gas from these lands."[10] Since that short-lived spurt in activity, outer continental shelf oil represents about 11–12 percent of all U.S. oil production.[11]

Economic benefits also spill over into the coastal states and local communities where drilling takes place.[12] For instance, Santa Barbara County receives sizable economic largesse from adjacent OCS oil and gas production. In 1996 the oil industry spent a total of $320 million in the county. This included employing about 1,200 workers, or some 0.8 percent of all jobs. The industry contributed $14.5 million in property tax revenues, or 5.4 percent of the total.[13] About one-sixth of national offshore oil production comes just from the waters off Santa Barbara.[14] Moreover, offshore development also reduces the nation's reliance on imported oil. The oil and gas industry in Santa Barbara produces a daily average of 182,444 barrels (7.6 million gallons) of oil and 105 million cubic feet of natural gas. That amount of natural gas is sufficient to provide enough energy to supply the needs of about 7.5 million homes daily.

On the other hand, the substantial ecological costs of offshore oil extraction must also be reckoned with. Accounting for such intangible *costs* is much more difficult than simply tallying up the dollar benefits. At the outset it should be noted that the industry is thankfully far cleaner than it used to be because of increased regulation. For instance, seismic surveys of subsurface strata offshore were once crudely done with dynamite blasts, which wrecked undersea habitat and killed fish, whose carcasses floated to the surface by scores of thousands. Surveys are now done with air cannons that seem to have less acute impacts, although (as with much else associated with marine ecosystems) even here the consequences of this activity are still largely unknown.

Yet despite these efforts to tread more lightly, offshore development necessarily has many negative impacts. Offshore drilling, for example, entails the massive use of "drilling muds," a complex mixture of substances designed to lubricate and cool the drilling bit, regulate pressure in the well, and carry back drill cuttings. These muds may contain barium sulfate, emulsified oils, chrome lignosulfate, and sodium hydroxide, among other components.[15] The muds may also be toxic for local marine organisms, although here again the matter is subject to considerable debate.[16]

Regardless of whether drilling muds are toxic, they do have a major impact on the seafloor. The sheer amount of muds is quite imposing; in the 1980s an estimated 200,000 metric dry weight tons were discharged each year into the waters off California. The EPA estimates that "up to 1.5 million barrels of drilling muds, fluids and other waste products could be expected to be discharged into federal waters off the state's coast from future oil development."[17] And that massive discharge comes from routine operations, not from unexpected accidents.

Drilling muds are only one cost associated with offshore oil development. There are of course the well-known problems associated with drilling, such as air and water pollution, assorted negative impacts on wildlife, fisheries, and tourism—and the ongoing risk of spills, whether during the development, production, or transportation phases.[18] There is also an aesthetic matter: people simply do not enjoy the sight of oil rigs in coastal waters. The public may associate the most widely publicized spills like that caused by the *Exxon Valdez* disaster in 1989 with offshore drilling, but such events are more relevant to the transport of oil. Nonetheless, catastrophic spills at sea are symptomatic of our heavy reliance on imported oil, and therefore intimately tied to the larger problem.

Unlike federal government, many local and state authorities see the environmental costs of drilling for offshore oil as burdensome. As a result, state-federal tensions over offshore oil are now deeply mired in a repeating pattern. Elected officials in most coastal states are responsive to fervent public concerns over the environmental impacts of pumping offshore oil.[19] With the exception of states bordering the Gulf of Mexico and Alaska, coastal states are opposed to any new OCS development.[20]

Despite opposition, federal officials charged with managing the outer continental shelf have been aggressive proponents of development.[21] Defending the national interest, as perceived by Interior Department secretaries like James Watt or Manuel Lujan, often meant overriding state resistance to increased exploitation of offshore oil. Not surprisingly, profound mistrust has taken the place of cooperation and consensus building.[22] Santa Barbara County, for instance, voted to reject most industry proposals for more offshore development. They did not do so because oil reserves beneath the celebrated Santa Barbara Channel were depleted: of the valuable known reserves, not even half has been extracted, and 1 billion barrels of oil remains at the undeveloped lease sites.[23] Voters were more concerned about the subtle long-term ecological costs of OCS oil than immediate economic benefits.

Moreover, state and local officials do not support new oil development because the costs and benefits are unequally distributed.[24] Local concerns, often not adequately perceived by policy makers in distant Washington, D.C., are that valuable environmental quality is degraded, traditional life styles are disrupted, and the jobs created at offshore rigs or refineries may not go to local workers but to experienced oil hands from other areas. Biliana Cicin-Sain and Bob Knecht observe, "The benefits of offshore oil production tend to be distributed nationally, while the costs tend to be concentrated locally."[25] Federal officials may see exploiting offshore oil as a way to reduce the nation's dependence on foreign oil as well as enriching the Treasury. For them, outer continental shelf development reduces the national debt and trade deficit, makes fewer oil shipments by tankers necessary, and provides a secure supply of fuel for the nation.[26] But it is often at the local community level that ecological costs are appreciated (though the Gulf of Mexico shows a rather unique case). What are most important are the exciting opportunities for improvement that can now be explored.

Offshore Oil Development and Total Energy Consumption

The question of further development of the outer continental shelf is placed in a new perspective if one asks whether demand for energy can sensibly be reduced. There are vast economies yet to be realized. At present, nearly two-thirds of domestic U.S. oil consumption goes for transportation, primarily for auto fuel.[27] Meanwhile, structural distortions in prices increase our reliance on the least efficient means of transportation. These include the many subsidies to the oil industry to keep prices artificially low, which in turn create incentives to expand the size and thirst of American cars. Further, the costs of air (and subsequent ocean) pollution caused by burning gasoline and building expensive roads are externalized (not properly accounted for), since they are paid for out of general tax funds. Such systemic, hidden distortions obscure the actual costs of our wasteful use of energy.

Remarkably, however, economic distortions that affect energy demand are almost always ignored in policy debates over whether to allow new offshore oil drilling. In the words of the *Economist*, which has persistently called for a more fiscally rational energy policy in the United States, "Failure to price road-use properly leads to an inefficient use of resources. One of the costs not being taken into account [is] pollution—an instance of collective damage resulting from the sum of individual choices."[28] The larger picture includes energy demand.[29]

Reducing demand for energy would not only be economical but also bring about ecologically better policies. Yet it is assumed that the only recourse is to increase the supply of oil, rather than temper demand. Funding for conservation and finding alternative energy sources has nearly dried up. That retreat did not occur by accident. It occurred because conservation initiatives entail a degree of planning that was felt in the 1980s to violate the principles of the "free" market.[30] Thus despite the clear advantages of alternative energy sources like hydrogen power and fuel cells, solar power, and advanced energy storage technologies, the federal government was regarded as having no role to play in solving the problem of energy supply and demand.

This strange view of free-market orthodoxy has stymied useful anticipatory action. Meanwhile economic tools that have long been accepted on the energy supply side, like subsidies for fossil-fuel industries, are strangely regarded as inappropriate for alternative fuels. Such sentiments, when coupled with antipathy to a comprehensive energy policy, leave little room for federal programs, even though energy efficiency and conservation would mean a stronger economy in the long run.[31]

Most significant, however, is that our thinking about continental shelf oil misconstrues the true energy situation. It is actually impossible for offshore drilling to relieve the United States of its massive imports of foreign oil, which now account for over half the energy supply. Offshore production is unable to overcome U.S. reliance on imported oil because the continental shelf might provide only about "enough energy equivalent to fuel the nation for about 1,300 days at the current rate of consumption, which is roughly 17 million barrels per day; . . . as long as the country is dependent on oil, it will remain dependent on foreign sources."[32]

On the other hand, the numbers tell a much cheerier story on the demand side, for great savings can be realized. While estimates of OCS oil and gas resources are put at roughly 21 BBOE (billion barrels of oil equiv-alent), it is estimated that the oil that could be saved just by implement-ing better efficiency measures could amount to 45 BBOE by the year 2020.[33] One approach is suggested by Bruce Babbitt, who writes:

> A green tax could be promoted as the ideal link between the environment and economic growth, and it might be imposed by reducing other taxes an equal amount for each dollar of green tax—a dollar up and a dollar down. The ideal candidate for tax reduction has already been identified in current congres-sional debates as the payroll tax designated for Social Security.[34]

Energy savings might be earned by raising the mileage standards for auto-mobiles through a corporate average fuel efficiency system—though this useful standard was actually lowered in the 1980s. Recently we even moved backward: for the first time, new cars rolling off dealers' lots are less fuel-efficient than the older cars being retired. Despite this fact, a host of useful options include constructing houses and buildings with better in-sulation and creating economic incentives for the manufacture and use of more efficient light bulbs and appliances. Experiences in Japan and north-west Europe show that market-based strategies for encouraging energy efficiency do not mean a lower standard of living.

Nonetheless, a certain scarecrow image has been attached to energy con-servation in America. That negative image was put forth by opponents of conservation during the Carter administration, and the image stuck be-cause conservation technology was still rudimentary. It is time now to per-manently lay to rest the notion that better efficiency means "freezing to death in the dark." Though we hardly stop to think about it, a wide array of technological advances since the late 1970s have already brought con-siderable positive changes in life style and energy savings. Such changes in-clude the wide availability of smaller, more fuel-efficient cars, like the beautifully engineered Honda Civic, widespread use of computers for stor-ing data (reducing the use of paper), and compact fluorescent lightbulbs. Such advances save both energy and materials.

Contrary to popular opinion, the unexpected and painful oil price shocks of the 1970s also carried a silver lining. Over the long term, they helped to bring about a more energy-efficient nation. By the 1990s, more fuel-efficient American cars were distinctly quicker, sportier, and better-handling than U.S. models designed just two decades before. Spurred by Japanese competition, U.S. manufacturers were forced to make their own cars more efficient, and the state of the art and quality of their products improved as well. Much more can be done to encourage hybrid vehicles, light-weight composite body materials, and the use of alternative fuels.

An idea worth considering is an incremental increase in the federal tax of 18.3 cents per gallon of fuel. To propose a tax increase is always painful, and (not surprisingly) a Clinton proposal for a 10-cent-per-gallon tax increase raised such an outcry that it is unlikely that an energy tax will be proposed again soon. But for reasons besides issues of air pollution and global warming from greenhouse gases, a carefully tailored green tax on energy could be an incentive to increase fuel efficiency and encourage conservation. "Finding" energy this way can slow the increase in demand for oil while causing fewer distortions than either the personal income tax or the business income tax, both of which have the effect of discouraging work. By shifting the costs of pollution back to the heavy users of energy, a proper energy tax helps to correct distortions brought about by externalities. Or the "green" tax can combine environmental benefits with deficit reduction. All this and cleaner air and seas to boot.

Of course, in practice almost any policy calling for higher gasoline taxes, whether offset by reduced personal income taxes or simply advanced to promote better conservation and fuel efficiency, is never popular politics. Where to spend the revenue that results from such taxes is also a hot-button issue. When the Clinton administration proposed to use already collected gas tax revenues as a means to reduce the federal deficit (rather than for highways), the normally fractious fifty-two-member congressional delegation from California was united in opposition. Citing California's notoriously congested highways, they opposed spending on anything but roads. Never mind the fact that the federal gas tax itself had been created for other purposes in 1969, when Lyndon Johnson needed funds to mask the costs of the Vietnam War. But where the revenue from such a tax should be spent is a side issue.[35]

What is clear is that an energy tax represents a radical shift from recently popular politics and that any such proposal is sure to encounter significant political opposition. For instance, many conservatives may oppose it out of a general distaste for new taxes of any kind. Yet an energy tax is less distorting to the U.S. economy than other revenue-raising devices like an income tax, and thus a broad energy tax could be acceptable to some conservatives. And liberals might argue that a gas tax is regressive because gas is inelastic: as with food, people will still buy gas despite increases in price. Thus many liberals contend that a tax on gas will hurt the poor more than those better off, since the poor can least afford it. However, there are ways to redress this problem.[36] But energy efficiency can also be achieved without a resort to energy taxes.

Government leaders must first move beyond the lingering notion that a high consumption of energy correlates with a high standard of living. By the 1990s, high GNP growth is no longer associated with profligate use of resources. Consider an Asian tiger like Singapore, with phenomenal economic growth, yet without natural resources to speak of. On the other hand, Russia, which consumes huge amounts of energy, is still mired in poverty. In fast-growing Japan and Germany, gasoline is priced dearly, which in turn has created market incentives for energy efficiency and conservation. This has led to technological innovations there, which will soon prove an economic advantage. Federal officials in the United States ought to do something that does not come naturally. They should look for ideas to other nations and to states such as California that are now adopting progressive incentives for finding alternative energy sources and promoting conservation.

The states ought to serve as models for more proactive federal energy policy. Indeed, where forceful state action is not preempted by weaker federal requirements, California is doing a lot. It is fostering a growing interest in the production of hybrid and purely electric cars as a unique way of tackling air pollution. In 1990 the California Air Resources Board initiated a quest for cleaner vehicles by adopting tough rules to reduce air pollution. California originally required that 2 percent of the cars sold in state by big auto manufacturers be zero-emission vehicles (ZEVs) by 1998, and the proportion was to increase to 10 percent by 2003.[37] While those requirements were later pushed back, they are still a major catalyst.

Though General Motors made an early attempt at an electric car when it released the EV 1, that model suffered poor sales because it used lead-acid batteries for on-board power. These batteries are clearly impractical, since they are heavy and give only lackluster performance in everyday driving. Since 1990, when it first showed its exciting Impact concept car at auto shows, GM has made strong statements about green technology, but its lineup of available products has been limited.

Contrast that with work now being done, for instance, at Toyota, Honda, and Daimler (Mercedes)-Chrysler. A new Toyota Prius is already on sale in Japan; this hybrid vehicle uses a small gas motor on the highway and switches to an electric powertrain for city driving. That approach significantly lowers emissions, provides for better gas mileage, and conveniently uses existing gasoline stations. For in-town commuting, Toyota is developing an entirely electric car that uses advanced nickel-metal-hydride batteries. And Honda is working on several projects, including a gasoline engine achieving close to zero emissions.

Perhaps the most exciting of new green technologies is the fuel cell. While the fuel cell concept was first described in 1839, this keen idea went neglected through the twentieth century because its use proved too costly for all but the most specialized of applications (such as powering spacecraft). The fuel cell is an electrochemical device that generates electric power by reverse electrolysis—that is, by combining hydrogen and oxygen. A key advantage is that the fuel cell works cleanly, without the combustion that produces pollutants. The only pollution from its operation is water vapor and heat.

A breakthrough recently occurred when a novel proton exchange membrane system was developed that allows fuel cells to be built far more cheaply than before, using a bit of platinum as the catalyst. Daimler (Mercedes)-Chrysler quickly partnered with a Canadian company that had developed this technology, and they now hope to bring out fuel cell–powered cars and buses early in the twenty-first century. Indeed, Daimler-Chrysler already has prototype fuel cell buses operating in Chicago and is fast improving its NECAR (new electric car) technologies that use methanol to supply hydrogen on board.

Such swift advances by Daimler-Chrysler has stirred interest among U.S. car companies. The Ford Motor Company took a large step in 1998 when it invested some $600 million in the company developing the fuel cell technology, partnering with that company and with Daimler-Chrysler (which earlier invested $450 million). And a subsidiary of General Motors is working on reactors that can strip hydrogen from gasoline, allowing existing gas stations to provide hydrogen fuel. Ironically, however, Daimler-Chrysler has seized a real lead in fuel cell–powered cars. After all, it was Daimler-Benz that first created the gasoline-powered car more than a century ago.[38]

Yet many obstacles remain. Popular automobile magazines for enthusiasts have been wedded to traditional internal combustion engines and until very recently were loath to consider alternatives. Their writings helped to fuel the demand for big, pavement-pounding machines whose thirsty engines are part of the petroleum-consuming status quo. More important is the unwillingness of most political leaders to break free of the cheap oil scenarios of the past. We have become accustomed to paying less for fuel at a gas station than for milk or even bottled water bought in a store. This culture helps explain federal efforts to encourage continental shelf oil production, despite intense opposition from coastal states and environmental groups.[39]

Whatever energy path is taken, and despite inevitable short-term price gyrations downward, gasoline will grow more dear in the next century. Over the long run, demand will eventually outstrip new finds like the oil fields discovered by the Caspian Sea. Indeed, the limits of the finite oil supply are certain to be felt in the twenty-first century. In the meantime, it is implausible to expect that the coastal states that have long opposed OCS development will embrace a push for offshore drilling. But federal ocean agencies could act now to build better partnerships with the states.[40] To accomplish this partnership, legislative amendments will be necessary. Part of any integrated ocean regime must be designed to better account for states' rights and ecological concerns.[41] Thus stewardship and good governance are intertwined.[42]

Challenging the Notion of Exclusive Federal Control

Ocean management is built on dual federalism, or a sharp division in authority between the states and the federal government whereby each remains supreme in its own sphere.[43] A geographic dualism has long been in effect in ocean management, demarcated by the three-mile line. But this

scheme encourages the assumption that coastal states have no valid interest in federal OCS activities. Why should states be largely prohibited
from authority beyond three miles? Two assumptions have propped up this
regime.

First, a divided ocean management may have intuitive appeal because
of its sheer simplicity. But finding the appropriate balance between state
versus national interests is not so easy.[44] Thus, "No fully satisfactory standard is at hand for locating the divide where the full sovereignty of a state
ends and that of the United States begins." Among ocean policy subsectors
are fisheries (management), endangered species (protection), and offshore
oil (development), each of which displays a unique pattern of state-federal
relations due to specific circumstances. To characterize all of these as best
represented by a particular dominant model of federalism is misleading.[45]
In this case it may be best to follow Einstein's sage advice that "things
should be made as simple as possible but never simpler." The present three-
mile state-federal division is just too simple. It belies the vast ecological
complexity of the fluid marine environment.

Along these lines was the Supreme Court's reasoning in its seminal 1947
decision in U.S. v. California (332 U.S. 19), in which it held that the federal government alone had paramount rights offshore. In the majority opinion, "The farther seaward the marine area lies, the more preponderant the
federal interest; the further landward the area, the greater the state interest." Yet, on the contrary, national interests such as defense do not grow
weightier with the distance seaward. Thus coastal states are sure of protection by a common military defense, whether attacked by land or sea.
And so a case for exclusive federal control offshore ought not be based upon
a presumed stronger national interest.[46]

A second assumption also has been key in justifying federal control offshore. Based on the idea of "uniformity versus diversity," it implies that
coastal waters beyond three miles need disinterested, uniform management. But this too is a flawed rationale for limiting states' rights. This argument holds that the federal government alone is capable of an objective
overview, yet it does not explain why a federal agency should be thought
of as disinterested. A federal agency might actually take a position "more
parochial, bureaucratic, or provincial than any that the states might wish

to pursue," writes Milner Ball.[47] Such a federal agency is not capable of "overviewing"; if federal officials have an "overview," are states considered to have an "underview"?[48] Whether or not they take positions less parochial than those of coastal states, federal agencies do not have a magic wand that makes them better run or less affected by pressures than states.

Finally, to assume that the federal government should have exclusive control beyond three miles overlooks several important instances in which diversity could serve U.S. national interests. The U.S. coastal sea is very long, varied, and heavily utilized in many places. Some areas require protection, for example, as genuine ocean sanctuaries where fishing is not permitted. To place everything beyond three miles under uniform control is to adopt a "one-size-fits-all" approach. This approach may cause U.S. federal officials to overlook the many local areas that merit special protection.[49]

Moving Toward Cooperative Governance

Near-term steps can be taken to move toward cooperative ocean governance. For example, a national commission might be created by Congress to examine the topic; the administration could set up a high-level working group; there could be a state-federal interagency task force; or a National Research Council committee might be commissioned akin to the earlier Stratton Commission.[50] This chapter will offer specific, narrowly tailored legislative changes designed to enhance the states' role. These suggestions would not necessarily mean an increase in continental shelf oil production. Instead, adding the states' perspectives to ocean management could result in complex planning, something even less streamlined than at present. Conflict might be formalized, as states opposed to development are allowed their say. Yet arguably these are justifiable results, given the positive role of dissent in a democracy and the importance of promoting healthy marine ecosystems.

Those who oppose extending state jurisdiction because it would disturb the current state-federal "balance" need only look at the situation as it now exists. While the federal government may seem to control the continental shelf, in reality this is hardly the case. The current supposed dual federalism cannot account for the fact that states are extremely effective in halting new federal development of the shelf through offshore drilling moratoria created in Congress and through the federal budget process.[51]

Members of Congress can insert language into appropriations bills that prevents spending federal dollars for new offshore exploration and development. This action, which shuts down offshore leasing, is an "end run" around the normal expectation that ocean policy should be made by the executive branch.[52] It allows the states, acting through Congress, to prohibit new development, although theoretically they do not play a key part in planning.[53] The fact that the states have found it necessary to oppose federal plans by a back-door approach strongly implies that current governance and its options for state input are inadequate.[54]

States are aided here by nongovernmental organizations that seek to work in the public interest.[55] Sally Fairfax observes that their joint success is owed to a new opportunism, a reorientation of federalism.[56] State governments are now in some instances seen as more competent, capable, and accessible than the national level. Defending states' rights was once a way to avoid federally mandated racial integration; to get to this point, southern states have thankfully "shed their malodorous affiliation with racial oppression" once sanctioned by state law.[57] Race relations gave such a bad name to states' rights that in 1964 it could be said that "if in the United States one disapproves of racism, one should disapprove of federalism."[58] But states are now "competent participants in policy making and implementation: an appropriate target of opportunity for [environmental] advocates dissatisfied by federal response to their entreaties or seeking a solution closer to home."[59]

The most appropriate role for the federal government could be to set minimum environmental standards for the nation as a sort of "floor" beneath which the less ecologically aware states would not be allowed to fall. Such a role would recognize and respond to the perverse economic incentives that might otherwise encourage waste and pollution. "Dirtier" states already permit relatively more pollution to promote cheap manufacturing and to lure businesses from other states. Only the federal government can prevent a further trend in that direction and a race to the bottom. With federal law serving as an environmentally stringent floor, states should then be encouraged by market-based incentives to function as fifty laboratories in which rigorous new policies are formulated.

Given such flexibility, the ways of extending coastal states' authority are limited only by one's imagination. Three possibilities are distilled here, all of which require congressional action. Note that little is expected from the judicial branch: in offshore matters, "the Supreme Court, more often than not, has tended to make judgments against the states."[60] This fact, coupled with a general sympathy in Congress for states' rights arguments and its ability to write desirable legislation directly, rather than wait for some new judicial departure, indicates that Congress is the most appropriate forum for enhancing the states' role.

The simplest method is to amend current law so that the federal government must share a greater percentage of OCS revenues with states. Along these lines, the coastal states have already reached a compromise with the federal government whereby they receive 27 percent of the revenues from the oil pools situated from three to six miles offshore.[61] The Coastal Energy Impact Program from the 1970s did allow the coastal states a portion of revenues from offshore drilling in response to the negative impacts of continental shelf development, but that program was curtailed in the early 1980s by an unsympathetic administration. Nonetheless, shared governance based on revenue sharing alone would be an unlikely objective. Because this option does not also give states any new *authority* beyond three miles, it would be a nonstarter for environmental NGOs and many coastal states.

A second and still moderate option is to extend, by act of Congress, limited authority for the coastal states beyond three miles. In essence, this is a more robust version of the powers conveyed by the Coastal Zone Management Act of 1972.[62] Such a change would create a new zone of shared state-federal jurisdiction extending three to twelve miles (a figure derived from the 1988 proclamation of a twelve-mile U.S. territorial sea).[63] Under this regime, the coastal states that wished to do so could share authority for ocean governance with the federal government.[64]

A third statutory option is to amend the Submerged Lands Act of 1953, as well as the Outer Continental Shelf Lands Act of 1953, to simply extend exclusive state control from three miles to twelve miles offshore. Moving state authority to a twelve-mile limit would displace the exclusive control that the federal government now enjoys between three and twelve miles. The major drawback is that the old geographic dual federalism would remain, with the division moved nine miles seaward. Clearly that is a poor option. It is also highly unlikely that inland states would agree to such a giveaway of ownership, because of the loss of OCS revenues that now flow to the federal treasury.

Over the near term, then, the second view is the best of the three. That approach calls for building a cooperative state-federal governance by making incremental amendments to existing statutes.[65] Initially this could be undertaken within the new three-to-twelve-mile zone created by the Reagan Proclamation. Later, with the benefit of experience, shared governance might be built throughout the 200-mile zone of U.S. authority offshore.

There will be opposition to giving such authority to the coastal states, partly because more environmentally activist states like Oregon, Florida, and California would probably seek to prohibit all new oil development within twelve miles. Coastal states might move en masse to ban new continental shelf oil and gas development within a shared three-to-twelve-mile zone. A huge swath of the shelf would be placed off limits. Yet shared governance is worth seeking. It provides equitable ocean governance that is cognizant of states' rights, and—what is more important—this joint approach can provide sounder protection for the marine environment. Shared governance will probably not increase offshore development, but then ocean governance policy should hardly be directed to that end, nor is it a proper measure of success.

Realistically, ecological arguments for shared governance alone would not be sufficient to persuade Congress to extend state jurisdiction. But one powerful impetus for overhauling the law is that cooperation is essential if OCS planning is to go smoothly. The states have blocked attempts to develop not just the frontier areas of contintental shelf, but also proven production sites. A case in point is Chevron's Point Arguello project near Santa Barbara. It cost $2.5 billion to build and sits on an oil field estimated at 300 million barrels, yet local opposition effectively postponed its start-up for a lengthy period.[66] Given the importance of improving this system, how, specifically, can management be improved?

Drafting Laws and Bureaucratic Culture

To arrive at a better direction for OCS governance, it is well to examine the mistakes in the Outer Continental Shelf Lands Act of 1953
(OCSLA). Just as important are the 1978 amendments to that act, which
effected substantial changes.[67] A leading goal of that new language was to
enhance the state role in planning offshore development. Drafters of the
amendments hoped they would provide "an opportunity for [states] to par-
ticipate in the decisionmaking process with regard to the overall leasing
program . . . involving states in the process from the beginning should
avoid time-consuming lawsuits later." The 1953 act had given the states almost no role in planning, creating virtually a closed-door process whereby
federal officials and industry made all decisions. By the 1970s it was felt
that a greater state role was needed.[68] But there were also many other pressing reasons for amending the law. The oil price shocks of the 1970s had
sent an outraged public to Congress demanding answers. The OCSLA
amendments were one response, and among other things their intent was to
expedite continental shelf oil development. But balancing a stronger state
role with a competing goal of facilitating development was no simple task.[69]

Now more than twenty years later, many members of Congress still feel
that the 1978 OCSLA amendments as implemented do not give the states
an adequate voice.[70] They have responded by persistently invoking moratoria, indicating that mechanisms designed for domestic cooperation have
failed. Like a canary in a coal mine, the moratoria show that this law has
not provided the effective state voice envisioned by the law. In hearings
held in 1989 on improving OCSLA, Leon Panetta, U.S. representative
from California, remarked:

> From the President to the Congress to the State Legislature and the com-
> munities, there is a universal sense that the OCS Lands Act does not work,
> and we are ad hocking day to day. That is not the right approach, as I see it.
> It makes no sense to continue this kind of guerrilla warfare when it comes to
> an important resource or the importance of trying to protect sensitive areas
> of our coastline. For that reason, I would strongly recommend that the Con-
> gress has to take another hard look at the OCS Lands Act. . . . Unless this
> Congress is willing to look at the entire law, we are going to operate on the

basis of two things: Leadership or crisis. Right now, very frankly, we are operating by crisis when it comes to the OCS Lands Act.[71]

Does this pessimistic evaluation of the OCSLA amendments mean they represent a failed policy? Success and failure are slippery, subjective concepts when applied to policy, but considering that the 1978 amendments were expected to provide increased OCS production and relief for a nation too dependent on foreign oil, then by almost any measure they have failed.[72] As Cicin-Sain and Knecht observe, "Uncertainty and delay are costly to the industry; the predictability that the federal government seeks in the oil program is elusive; and other ocean users, state and local governments and the interested publics, must expend inordinate amounts of time in virtually continuous maneuvers of one sort or another."[73]

Moratoria are regarded by proponents of offshore drilling as a major problem. Yet it should be recalled that even if development were accelerated, this would not resolve the nation's continuing dependence on foreign oil. A congressional subcommittee on fixing the problems of the OCSLA amendments opened a session with this comment:

> The Subcommittee will proceed today from the presumption that the objectives of the OCSLA are not being met. Despite the need to harness additional energy resources, despite the need to reduce our imports of foreign oil and the widely recognized need to reduce our dependence on tanker-transported oil supplies, the OCSLA program is essentially shut down. The Act is not guiding the orderly and timely development of the OCS while providing for the protection of the marine and coastal environment. Whether or not the fault lies with the Act itself or elsewhere, the OCSLA program is essentially shut down.[74]

Tension on this issue stems from a perception that states do not have an adequate voice.[75] However, this raises a dilemma both as to the actual intent of the OCSLA amendments and the best scheme for intergovernmental relations offshore. Did the amendments' drafters intend to give states a truly effective voice in planning? Or were the amendments intended to limit the states to a mere advisory role in national decision making? This is difficult to answer, for the law is ambiguous.

The range of opinions on this issue is diverse. In the 1989 hearings on improving OCSLA, Rep. Leon Panetta of California lauded states' rights provisions in the amended act but criticized its national implementation: "The basic philosophy, the basic intent of the OCS Lands Act was a legitimate one and its basic goal was a legitimate one. Unfortunately, what happened was that in the process of trying to implement that Act, it has become grossly distorted." But a representative from Massachusetts claimed that structural defects in the amendments give states an inadequate role, citing the inherent "imbalance that exists between [national concerns for] development and [state concerns for] environmental protection." Ralph Regula, representative from Ohio, faulted various coastal states for allegedly seeing greater states' rights provisions within the act than were actually there, declaring, "I would remind the members of the Committee that the operative law at the moment says that the OCS is a vital national resource."[76]

Perhaps the most accurate interpretation of the amendments is that they were meant to denationalize what had been almost exclusively a federal process.[77] Congress clearly did not intend the amendments to give coastal states a role equal to that of federal officials, but they were also not to be relegated to mere supplicants in a largely federal process, either.[78] The states' role in outer continental shelf management is less than some proponents bargained for, but this need no longer be so.[79] Members of Congress have again begun to consider specific problems and identify changes that would strengthen the states' hand.[80]

The Problem of Ambiguous Program Objectives

The 1978 OCSLA amendments were so vague that they could be interpreted to give the states only limited power to object to offshore development on environmental grounds. Whereas they contained ample latitude meant to give the states a stronger role, federal officials did not interpret them that way. A policy model framework created by Paul Sabatier and Daniel Mazmanian helps to explain why specific language in the amendments failed to give the states a stronger voice.[81]

According to Sabatier and Mazmanian, to be most effective a regulatory program should include specific criteria. First, the legislation should mandate "policy objectives that are clear and consistent or at least provide substantive criteria for resolving goal conflicts."[82] Put another way, ideal performance is difficult when statutory objectives are in conflict, ambiguous, or lack priority ranking.[83] Yet objectives are rarely precisely stated. Because of political pressures, lawmakers often phrase the language of a proposed law in general terms to achieve consensus. Allowing some ambiguity in a statement of objectives is a simple way to avoid the political opposition that could defeat a bill.[84]

The objectives of OCSLA, as amended, are neither clear nor consistent. National interests are given some priority, but how far the state can influence new development of the continental shelf is unclear.[85] This ambiguity is evident in the act's statement of objectives, and the result is much confusion. While the amendments were intended to enhance the states' role offshore, ambiguity has led to a policy breakdown. For instance, the amendments provide that if federal aims should conflict with state interests, the ultimate decision rests with federal officials. Even when the goals of a statute are internally consistent (which is not the case here), some qualitative and/or quantitative standards may still be helpful for measuring the full performance of implementors.[86] Moreover, if federal officials oppose a state's conservation efforts, the potential for state participation in offshore planning is significantly reduced. Problems thus rest not only with ambiguity, but also (from the states' perspective) with the goals themselves. Objectives must be clarified to make the states' role clearer.

Incorporating State Concerns into OCSLA

The law should be designed so as to compel officials to implement it as required.[87] Thus this law should structure the OCS planning process so as to incorporate the states' perspective; this approach would mean less state-sponsored litigation and a generally more cooperative relationship. Three major conditions are necessary: (1) a statute should assign implementation to an agency that supports its objectives; (2) it should minimize the number of veto or clearance points by providing enough inducements and sanctions to assure acquiescence by target officials or agencies; (3) it should bias decision rules of the implementing agencies in favor of adhering to statutory objectives.[88]

The first condition means that the OCSLA amendments should assign implementation to an agency whose officials are at least sympathetic to the desired goal—in this case, extending state regulation beyond three miles. A case study of the California Coastal Commission indicates that this condition was there adequately met. An activist commission showed concern for the environment from the start, so that the Coastal Act was carried out by an agency that gave conservation goals some weight. Of course, the political appointment process for commissioners has meant that the California Coastal Commission has gyrated between rather strong environmental protection to periods of antienvironmental sentiment; however, compared to the federal Minerals Management Service (MMS) it has often been a friend of environmental protection.[89] In the case of federal management of offshore oil and gas resources, however, the results are radically different.

The federal agency now administering the development of the continental shelf is the Minerals Management Service within the U.S. Department of Interior.[90] Like the California Coastal Commission, the Minerals Management Service, created in 1982, is a relatively new body. But unlike the Coastal Commission, whose goals included protecting the environment and assuring public access to the beach and to the sea (new concepts for a state agency), the MMS primarily administers oil and gas production. Hence its forerunners were the federal agencies that had overseen offshore development during the Tidelands Controversy of the 1930s through 1950s. Even the same personnel were transferred from those agencies when the Minerals Management Service was created. Some background about these forerunner agencies provides some clues as to the MMS's current organizational goals and ethic.[91]

Responsibility for supervising exploration and development had formerly fallen to the Conservation Division of the U.S. Geological Survey. The Geological Survey brought a predominantly scientific orientation to its work, revealed by how it administered OCS development until the creation of the Minerals Management Service. At that time, the supervision of lease auctions and revenue collection was transferred from the

Bureau of Land Management to the Minerals Management Service in 1982.[92] Because its staff included scientists carried over from the Geological Survey, the Minerals Management Service was staffed from its birth with career personnel who favored relying on scientific expertise in decisions about offshore leasing. They generally distrusted the power of the free market alone to allocate the size and location of oil tracts. However, the high value they placed on science and government planning was soon challenged.

Significantly, the birth of the Minerals Management Service in 1982 coincided with the Reagan administration's emphasis on freeing up market forces. This objective was emphasized at the new agency.[93] Federal policies regarding the continental shelf suddenly shifted away from government planning and toward greatly expanding industry's influence over leasing allocations. The unsurprising result was a split in the agency's organizational ethic. At the top, political leaders installed during the Reagan years placed an unprecedented emphasis on developing natural resources in an accelerated fashion. Market forces were more important to agency heads than pursuit of exacting scientific management by geologic specialists.[94] Because political appointees took a less selective approach to offshore management, tremendous offshore leasing tracts were soon being offered at very low prices. Soon the MMS initiated a novel "areawide" approach to leasing that was designed to give the oil and gas industry new access to tremendous swaths of the continental shelf at very low cost per acre.

The consequence was an avalanche of criticism and widespread charges in the 1980s that leasing had become "a disposal program whose success might be measured by the extent of transfers to the private sector."[95] No longer guided by its earlier organizational ethic steeped in respect for scientific expertise and selective leasing, and showing a newfound affection for areawide leasing and profits, the agency generated billions of dollars for the U.S. Treasury. The various taxes, rents, and royalties from offshore oil production became a significant source of federal revenue, which made expanding offshore oil production doubly important at the MMS. Significantly, at the powerful Office of Management and Budget, revenue generated by outer continental shelf leasing, not sensitivity to coastal states' objections to offshore development, was regarded as a key indicator of the agency's overall performance.[96]

The United States' enormous dependence on oil, together with the treasury's reliance on OCS revenues, contributed to a singularity of purpose at the MMS.[97] Its performance was often viewed in terms of efficiency, meaning efficiency in leasing offshore oil tracts to a willing industry. Yet MMS performance could also be measured in terms of the tracts not leased—for instance, out of ecological concern. The agency's objectives ought to be diverse enough to prevent it from being forced in a single direction by powerful economic forces.

In encouraging development of the outer continental shelf, the MMS was only acting in accordance with its mandate and the overall intent of the OCSLA amendments. But when it comes to sympathetically implementing aspects of the law highlighting environmental protection, then arguably the agency falls short. One problem is that OCSLA assigns to the MMS alone the task of judging states' objections to offshore development —and by its design and culture the agency is likely to favor, not resist, new development. The MMS is clearly no Environmental Protection Agency, and it would be extremely hard for it to act like one. But because it is assigned the difficult task of balancing state and national interests, its organizational ethic and values are vital issues.

The MMS has little incentive to give coastal state policies the consideration they deserve. Lacking a very clear statutory directive, the agency is unlikely to see requests from assorted environmental NGOs, coastal states, and others to set aside large areas of the continental shelf as viable or reasonable options. The agency's organizational ethic attracts a certain type of manager, which constrains the range of options considered feasible. Adding to the problem, the goals of the agency are already weighted toward resource extraction. In a classic study of the U.S. Forest Service, Herbert Kaufman analyzes the impact of organizational ethic on agency officials. He concludes that agency personnel conform to policy by doing "as a matter of personal preference the things that happen to be required."[98]

A similar situation occurs at the Minerals Management Service, where persons drawn to that agency typically seek to do what the agency considers right: to expand offshore development. In another work, Kaufman discusses why organizations tend not to change. Inertia is created not only by the preselection of specific types of individuals, but also by the way in which proper behavior is programmed within the group. Kaufman observes,

> Important as preservice and selection processes are in producing personnel with the appropriate predispositions and abilities, it is within the organizations that the fitting of the individual to the requirements of the system takes on particular intensity. The organizations proceed methodically to try to shape the values and perceptions of new members, and to instruct them in what they must do if they would like to get ahead. The initial match of candidate to system is at best a rough approximation; the fine adjustments take place later on.[99]

Given the vagueness of the act's goals regarding what weight should be given to states' objections, when push comes to shove the MMS favors new OCS activities. The MMS already has several reasons for permitting the expansion of offshore oil production, such as reducing imports, securing energy supplies, and bringing in revenues; as a result, it has less incentive to encourage compliance with another objective, giving states a stronger voice in governance. There is no simple legislative fix here other than to let the bureaucratic culture evolve, such as through future OCSLA amendments that would be designed to facilitate cooperation in ocean management.

Obtaining Target-Group Compliance

Another issue concerns this law's "veto/clearance points," which means that future changes to the OCSLA should be designed so as to minimize resistance by federal officials or should contain inducements to encourage their attention to state ocean policies.[100] Yet two primary veto points in the law now frustrate the states' attempts to achieve more than a supporting role. One is Section 18, which is ironically intended to give states influence in decision making early on, at the lease planning stage. The section requires federal officials to design a five-year plan consistent with "laws, goals, and policies of affected states," as identified by state governors.

In practice, however, Section 18 has not been an effective tool. Although designed to involve states in the planning process, it only requires the interior secretary to accept state recommendations if they are determined by the secretary to be in the national interest.[101] In practice this has meant that under a pro-drilling secretary like James Watt, even forceful objections to new offshore development at the program stage can be too easily rejected. Section 18 has thus not had its intended effect. A solution would be to mandate greater emphasis on state concerns.

A second veto point is Section 19 of the amendments to OCSLA, intended to give coastal states a voice regarding specific lease sales.[102] It requires the secretary to accept a state's comments if determined to be a "reasonable balance between the national interest, and the well-being of the citizens of the affected state."[103] When comments were rejected, opponents have resorted to litigation, often successfully.[104] However, as with Section 18, the interior secretary ultimately has final say as to whether to accept a governor's recommendations. For this reason, OCSLA needs to be further strengthened. Protecting both states' rights and the environment are important enough objectives to be written into a law that should be amended once again.

Incorporating Supportive Decision Rules in OCSLA

A final goal is to put useful decision rules in a statute that bias an implementing agency toward a desired outcome. One way to get favorable results when drafting a statute is to pay careful attention to the burden of proof.[105] If a secretary of the interior denies a state's comments under Sections 18 or 19, the outcome of a lawsuit challenging that denial will depend heavily on where the burden of proof is placed—and how stringent it is. To an attorney this is no surprise, as many a lawsuit hinges on burden of proof. Yet the public is not aware of that fact. Here, significantly, the burden of proof falls on the state: a state must demonstrate why a secretary's decision to deny its objections should be reversed by a court. Yet to do so, a state must demonstrate that the secretary's decision is "arbitrary and capricious."[106] It is difficult to meet this standard, since it requires a state to show that a secretary's decision lacked a sound basis. (To rebut the allegation of "arbitrary and capricious" action, an interior secretary need only show that some consideration was given to the state's objections before they were rejected.)

This difficult standard was not written in by Congress but was imposed later by the courts, which substituted it for the original law's more easily met "substantial evidence" requirement.[107] As a practical matter, being held only to an "arbitrary and capricious" standard does little to encourage an interior secretary to accept a state's recommendations. This makes it easier to come down in favor of federal policies for new offshore development, even if that view conflicts strongly with the state's position. Amending legislation has been introduced in Congress to overturn this standard regarding the burden of proof and to require the secretary of the interior to accept a governor's recommendations unless it can be shown that they do not provide a reasonable balance of state and federal interests. This change would place the burden on the secretary to show why a state's recommendations are unreasonable. Hildreth suggests a prioritized list for determining the fate of state objections. The secretary would "give greater weight to traditional state concerns such as the risks of oil spills, the lack of onshore support facilities, and conflicts with commercial fishing activities."[108] Prioritizing may enhance states' input by compensating for the vagueness of statutory objectives; it could also constrain the secretary's discretion to act as a veto/clearance point.

Certainly, the law needs to better recognize the fact that federal bureaucrats may be less responsive to concerns over ecological degradation than state and local leaders, who are much closer to the problems caused by offshore development and pollution.[109] Given the aggressive prodevelopment approach of the 1980s, when federal officials largely ignored states' rights provisions, such vagueness is especially fatal. The act needs to specify more exactly "that preserving our environmental and coastal resources is as important as finding oil and gas."[110] Similarly, Section 18 should be amended to make it clear that "in preparing a leasing program, protection of the environment and of coastal resources is to be given as much weight as the recovery of hydrocarbons."[111] And states ought be allowed to require that any new leasing plan make more rigorous provisions for environmental protection. Van de Kamp and Saurenman suggest that the secretary should "be required to accept [states'] reasonable recommen-

dations concerning the leasing program. [Further,] these alterations to Section 18 should lead to leasing programs which are far more specific and
which, because of the increased role played by the states, are more free
from controversy and thus easier to implement."[112]

In sum, the energy scenario of the 1990s is far different from that of the
1970s, when energy price shocks sent a vulnerable United States and a
startled Congress searching for ways to expedite domestic oil development. The outcome was the 1978 amendments to OCSLA, which paid
only modest attention to states' rights and environmental protection. The
political and energy scene has shifted markedly since then. The states'
rights movement, as well as better conservation and efficiency technologies, can point toward beneficial changes that should be made in ocean governance. Over the short term, change will be only incremental. But
observers of ocean governance now recognize that it is time to go back and
amend the OCSLA amendments.[113]

Toward Integrated Governance

Look back to before the oil shocks of the 1970s shattered U.S. compla-
cency. Before that watershed event, when Mercedes-Benz of Germany designed its own "muscle" car, it called this most American of its creations
the "6.9" after its nearly seven-liter engine. Yet while this was a remarkably thirsty engine for Europe, it was still smaller than many U.S. muscle
cars of the period. When it came to American cars, it almost seemed as if
fuel inefficiency was desirable. Of course, this was all made possible by gas
prices far lower than those in other industrialized nations. Few Americans
realized that more efficient cars like Britain's famed Mini or Lotus were
quicker and handled better than cars built in the United States.

With the Yom Kippur War of 1973, the Arab nations stopped selling
oil to nations that supported Israel, including the United States. Then
OPEC (the Organization of Petroleum Exporting Countries) was able
to demand tremendous price increases. In 1973 the price of a single barrel
of oil skyrocketed from about $3 in October to more than $11 in December. An immediate consequence was uncertainty over the nation's energy
supply. Long lines at gas stations led to popular anger and frustration.

Disruption returned in 1979 with the Iranian Revolution and the Iran-Iraq War. World energy markets were again thrown into chaos, as oil prices soared from $17 to $34 per barrel. Interestingly, America's two worst economic recessions of the late twentieth century came in 1973–1975 and 1980–1982. The timing was no coincidence. Both recessions were partly an aftermath of the severe and unprecedented rise in oil prices of 1973 and 1979. Indeed, a report for the secretary of energy from the oil industry lobby claims that these sudden energy price shocks actually shrank the American economy by about 2.5 percent and 3.5 percent, respectively.[114]

The petroleum industry is surely right to conclude that the oil price shocks of 1973 and 1979 caused immediate and vary painful contractions in the U.S. economy. And the nation's reliance on foreign oil is also a most vexing problem. But the oil industry is wrong about the lessons to be learned. Difficult as they were, the oil shocks of the 1970s ironically helped to strengthen America by encouraging energy efficiency. Once the nation had time to adjust, shortages encouraged consumers and manufacturers alike to consider (many for the first time) improving efficiency and conservation to reduce demand. U.S. energy consumption dropped dramatically after the shocks as Americans adopted different and often better ways of living. But on the heels of these welcome developments came dissension in OPEC, an oil glut with sharp drops in the price of gasoline, and the election of Ronald Reagan in 1980. The new administration's policies focused narrowly on increasing the supply of oil (while ignoring the recent advances on the demand side), and the trend again was toward wasteful and inefficient use of fuel.

In the late 1980s and into the 1990s, the federal government under Presidents Bush and Clinton followed a rather different course. Bush recognized that ongoing moratoria would continue to stymie federal development and, because of promises made during the 1988 campaign, he issued an order in 1990 that abruptly halted much new leasing of offshore development tracts. Bush directed the federal government to

* cancel all scheduled leases in the OCS off California, southern Florida, Washington, Oregon, and in the North Atlantic until the year 2000— except for eighty-seven tracts off the coast of southern California, which could be considered for leasing;

* begin a process that might lead to buyback of existing leases in the east-ern Gulf of Mexico OCS planning area, off Florida's Gulf Coast;

* approve the proposed Monterey Bay Marine Sanctuary and ban oil and gas activity there;

* prepare a legislative initiative to allow the coastal communities affected by OCS development a greater share of revenues and a larger voice in decision making.[115]

Those actions were all laudable, yet if the 1990 directive was intended to keep coastal states from seeking moratoria in Congress, it failed. Areas set aside by moratoria grew from 84 million acres in 1990 to 284 million acres in 1991 and fell only slightly, to 266 million acres, afterward.[116] Thus even with the marked shift to a Republican-controlled Congress in the mid-1990s, the OCS moratoria were reenacted with bipartisan support. Coastal states continued to seek moratoria in Congress because they felt that Bush's directive was only a beginning and could be revoked at any time. Moratoria were a last-ditch resort, but they were the only weapon available to block new development.

What does the future hold? The crucial tactic of using the moratorium may not be available much longer. With the passage of legislation grant-ing the president the line-item veto, a president might be able to delete moratoria language if this provision eventually passes constitutional muster. Whatever the fate of moratoria, possible trends can be gleaned from the recommendations of an advisory board to the Minerals Manage-ment Service. That board has a subcommittee on legislation made up of representatives from the oil industry, the states, and from an environmen-tal NGO (recently the Center for Marine Conservation). The subcom-mittee's report points toward some possible alternatives.[117]

The report concluded that it is time to move from state-federal conflict toward consensus. Its chief recommendations were to (1) create regional task forces that are designed to seek consensus by better involvement of various stakeholders, perhaps obviating the need for moratoria; (2) leave in place the existing safeguards for industry that make it difficult for the federal government to buy back existing leases; (3) allow coastal states a portion of revenues from adjacent offshore production activities; and (4) provide further incentives such as tax breaks, royalty reductions, and deep-water "holidays" that all reduce the costs of deep-water drilling so as to encourage the oil companies to expand exploration and production.[118]

In response, the Natural Resources Defense Council (NRDC, a leading environmental NGO) has pointed out several ways to improve the subcommittee's recommendations.[119] First, it observes that the proposed regional task forces are not needed; a consensus on offshore development has already been achieved. However, for many states the consensus is *against* new offshore drilling and *for* moratoria, something federal officials refuse to accept. The NRDC statement aptly observes regarding Florida: "Support for the current leasing and drilling moratoria has recently been expressed by the Governor, the Florida Cabinet, the Florida House of Representatives, the entire United States House delegation and both senators. Does this not represent consensus?"[120] Also problematic is that the task forces must ultimately defer to the secretary of the interior. The NRDC argues that creating regional task forces cannot be a solution if the secretary still has unbridled authority, for this is the root of the problem.

The OCS subcommittee's report further recommends leaving intact the statutory provisions that make it difficult for the federal government to buy back existing leases. Hypothetically, a buyback can occur if the government determines that it is contrary to the public interest to develop offshore sites already leased to industry. The NRDC observes that existing provisions have so far have prevented buybacks, and the fact that no leases have been canceled in the program's forty-year history strengthens this argument. The NRDC also recommends adding new language to the OCSLA amendments to clarify the provision that a substantial threat to the marine environment can be adequate grounds for canceling an existing lease.[121]

Regarding the OCS subcommittee's proposal for renewed revenue sharing as coastal impact assistance, the NRDC findings disagree with many specifics. In theory, revenue sharing may be an attractive way to move toward integrated governance. But the NRDC observes that the subcommittee nowhere requires that revenues from development shall be used to offset adverse environmental and social impacts of that activity. Therefore, there is no way to prevent states from spending impact assistance funds for exactly the wrong purposes, such as for projects that lead to increased demand for offshore oil, or even for more development in the coastal zone.[122]

To operate properly, OCS revenue sharing with the states must be carefully restricted. The funds coming into state coffers as coastal impact assistance must be designated to preserve or rehabilitate environmental quality or to redress the damage caused by continental shelf development; they must be earmarked for coastal uses. They should not be dumped into a general fund to be used for a potpourri of projects such as more coastal highway construction.

Another drawback of revenue sharing is that it would create incentives to expand offshore production so as to receive coastal impact assistance funds. The NRDC notes that suggested criteria for deciding which states will receive assistance turn on the presence of coastal energy development facilities and offshore oil and gas activity. While this makes sense from the standpoint of compensating for ecological damage due to offshore development, revenue sharing could also create perverse incentives that encourage some states to fight moratoria efforts. Finally, the NRDC opposes government subsidies and incentives that encourage new offshore development. This also makes good sense. If federal incentives must exist, they should first go toward reducing demand and improving energy efficiency as well as finding less environmentally damaging sources of energy.[123]

One type of action that can be taken now is to encourage the use of natural gas as a fuel. This makes sense as an interim step for several reasons. Natural gas can be taken from beneath the ocean floor more safely than oil. Unlike drilling for oil, extracting gas is environmentally more benign, with less potential damage from blowouts. And gas supplies in the United States are relatively abundant: imports account for only about 8 percent of gas consumed.[124] A significant supply of offshore natural gas is now being profitably taken from the central and western Gulf of Mexico, where there are currently no OCS moratoria, so drilling may be continued with relatively little opposition.[125]

Once extracted, natural gas can be used instead of oil for many residential, commercial, industrial, and transportation purposes. It can even be adapted to the conventional internal combustion engine. Needed infrastructure for expanded use of natural gas may be built rapidly, especially if large-scale purchasers of fleet vehicles like the U.S. government switched to natural gas.[126] Most important, compared to oil or coal, natural gas when burned creates less emissions of carbon monoxide, sulfur dioxide, nitrogen oxides, and particulates. Nonetheless, natural gas does cause pollution and it is a nonrenewable fuel.

The fact remains that although the big U.S. auto companies have allowed themselves to fall behind, by long opposing more efficient vehicles, there are fortunes to be made in energy efficiency and entrepreneurial opportunities abound. Not to be at the forefront in the search for alternatives to oil-burning cars is unhealthy for the nation and will ultimately bring more, not less, reliance on imported oil. The respected international news journal, the *Economist*, unmistakably devoted to free-trade principles, points up the advantages of pursuing alternative fuels and more efficient vehicles. When at last pushed into working on alternative vehicles, reports the *Economist*, major U.S. auto companies have done so

> rather grudgingly and certainly not with the zeal of the [smaller] entrepreneurs. Clean-air provisions, fuel efficiency and recycling are all too often seen as the annoying requirements of politicians rather than as market opportunities. Just as much effort is put into lobbying against new rules as meeting them. . . . With massive investments in their existing factories and the old ways of doing things, there is little incentive for car producers to rush any changes. And why, they retort, should they? With present technology, there is nothing to match the reliability, range, performance and low cost of a gasoline-powered car. A hundred years ago people made exactly the same claim about the horse.[127]

Hybrid vehicles powered by a combination of gasoline and fuel cells and made of ultra-light materials are already on the horizon; indeed, a few have already arrived. For the good of both the nation and the environment, the federal government should offer incentives to encourage U.S. auto makers to build the best of them sooner rather than later.

Given political pressures and the impact of the oil industry lobby, it is difficult to get even incremental goals transformed into law.[128] But times change. Providing market incentives to achieve higher fuel efficiency is a useful role for government, given the market distortions that mask the true cost of gasoline-powered cars. Improving efficiency makes good economic sense in its own right and reduces the demand for carbon-laden fuels, thus allowing the nation to leave its oil and gas resources where they belong—

in reserve, in the earth. In sum, contemplating changes in governance toward states' rights and ecological stewardship is not to be feared. Leaving some real authority with the states is, after all, what federalism and
basic American political principles are about.

Climate Change and Energy Use

As a separate matter, the threat of global climate change may profoundly
change how we look at energy consumption. There is now a growing consensus among scientists that human activities are causing a discernible
warming of the earth's lower atmosphere and altering its climate, with potentially damaging effects. Although many thorny questions remain as to
the causes, there is increasing agreement that robust steps must be taken
now to reduce the production of "greenhouse gases" like carbon dioxide.
Such energy policies also make good economic sense. They include mandating that oil be used more efficiently, selling fuel at more realistic prices,
and undertaking research into renewable energy. In 1997 more than 2,000
economists, including six Nobel laureates, signed a declaration stating:
"There are many potential policies to reduce greenhouse gas emissions for
which the total benefits outweigh the total costs."[129] Concern over climate
change could in fact be the catalyst that forces adoption of smarter energy
policy.

Yet so far there has been little action. Rather than stabilizing emissions
at 1990 levels by the turn of the century, the United States will exceed
that level by some 13 percent in one decade. Nonetheless, attention to the
issue is growing. Looking ahead, the best policies for combating global
warming will be those that make good sense, regardless of whether climate change occurs. This said, an ideal target for pruning is the roughly
$230 billion that world governments spend annually in subsidies for fos-
sil fuels. While cutting back subsidies is politically very difficult, such a
tactic can both improve global efficiencies and cut energy use by an impressive 10–30 percent.[130]

The threat of human-induced climate change can also be an impetus for
faster development of renewable energy sources. There has been a small in-

crease in research among the world's richest nations, from $784 million in 1993 to $878 million in 1995, but consider that this sum has been dwarfed by over $5 billion per year spent on nuclear power research. The latter figure is more than half the total public research funding spent on all energy research. Nuclear power is not generally considered a source of renewable energy because of the waste problem, nor is it a politically viable response to global warming, yet it has dominated research efforts. This is due to intensive lobbying by that industry and its nexus to weapons of mass destruction.[131]

Given the substantial political power of the oil, coal, and nuclear power industries, governments will no doubt go on offering subsidies to those industries for some time to come. British efforts to wean coal producers from decades of subsidies reveal the difficulty of trying to change policy. However, the growing threat of climate change is increasingly grabbing public attention and introducing a new element into the energy debate. In the late 1990s a senior official at British Petroleum even broke ranks with oil giants when he expressed concern about the potential for global warming: "If we are all to take responsibility for the future of our planet, then it falls on us to begin to take precautionary action now."[132] The specter of damaging climate change can force a change in entrenched habits and public policy.

Conclusion

Most legislative measures designed to protect the environment are typically narrow in scope. Indeed, because making substantial changes is always an imposing proposition, some specific amendments are offered here as ways of slowly building up shared governance over the coastal sea between the states and the federal government. Fine-tuning is all that can be expected in the near term. However, such changes can only work at the edges of problems and merely treat symptoms rather than addressing the underlying causes for lost marine biodiversity and degraded ecosystems. The next chapter reveals fresh solutions that are a sharper break from the past. The focus should be on preventing pollution in the first place, building improved policies that adopt precautionary action.

5

Prevention Rather Than Cure

An ounce of prevention is worth a pound of cure.

Poor Richard's Almanac

CONSIDER THE MOST SENSIBLE path ahead for ocean governance, and a new principle readily suggests itself. The precautionary ideal embraces a more integrative and conservationist perspective—something wiser than traditionally divisive boundaries like a three- or twelve-mile jurisdictional limit. Not surprisingly, then, this new thinking is increasingly cited in international accords, since it is an attractive means to improve marine policy. At its heart, the principle is based on the conviction that it is no longer valid to assume that the sea has a vast capacity to absorb a variety of harms.[1]

Precautionary action seeks to prevent pollution from land-based sources, thereby reassessing the thicket of pollution controls that operate at the "end of the pipe."[2] Unlike most current policies, precautionary action would *prevent* ecological harm before it occurs. For instance, it would avoid discharges into the marine environment and prevent damage from overfishing. Likewise, it would minimize the destruction of wetlands or other essential fish habitats that serve as breeding grounds. On a legal front, it would shift the burden of proof off nature and onto those who are proposing significantly harmful activities.[3]

The United States brims with exciting opportunities for preventing pollution. Money-saving options run a wide gamut from new manufacturing processes that replace toxic substances with benign (and often less expensive) substitutes[4] to educating consumers on nontoxic and organic household cleaning agents.[5] There are an array of economically sensible ways of pursuing these ends. However, such prevention-based goals will not be easily achieved because of the vast inertia surrounding most environmental regulations.

The direction taken in U.S. environmental laws is instructive. The core environmental legislation that began in the late 1960s at first represented a challenge to the power of traditional government. Rapid change was precipitated by opposition to the Vietnam War and efforts to raise public consciousness such as Rachel Carson's *Silent Spring* (1962), which alerted the public to the damage caused by pesticides, the Santa Barbara oil spill of 1969, and a broadening realization that the global ecosystem needed protection. These events and others grabbed the public's attention and thus the notice of politicians. In the space of a few years, sixteen major environmental laws (albeit narrowly defined and usually single-purpose) were enacted in the United States.

Countless regulations spawned by these basic laws have built businesses in areas like pollution control and waste management. Meanwhile, the rising number of consulting firms attests to the profits that can be realized by after-the-fact pollution monitoring and cleanup. The immense sums that are spent in attempting to clean up toxic waste sites illustrate this institutional mind set.

Yet there is a flaw woven into these laws, policies, and regulations: most environmental statutes rely on end-of-pipe control strategies. The assumption that the natural environment has an almost limitless capacity to absorb pollution has prevailed for so long that it goes unexamined. Starting from this assumption, most regulatory efforts focus on after-the-fact pollution controls, while ignoring prevention.

Control techniques have made impressive strides, as illustrated by new sophisticated filtering technologies. Catalytic converters used globally in automobiles are a case in point. They have caused a sharp decine in pollutants from exhausts of individual cars. Nonetheless, this case also demonstrates a problem with control strategies: although pollution from each car has dropped, the total number of cars on the road has increased exponentially, far outstripping any initial declines in pollution levels. Similarly, the growth of many industrial activities means that after initial declines, many pollutants are again defying all control efforts. After early encouraging signs, the measured totals of numerous pollutants are now dropping only modestly, if at all, and in many cases are worsening. Meanwhile, a broader loss of ecological integrity continues.[6]

Hence, despite a few successes to the contrary, the goal of these laws—to "save the environment"—still remains elusive. This has happened largely because environmental laws have emerged in startlingly piecemeal fashion; they are not integrated so as to wisely prevent harm, nor do they address the causes of ecological harm at the source. Because regulations have not yet recognized that prevention is far more successful than remediation after harm is done, control strategies have stayed locked in place. Thus the dominant paradigm is still to dilute pollutants, such as by releasing them into coastal seas, or secreting wastes away in the depths of the ocean. But those short-term responses will in time come back to haunt us: merely diluting or hiding waste is not the answer.[7]

On the other hand, if pollution is regarded as a form of inefficiency, which in fact it really is, then new attention to upstream preventive measures makes great sense.[8] Why then is prevention overlooked? Part of the explanation is inertia. The *Economist* observes that when a smart, inexpensive technology was introduced to enable certain industries to reduce pollutants while also operating on 30 percent less electricity, the one source selling this novel technology generally met with stubborn resistance to its product. Only a few companies were willing to switch operations immediately. "To understand why [the] technology spread relatively slowly despite promising such huge savings, think in terms of work psychology. Big companies are conservative; engineers are hard-put to believe that their traditional approach to design can be bettered so easily."[9] Oftentimes large firms seemed to assume that if alternative "greener" technologies really were so much cheaper and better, we would all be using them by now.[10]

Resistance to new preventive technology includes a sentiment that government intrusion in manufacturing choices is tantamount to "command-and-control" economics, reminiscent of Soviet-era communism. Clearly, governments in a free-market economy should not be in the business of picking winning technologies. Nonetheless, where new subsidies or "green" taxes make ecological and economic sense, they ought to be considered. For although government-industry partnerships (made for "green" ends) are often painted as un-American, many industries like coal, petroleum, and nuclear power already enjoy a host of subsidies, tax relief, and other indirect government aid. Those many incentives, created before the environmental protection ethic entered the national consciousness, ought to be reconsidered.

Yet another reason why pollution prevention strategies are so far disregarded is that the economic benefits may accrue over the long term and thus do not show up immediately in ledger books. Economic incentives currently work against prevention because under generally accepted accounting practices, it is typically cheaper to create ecological harms (pollution) and then to disperse the costs so that the broader community bears the burden. If environmentally harmful activities are borne by the commons and if producers can shrug off ecological responsibility, there is undeniably an economic incentive to do so. A result is that inefficiencies (pollution) are shifted from the polluter to the public, and the cost of cleanup falls to future generations.

Another reason for precautionary measures stems from the fact that our scientific understanding of marine ecosystems is still rudimentary and hindered by a host of factors.[11] Recently, for example, genetic studies of a common mussel species off the shores of southern California underscores how little is known about marine ecology. For many years a species of mussel was thought to be among the better-studied marine organisms. This was because it inhabited the waters adjacent to marine science laboratories. Yet scientists recently discovered that this particular species may have sharply declined in numbers decades ago, when its original populations were replaced by a nonendemic (foreign) species, a subtly different invader from the Mediterranean.[12] Without our realizing it, a mussel species may have crashed, and right under our noses. Given such levels of uncertainty, precautionary action encourages a restraint to protect marine biodiversity.

A core element of this principle is proved by the few successful cases in which pollutants have been most effectively reduced, as with airborne lead, DDT, mercury in surface waters, and radioactive fallout from atomic bomb tests—these successes were owed to the *elimination* of the offending substance or activity at its *source*.[13] Precaution thus means avoiding or minimizing an offending activity upstream, or finding new means to replace a harmful substance or activity with more benign substitutes. Both the precautionary principle and pollution prevention look upstream to avoid the use of dangerous substances like organochlorines.[14] They are not intended to replace all end-of-pipe control technologies, but rather to provide efficient concepts for better protecting the marine environment. Both precaution and prevention would offer more than the old shell game of just shifting pollutants from one environmental medium to another.

Precaution also responds to a vexing problem: how should environmental policy be made in the face of scientific uncertainty? The sciences rightly engage in rigorous objective studies in order to better understand the workings of nature.[15] And yet that academic, time-consuming process of seeking scientific agreement is rarely available to policy makers, who are under pressure to make rapid decisions.[16] Without a common yardstick for "good" governance, the swift extraction of nature's resources may be regarded as a preferable goal (nice economic miracle—shame about the environmental costs). Given the exigencies of making policy under such conditions, government leaders tend to ignore preventive strategies and leave it to the environment to assimilate damage. The precautionary principle would respond to this dilemma by encouraging *conservative* decisions in the truest sense of the word.

A Case Study in Pollution Prevention

The economic possibilities of pollution prevention is seen in the case of Dydee Diaper Service, once the largest cloth diaper service in New England, with eighty-five employees.[17] In a typical week Dydee washed about 200,000 pounds of soiled baby linen and diapers. To act in an environmentally conscious fashion and to conserve water, Dydee used a special eighteen-chamber continuous-batch tunnel washer that required only 20–25 percent of the water used by a conventional washer. However, a major drawback to this conservation effort was that contaminants in the waste water were more concentrated. Ironically, by using less water, Dydee Diaper found it more difficult to meet effluent guidelines.

Soon the effluent exceeded the maximum of 1 part per million (ppm) for zinc set by the Massachusetts state water resources authority. In January 1992, Dydee was cited for exceeding zinc discharge limits, a violation widely reported in the local news. Concerned customers, many of whom had chosen to use cloth diapers rather than disposables, were outraged and many canceled their accounts.

Dydee Diaper was puzzled by this effluent problem, since the company did not use zinc in any of its cleaning processes. Tests showed no zinc in its cleaning chemicals or water supply. It was discovered that the zinc came from the diapers themselves, from the zinc oxide–based baby ointments commonly used to treat diaper rash. Zinc was also an ingredient in various baby skin creams.

Dydee's president next considered three alternatives to resolve this zinc problem. The conventional answer, a classic control approach, would be to purchase a water treatment system, costing about $150,000 for purchase and installation and another $30,000 per year for chemicals. Additional expenses were required to pay a licensed operator. The second alternative was to purchase "closed-loop ozone activated" laundering machines. Dydee's president was impressed by the concept of closed-system technology, which can almost eliminate water discharge altogether, but applications of this new technology to diapers were still being developed. Because that option might be adaptable for Dydee's special needs in several years' time, the company was reluctant to spend over $150,000 up front for the more conventional waste water treatment system.

The third option was the most unconventional—and the one Dydee chose. In a pioneering decision, Dydee opted to try to reduce the problem at its source by convincing its customers to voluntarily alter habits at home. The main question was whether its customers would do so. In an unconventional route for U.S. business, Dydee reached out to customers, informed them of an environmental problem, and provided them with education and assistance to make the solution work. Dydee sent out a letter explaining the problem and asking customers to use zinc-free ointments. It offered to pay customers $1 per container for their zinc-based ointments and to sell them zinc-free products—such as diaper rash ointment and baby skin cream—at about half the retail cost. Customers were sent free samples of zinc-free products and the zinc-free campaign was promoted in a monthly newsletter, "Bottoms Up."

The results were highly positive. The company immediately witnessed a substantial reduction in total zinc discharge. Before this outreach campaign began in 1992, zinc concentrations typically ranged between 2 and 4.5 ppm. Following the campaign, its zinc discharge was consistently held below the 1 ppm limit. In this way, Dydee was able to comply with zinc discharge regulations, and even save money, by preventing pollution.

The benefits exceeded the costs. Dydee spent about $1,000 to buy back zinc ointments and another $7,000 for 20,000 samples of zinc-free products. It sold some 2,000 containers of zinc-free ointments and creams and larger zinc-free containers at a loss, costing Dydee $250. This total campaign cost less than $10,000. On the other hand, the education effort saved Dydee Diaper from spending about $150,000 in start-up costs for a treatment system plus $30,000 per year for treatment chemicals, sludge disposal fees, and an operator. Through prevention the company was able to realize substantial savings.

This example suggests that if more companies actively considered prevention, the results could be not only cost savings but also reductions in global environmental problems. Yet current U.S. campaigns for advancing pollution prevention and precaution are only at an embryonic beginning.[18] And although we rarely think of such upstream activities as related to the state of the seas, there is a direct connection. Pollution prevention will be rewarded by better protection of the ecological integrity of the sea.

The Precautionary Principle in International Law

While clean production strategies will grow more popular as industry discovers that new techniques can lower costs while reducing pollution, there are at present strong disincentives that must be overcome. Perhaps most daunting is that humanity has grown accustomed to assuming that the ocean is endlessly capable of absorbing the land's wastes. But in recent multinational accords for protecting the environment, the precautionary principle (and thus prevention) is receiving increasing attention from industrialized nations. Initially put forward in an international setting at a First Ministerial Conference on North Sea Pollution in 1984, the precautionary principle was strengthened in London at a Second North Sea Conference in 1987 and reinterpreted at a Third Conference in 1990.[19]

The principle has since provoked a variety of responses from the industrialized nations. Views currently range from cautious resistance, as in a case of Britain, to much more sympathy toward precaution, as shown by Germany and the Scandinavian nations.[20] Hence the concept is at a crossroads, and a meaningful question is whether the nascent principle will be embraced in future international agreements. Recent trends suggest that precautionary action may slowly become more mainstream thinking. References to this concept are on the increase.[21]

The principle, for example, is noted approvingly in the 1991 Bamako Convention for Regulation of Pesticides and Hazardous Wastes (Africa), in Principle 15 of the Rio Declaration (UN Conference on the Environment and Development, 1992), and also in Article 2 of the Convention for Protection of the Marine Environment of the Northeast Atlantic (OSLO and Paris Commission, 1992).[22] Other key instances of precautionary action include the 1987 Montreal Protocol on Substances That Deplete the Ozone Layer, the moratorium against whaling, and suspension of disposal of low-level radioactive wastes at sea without approval of the consultative parties to the London Dumping Convention.[23] A UN resolution against drift netting on the high seas, together with a vigorous policy statement on this resolution, are likewise precautionary, since they shift the burden of proof.[24]

These resolutions suggest that the precautionary principle is moving toward acceptance in international law. But closer examination of this principle as implemented reveals a different picture. Precautionary thinking seemed to have found some early consensus in 1987 at the conclusion of the Second North Sea Conference, when success injecting the principle was regarded by many within the environmental movement as a breakthrough. The progressive northern European and Nordic nations appeared to be seriously grappling with the vexing problems of North Sea pollution and genuine, forceful precautionary policy seemed about to be implemented.

Since that time, however, there has been a notable absence of robust new policies. Irresolute efforts to instill precaution have fallen short of environmentalists' expectations. A shadow report by an environmental group argues that efforts among nations represented at the Second North Sea Conference still shy away from precautionary measures.[25] This resistance might be explained by certain common characteristics of the northern European nations. Divided by dissimilar customs, they all have mature market economies and are linked by competitive free trade. Although a spur to economic development, that competition as currently framed may cause people to undervalue the costs to the earth of economic activity.

Industrial nations have understandably resisted making economic sacrifices to avoid harm to the environment, for fear of allowing others a comparative advantage. It is difficult even for the "greener" Nordic nations to lead the cause of environmental protection because of the "lowest common denominator" factor in international negotiations, whereby a single unenthusiastic nation can stymie agreement on progressive treaty goals. In the aggregate, this is a collective free-rider problem with the health of the global environment at stake. As a result, opponents of precautionary action can claim that to expect more aggressive measures from Second North Sea Conference nations is romantic but unrealistic.[26]

Although the United States often sets an example for environmental regulation, it usually resists the precautionary approach. Such resistance was evident in U.S. opposition to the 1990 Bergen Conference and again at the 1990 Second World Climate Conference.[27] This opposition of course is articulated in the best light possible. In the words of James Baker, secretary of state under President George Bush, "While the U.S. continues to support scientific research into the greenhouse effect, [we] are prepared to take actions that are fully justified in their own right and have the added advantage of coping with greenhouse gases. They're precisely the policies [the United States] will never have cause to regret."[28]

This "no regrets" position seems reasonable and beyond reproach. It even seems to support government incentives to encourage industries to use more efficient production methods that will produce fewer environmental harms—a key aim of the precautionary principle. Yet paradoxically, the United States adopted a unique version of this "no regrets" position that defends policies still rooted in the assumption that nature can assimilate pollution.[29] Despite its increasing favor, one of the major criticisms leveled at the precautionary concept by opponents, including the U.S. government, is that the principle is just too idealistic. They claim that this principle—at least, as they envision it—cannot be applied in real-world situations in which some risk in exploitation of resources is inevitable.[30]

But precautionary action need not be taken to extremes. The principle can be applied in various degrees. The rigor with which it is applied can depend on the danger of some proposed action. Indeed, just such a scaled approach is commonly used, for instance, for interpreting the constitutional protections written into the Bill of Rights. The degree to which an individual is shielded from discrimination will vary according to just how fundamental is the right that is being protected.

Critics further complain that ecological harms are not always foreseeable and therefore it is impossible to guard against them. That criticism carries substantial weight. Many substances or activities now recognized as harmful had once seemed to pose no risk. Seemingly benign chemicals like chlorofluorocarbons (CFCs) are an example. Despite their inert nature (or more accurately because of that quality), the release of CFCs into the atmosphere has led to a thinning of stratospheric ozone. Other unexpected outcomes have resulted from the spraying of DDT, marine habitat destruction, or overprescribing antibiotics, which in turn hastens the rise of resistant strains of bacteria.

To be sure, precautionary action cannot prevent all dangerous activities, and ecological damage is not always foreseeable. Yet that argument does not discredit the concept. Rather, on closer inspection, it reemphasizes the opposing view: with rapid changes to come in the twenty-first century, there is a growing need for precaution. For instance, machine-driven meat production in Britain has led to a fear that "mad cow disease" could jump across the species barrier. Indeed, bovine spongiform encephalopathy (BSE) may now be transmissible to humans, as manifested by Creutzfeldt-Jakob disease. It is often prudent to take readily available, economically sensible steps that reduce risk.

Another criticism of precautionary action is that the principle is still such an ambiguous legal concept that it cannot bind nations.[31] However, the principle may be given more concrete form as it is increasingly applied and thus evolves. Yet it can be interpreted in unintended ways. Some make the case that most environmental policies are already precautionary at base. That is a tactic meant to define away precaution. At this early stage in defining what the precautionary principle should mean, some may prefer interpretations that weaken the concept. A variety of nations and non-governmental organizations have thus "decided that the best approach is to try to undermine it while ostensibly endorsing it." By capitalizing on the lack of legal definitions for the precautionary principle, they may derail recent momentum for establishing this concept.[32]

Finally, the precautionary principle has been criticized for its simplicity, but—as with the U.S. Constitution—its strength lies in brevity and simplicity. Precaution is like the First Amendment, for example, which holds that Congress shall make no law abridging the freedom of the press. For more than two centuries, that one pithy line has had an impact out of proportion to its size; the free-press principle has built a wall against censorship. The precautionary principle can similarly inform our thinking. An abstraction may be fleshed out by interpretive rulings over time. Thus the vagueness of current definitions of the precautionary principle is not a fatal flaw; what is required is greater consensus on what the principle entails.

This discussion will review a wide assortment of U.S. environmental regimes as to their capacity for precautionary action. Where the idea of precaution is absent, ways are suggested for introducing it. As is shown, current U.S. policy does not emphasize the prevention of harm. Precautionary action requires the greater application of science in policy making and prefers prevention to cure.[33] As a matter of efficiency, it shifts the burden of proof toward improved environmental protection.[34] By exploring some ways in which precaution could inform our thinking, I will suggest what a second-generation precautionary regime should look like.[35]

The National Environmental Policy Act

The National Environmental Policy Act of 1970 (42 U.S.C. Sec. 4332 [2][C][1976]), commonly known as NEPA, was a milestone in the early history of U.S. environmental law.[36] It is one of the least understood yet most important environmental laws. NEPA clearly forged new paths by creating novel protections for the biosphere, including the oceans. As currently interpreted, NEPA is a "stop and think" statute, mandating that environmental assessments be written in cases of any proposed major federal actions that would significantly affect the environment.[37]

The authors of NEPA intended that federal agencies should for the first time be required to proactively consider the environmental consequences of their activities before they sent bulldozers into action. Its unique action-forcing requirement of an environmental assessment was born of the reasonable fear that because of inertia, once a bureaucracy decided to move ahead with a project such as a dam, a superhighway, or a toxic waste dump, the project was unstoppable. Among other things, NEPA was meant to nip ecologically unwise ideas in the bud.

That wisdom of considering environmental impacts before a project is begun is now taken for granted. Yet until NEPA was passed, few agencies had thought it necessary to think in ecological terms. For instance, immediately after the act was passed, an unyielding Atomic Energy Commission (AEC) vigorously challenged this requirement in court, arguing that NEPA did not apply to the construction of nuclear plants. In the first major interpretation of NEPA, Judge Skelly Wright ruled that the AEC's crabbed view was a clear violation of the statute and that NEPA bore a rigorous stop-and-think purpose.[38] That ruling set up many basic criteria for interpreting NEPA that still exist today.

But just as important was what Judge Wright chose not to do. He did not interpret other NEPA language that went beyond its procedural stop-and-think function. Remarkable language in NEPA went beyond the requirement to list the impact of proposed action; in addition, it implied that project planners should also favor an ecologically superior course of action.[39] If more attention had been given to this substantive function in judicial interpretations of the act, NEPA would have a far broader scope today. Thus Judge Wright's decision gave NEPA considerable force by fortifying its environmental assessment provisions, but if he had gone further and fleshed out NEPA's aspirational language, his decision would have provided broad stimulus for substantively "green" decision making.

The door had been opened for substantive interpretations of NEPA, but it was soon shut. For example, the law states in Sections 101 (a) and (b) that it is U.S. policy to "maintain, wherever possible, an environment which supports [biological] diversity."⁴⁰ Although NEPA could have been interpreted by the courts to mandate substantive review, and therefore projects should be shown to be environmentally sensible before they were allowed to proceed, a hostile Supreme Court in two crucial decisions (*Vermont Yankee* and *Strycker's Bay*) summarily held that federal agencies do not have to promote environmental concerns.⁴¹ The law was emasculated, enforcing only a duty to stop and think.⁴²

In theory, NEPA could be reinterpreted by the Supreme Court to give it more power, to create a regulatory regime akin to precautionary action. Yet that is highly unlikely. Alternately, it might be amended by Congress to mandate a substantive review of the ecological impacts of proposed projects, but neither is likely in the present political climate. As it stands, NEPA sets up a series of time-consuming hoops that agencies must jump through on the way to approving a given enterprise. To be sure, the jumping has not been easy. Environmental assessments are often exceptionally voluminous and detailed to avoid litigation over errors or omissions. That problem was corrected to some degree, but these reports are so complex that the public rarely hears of them. Impact statements fail to be the concise interdisciplinary reports suitable for public consumption, as intended.⁴³

Moreover, NEPA as implemented is not precautionary in nature because it addresses only the narrow issues, such as whether to build an individual nuclear plant or new superhighway. It does not require any substantive large-scale review of policy making with an eye to precaution in general or pollution prevention. If it did, this law could then fill an important new role. For instance, NEPA might require planners to consider whether it might be preferable to find alternatives to reduce traffic than to build another superhighway. Yet NEPA as now interpreted allows many unwise policies to emerge from a tyranny of small decisions. This need not be so. Lynton Caldwell, who played a major role in drafting NEPA, argues that the law does authorize consideration of substantive policy alternatives like precautionary action, pollution prevention, reduction of pollution at the source, and clean production strategies, but this goal has not been met.⁴⁴

Thus, as Caldwell points out, NEPA has been misinterpreted. He believes it was not meant to be a regulatory or procedural statute, but rather a declaration of ecological policy that includes an action-forcing provision. However, unlike U.S. civil rights laws that are backed by constitutional mandate, courts are often reluctant to rigorously interpret environmental laws or overturn executive decisions regarding the environment. Caldwell observes, "No law is more effective than the will to enforce it," and NEPA has thus far had very weak support in the executive and legislative branches.[45] Were this statute given a broad new element requiring federal proposals to consider new opportunities for precaution or pollution prevention in the first place, then NEPA could offer much. But because such expansion is unlikely in the present political climate, NEPA promises little for instilling precaution in domestic policy.

The Magnuson-Stevens Fishery Conservation and Management Act

Unlike the broad brush of NEPA that can apply to many actions on land and sea, the Fisheries Conservation and Management Act of 1976 is devoted exclusively to fisheries management.[46] Now known as the Magnuson-Stevens Act (see chapter 3), this law has been a failure from most perspectives. It was originally a response to foreign fishing off U.S. shores. Thus the law codified what became a 200-mile exclusive economic zone (EEZ).[47] Most important, the act served to oust foreign vessels and favored the small domestic fleet, which greatly increased in size.

Over twenty years after passage, the Magnuson-Stevens Act is most notable for what it is not doing—it is failing to conserve fishery resources. A so-called fishery conservation zone has proved to be anything but: it has brought about neither effective conservation of valuable stocks nor significant reductions in the total fishing effort. Instead, it has merely replaced overfishing by foreign vessels with a clearly home-grown problem.

Immediately following the passage of this act, foreign fishing within 200 miles of the United States declined precipitously from 3.8 billion tons in 1977, or 71 percent of the total catch, to just 12 million tons in 1991, or 0.2 percent. Meanwhile domestic fishing capacity increased dramatically. The U.S. catch jumped from 1.56 billion tons in 1977 to more than 5.78

billion tons in 1991. Foreign boats were allowed to capture fish only when U.S. boats failed to reach the total allowable catch.[48] Despite the new U.S. management scheme, an alarming percentage of fish stocks have fallen to depleted levels over the same period. According to the U.S. National Marine Fisheries Service (NMFS), the agency charged with monitoring the nation's 200-mile zone, fully 45 percent of fisheries whose status is known are in danger. Some stocks plummeted to less than 10 percent of optimum size.[49]

In a worrisome sign of things to come, the once abundant stocks of haddock and cod off New England have crashed. This is forcing New England fishermen, with their overcapitalized fishing fleets, to switch their efforts toward the less desirable species that have come to dominate altered marine ecosystems. As a result, the ecosystems on the northwest Atlantic continental shelf are being transformed by overfishing. Relatively valuable fish like mackerel and herring are in decline, while commercially less desirable sand lance take their place.[50] Desirable haddock and cod are threatened, which allows "trash fish" like dogfish and skate to proliferate.

Several broad factors responsible for the act's failure are listed in chapter 3. But in light of goals of precautionary action, some other points are notable as well. At the outset, this act is failing because it is being driven by short-term economic interests that fail to put the health of the resource first. It functions as a development regime, not the conservationist regime that it should be and is demanded by the precautionary principle.

Precaution is ignored partly because of the makeup of the eight regional fisheries management councils (FMCs).[51] These councils were established by the act to peg allowable fishing efforts. Yet council members represent the same fishing industry this law regulates. At NMFS, well-meaning scientists attempt to forecast maximum sustained yield, a difficult task in its own right. But when presented with various possible scenarios (scientists must draw up various estimates because of uncertainty), too often councils attempt to wring from the data the highest take possible. It is too much an instance of the fox watching the henhouse. Keen observers of ocean management like Sylvia Earle conclude that the councils have been a failure in theory and practice.[52]

Such problems with U.S. fisheries management are hidden from the public because declines in domestic stocks are masked by imported products. Fish and other seafood are abundant in local markets. Moreover, a lack of popular concern for the plight of crashing stocks may be explained. Fish simply do not inspire sentimental identification like other species. They are usually rather small, cold-blooded, scaly creatures, unlike "cuter" air-breathing marine mammals such as seals, whose very countenance seems to beg for human empathy. Moreover, they care not a whit for their young: many species release eggs by the million to be fertilized at random and eat their own young fry. Finally, the threat of commercial depletion is rather different from extinction; people are not alarmed.

Nonetheless, the tragedy of overfishing is now beginning to catch the public eye. Critics of the act are at last starting to be heard. Even a few FMC members say the councils are becoming their own worst enemies by institutionalizing overfishing. A front-page story in the *New York Times* notes that "overharvesting has helped to bring about the fishing industry's drastic decline."[53] One solution is clear: membership on fisheries councils should be more diversified so that they are not dominated by the fishing industry whose short-term interests lie in overharvesting the resource.[54]

Action must be taken soon. Worldwide total marine fish catch peaked at 86 million tons in 1989 and has since gone into decline; thirteen of the seventeen major global fisheries are now in serious trouble.[55] The causes are complex and will be nettlesome to resolve. One problem is pollution. Others stem from devastatingly effective fishing methods. Vessels that produce large bycatches (unintended catch of species not targeted) or that cause habitat destruction are tremendously wasteful over the long term, although this fact seems unacknowledged, given their ongoing use. So declines in many stocks will continue for many reasons, including deference to national sovereignty, a "tragedy of the commons," and the unceasing world demand for protein.[56]

Although wise ocean governance requires extensive knowledge of marine ecosystems, scientific understanding is still rudimentary. Only a few decades ago, it was widely assumed that most marine ecosystems were characterized by a balance of nature. Biotic communities and individual fish stocks were conceived as though centering on some ascertainable, knowable equilibrium. As recently as the mid-1970s, some scientists still regarded marine ecosystems as stable, closed, internally regulated, deterministic, and fathomable.[57]

The optimistic assumption that fisheries were not exceptionally complex systems led to the idea that a targeted species of fish (such as coho salmon) could be readily managed to produce its maximum sustained yield. It was believed that regulators could obtain the greatest possible take of salmon, for instance, by simply manipulating fishing pressures alone. Fish populations were seen as tending toward a steady-state equilibrium, and so susceptible to predictive modeling techniques.

Today the management of resources is undergoing radical revision. As that static "balance of nature" idea fell into disfavor, another school of thought has arisen that portrays the marine environment as characterized by change and turmoil. As noted by G. Carleton Ray, marine ecosystems are now seen as in a chaotic state of disturbance and fluctuation. Instead of stability, there are discontinuities and synergisms that "are devilishly difficult to predict."[58] This paradigm sees marine ecosystems as open and in constant flux, affected by both human and natural factors often originating far outside the ecosystem.

Given this revolution in attitudes, the classic aim of maintaining fisheries at very high levels of exploration, supporting large numbers of fishing boats from year to year, becomes all but impossible. Our very way of thinking is shifting. The assumption of a closed "symmetrical predator-prey relationship and bumper fish population become transient conditions at best, even in the absence of human intervention."[59] We have just begun to recognize that it is impractical to manage a fish stock as if it exists in isolation; it is folly to ignore the effects of fishing pressures on related stocks and the complex and cascading impacts of marine pollution. Precautionary action is essential.

How can the Magnuson-Stevens Act be altered so that it works toward the goal of precautionary action? This is admittedly pioneering work, for "to date there is no generally accepted definition of what elements should characterize a precautionary approach in the context of fisheries."[60] However, it is now clear that we should begin by identifying the stocks under the most grave pressure and by mandating reductions in total catch efforts. Because so little is known about marine stock fluctuations, a precautionary approach requires more conservative governance than is currently the norm. A report by the UN Food and Agricultural Organization recognizes that errors may be rife in fishery management: there are (1) measurement errors in basic fishery data used for analysis such as for catch, efforts, and sizes landed; (2) errors in estimation of stocks; (c) process errors caused by imperfect understanding of the interactions between elements of the ecosystem; (d) modeling errors; (e) decision errors; and (f) errors in implementation.[61]

That errors are rife throughout fisheries management ought to have significance. It should mean that "for modest levels of catch relatively little information is needed to ensure that the risks to a stock are held below a given level, but the required amount of information escalates rapidly when the resource is pushed to its limits."[62] Injecting the precautionary principle into the Magnuson Act would mean mandating types of fishing gear and methods least disturbing to marine ecosystems and strictly regulating or banning destructive practices.[63] (See figure 8.)

Precautionary action also mandates strenuous efforts to prevent the inefficient loss of nontarget species, known as bycatch.[64] Large numbers of unwanted fish, birds, marine mammals, and other creatures are simply thrown over the side dead and dying. Such bycatch can induce stress that radiates throughout an ecosystem. Other animals too are destroyed outside the nets. This ecological disaster occurs in part because there are no economic incentives to prevent it: bycatch is regarded as a mere externality outside cost-benefit calculations. Precautionary action would follow from the recognition that high bycatch is actually costly because it is degrading to the long-term health of an ecosystem.

Excessive catch levels will have to be defined, and fishermen must have reason to avoid them. This can be accomplished by selective means. For instance, the few ultramodern vessels that can stay at sea for long periods and bring in a huge catch should be prohibited, as should the most destructive fishing methods, if stocks are to be restored. Trade magazines like *National Fisherman* now exhibit a heartening willingness to consider boat buybacks and retraining of crews. Only a few years ago, these measures were regarded as unacceptable.[65]

Moreover, productive marine habitat must be set aside as protected re-

Figure 8. Trawling can obliterate bottom habitat necessary for many marine species, yet large areas may be trawled between two and ten times per year. *Artist: Jill Townsend*

serves. This is necessary to encourage the essential recruitment of new year classes and to maintain critical biological diversity. Carefully delineated and strictly enforced harvest refugia, where fishing would not be allowed, are an idea whose time has come. Yet so far amazingly few areas have been set aside. Off the California coast, with its 220,000 square miles of state and federal ocean, only 14 square miles, or just .006 percent, have been set aside as marine protected areas off-limits to fishing. By contrast, of 156,000 square land miles that make up terrestrial California, fully 6,109 square miles, or 6 percent of the total, is protected park land.[66]

Few of the existing marine sanctuaries or reserves are genuinely protected areas off-limits to fishing. Instead, because of political pressures from commercial and sport fishing interests, fishing is generally allowed even in national marine sanctuaries and state marine reserves in California. Indeed, even the idea of small test refugia has met with vitriolic opposition from commercial fishermen. When citizens of Monterey tried to create a tiny marine refuge less than a half mile in size off Cannery Row in the late 1990s, the combined opposition from sport and commercial interests were enough to defeat the proposal. Even though this area was not even being fished, local fishermen were organized in their rejection of any harvest refugia, which translated into opposition by local officials. Fearing an expansion should the refugia idea prove to be popular, and already facing declining catches, they saw little reason to support the proposal.

Nonetheless, this concept of harvest refugia will likely gather increasing support. Potential sites for harvest refugia include an area off of Malibu that has lately been proposed as a new "no-take" sanctuary. More such proposals will follow. It will take many years of effort, and much consensus building with the assorted fishing interests, naturally wary of losing any fishing grounds, but it can and should be done.[67]

Sport fishing should receive more attention also. Once of relatively minor impact, recreational fishing now entails unprecedented new technology for finding fish. As with commercial fishing interests, the concordance of sport fishermen is necessary for long-term conservation. And environmental groups should not demonize sport or commercial fishing, which are both honorable, age-old pursuits. But because of new technology, fishing pressures are making it difficult to maintain a fishery such as squid off the California coast at optimum levels; serious restrictions or even short-term moratoria are needed to protect the long-term health of stocks.

At heart, management of fisheries means managing fishermen themselves, which is where the difficulty arises.[68] A fishing community on the brink of precipitous decline has substantial political leverage. Environmentalists should learn a lesson from the vicious spotted owl controversy: the support of loggers themselves is needed to truly conserve forests. Conservationists will have to find incentives to get fishermen to support their aims, as difficult as that may be.

The precautionary principle is moreover a useful means to increase funding for scientific studies because of the considerable importance it attaches to high levels of confidence in fisheries data. Under precautionary action, the total allowable catch of a given species must be lower when data are sparse; larger catches should be permitted only if there is better information and thus greater certainty about stock levels. Hence, there are economic and political incentives for the government to improve the state of marine sciences. Such a marked turnaround in thinking toward ocean governance ought to open a door for better data collection. This includes new programs financed by the large-scale resource users, since sparse data becomes relevant to total allowable commercial catches set by government.[69]

The Outer Continental Shelf Lands Act

Just as the Magnuson Act misses the boat with respect to the precautionary principle, so too has the important Outer Continental Shelf Lands Act (OCSLA) failed to embody the thinking called for. Simply put, OCSLA is devoid of precautionary action. Yet it was given a significant task: to establish national goals for the exploration and production of oil and gas on the federal outer continental shelf extending 3–200 miles offshore.[70]

OCSLA in 1953 had little to recommend it from a standpoint of good governance. It initiated a closed-door process behind which industry and federal officials charted the course of offshore development. Critics of such development were to have almost no voice. After the oil shocks of the 1970s, Congress rushed to reform this statute. Amendments to OCSLA in 1978 attempted to correct the law's many defects.[71] But they only muddied the planning process. While the changes permitted somewhat greater involvement by the opponents of drilling (mainly coastal states), they were also designed to expedite new offshore oil exploration and development. The result is a contradictory mess dominated by resort to OCS moratoria. Greater consistency is needed to reconcile the two goals of rationalized energy policy and giving the coastal states an equal voice in the planning process.

One way to do this is to amend OCSLA again—but this time to embody clearly precautionary ideals. For instance, the statute should not enable new offshore oil drilling to "trump" all ecological concerns. Instead of giving priority to drilling, the law should make it clear that when a new leasing program is prepared, protecting coastal resources should be given as much weight as the recovery of hydrocarbons.[72] Precaution means that federal officials should listen to objections from state governors opposed to offshore drilling.[73]

The present emphasis on expanding new oil production also ignores compelling arguments for reducing the demand for energy.[74] Eco-businesses and technologies to improve fuel efficiency are being pursued vigorously in Japan and the Nordic nations. Reflecting this, a Japanese poll revealed that the two highest expectations for science and technology in Japan were preservation of the environment (68 percent) and development of more efficient sources of energy (62 percent).[75]

The catalytic converter exemplifies traditional thinking toward energy use, pollution, and the power of the natural world to assimilate harm. Converters do filter out much pollution, but the benefits of this end-of-pipe device are more than offset by a broad array of government subsidies that have encouraged the aggregate reliance on internal combustion engines.[76] Rather than investing in cleaner technologies, our policy is sisyphean. It is similar to the "taller smokestacks" response to acute air pollution: simplistically "fixing" the problem by dispersing atmospheric contamination over a wider area.

Injecting precautionary action into OCSLA means that new offshore drilling should not be undertaken until significant efforts have been made to reduce energy demand.[77] In sum, OCSLA fails to reflect the precautionary approach in two basic ways. First, it does not give the coastal states an effective voice in governing ocean resources. Second, it fails to address what can be done by conservation and working toward fuel efficiency.[78] However, some domestic laws have begun to be fashioned in ways that incorporate the principle of precaution.

Antecedents to the Precautionary Principle

THE ENDANGERED SPECIES ACT

The Endangered Species Act of 1973 (ESA) broke with the permissive thinking of the past. The act seeks to save from extinction certain forms of life that are disappearing at a rate comparable to what fossil records show occurred only during catastrophic events in the earth's history. The act helps to protect marine biodiversity by emphasizing caution and foresight. During the congressional debate on the bill, an advocate observed, "Sheer self-interest impels us to be cautious. It is institutionalization of that caution that lies at the heart of [this law]."[79] The act attacks the assumption that the environment is infinitely capable of absorbing harmful influences; it cannot, for human actions are destroying a diversity of flora and fauna. It asserts that the extinction of any species is alarming and rejects the idea that there is a surplus of life on our planet that can be depleted without harm to all living creatures.

The Endangered Species Act incorporates precaution by mandating substantive protections for animals and plants on the brink of extinction. The act's requirements are laid out in absolute terms. When a commerce or interior secretary determines that a species is in danger of becoming extinct, given the best scientific data, that species is "listed." Its critical habitat is defined and a recovery plan is devised. Unlike the National Environmental Policy Act (interpreted as only procedural), ESA provides substantive protections, although only for those unfortunate members of species clearly threatened with extinction.

The act prohibits actions that harass, harm, or kill a listed species in the United States and extends to persons subject to U.S. jurisdiction anywhere at sea. However, its precautionary elements are somewhat narrow. First, it aids only those species listed by federal officials. The current political climate is palpably hostile to the act, so species that appear undesirable to us (regardless of their ecological service) may find little support for listing. The Endangered Species Act continues to be a lightning rod for intense political opposition.[80] Section 7, which provides judicial review for federal actions that jeopardize the existence of a species, has been subject to innumerable attacks. Moreover, opponents have succeeded in curtailing the necessary discretion to list species; in an effort to hobble the act, extensive language was added so that this section grew from the original two sentences to ten pages of statutory text.[81]

In the first year of the unsympathetic Reagan administration, the listing process ground to a halt. Only two species were listed as endangered in 1981: a Texas orchid and a crustacean (Hay Springs amphipod) found only in the National Zoo.[82] Perennial political opposition and severe lack of funding for the Interior Department has since crippled the act. Interior has been able to process only about fifty listing decisions a year, yet it has identified 3,600 U.S. species that it believes should be listed. The Nature Conservancy estimates that up to 9,000 species should be listed, just in the United States.[83] Nonetheless, plans to list some 2,000 new species were dropped because it would have been impossible to satisfy the new listing procedures established by Congress. If the act is to forestall what Harvard biologist E. O. Wilson calls a global crisis of extinction, the law falls badly short. Wilson estimates that some 1,000 species are lost per year as a result of human activities.[84]

The Endangered Species Act does contain precautionary thinking, since it seeks to slow currently disastrous rates of extinction. This law has halted some development plans that would otherwise have pushed threatened species over the edge, although it often seems that the act itself is most endangered. The fact that it is partly based on science has helped to overcome politically motivated pressures to permit activities that threaten the fragile balance of nature.

THE CLEAN WATER ACT

The Clean Water Act of 1972 shows how an idealistic and aspirational environmental law can founder on the rocky shoals of implementation.[85] The law set up breathtakingly ambitious goals. It sought to virtually eliminate water pollution in the United States, regardless of cost. It aimed to make U.S. waters fishable and swimmable wherever possible by 1983— and to greatly reduce all discharges of pollutants into U.S. waters by 1985. To achieve such ambitious goals, the Clean Water Act built on a rigorous standard: that the best available technology (BAT) economically achievable should be applied to reduce pollution at the source. Proponents of this standard hoped it would lead to preventing pollution throughout U.S. industry. Their belief was that to attain the act's stringent no-discharge goals it would be necessary to avoid pollution in the first place.[86]

To be sure, the act has led to many marked improvements in U.S. surface water quality.[87] But far more improvement was expected. The law was designed to provide uniform standards for industrial effluent categories based on BAT. Yet after only a few years of attempted implementation, it was clear to EPA administrators that as a new agency with limited resources, the EPA could not meet statutory deadlines for issuing guidelines on categories of pollutants. Since that original failure, implementation has been blocked by extensive litigation, missed deadlines, court orders, and in the end, lowered expectations. As a result, tough BAT standards are repeatedly pushed back. The EPA is not able to promulgate effluent guidelines as fast as necessary and those that have been issued are far from comprehensive.[88] Nearly 80 percent of toxic industrial discharges are still not covered by a rigorous BAT standard. In *Natural Resources Defense Council v. Reilly* (1991), it was pointed out that of 74,525 discharges, 59,338 were not covered.[89]

There was notable progress at the beginning. As a result of a 1976 consent decree, the EPA sought to list criteria for ambient water quality and specifically identified numerous pollutants known to harm human health. These were designated toxic pollutants under the act's Section 307, and 126 of these key chemicals or classes were given priority status. Yet there has been little success since that time. Because of limited funds, the EPA has established necessary human health criteria for just 70 percent of these 126 priority pollutants. Criteria have been established for less than one-quarter of these priority pollutants to protect aquatic life—and most criteria that do exist are based on studies over thirteen years old. The EPA clearly faces an enormous task and is hampered by a severe lack of funding. About 1,100 nonpriority pollutants are thought to be entering the nation's surface waters; meanwhile, an underfunded EPA still has to establish the "required" standards for 126 pollutants listed as priority contaminants.[90]

Difficulties arise partly from the sheer number of chemicals, old and new, being used and produced by industry. Methodological problems also stem from inadequate risk management techniques.[91] Classic risk-benefit analysis often does a poor job of predicting environmental (nonhuman) risks.[92] Furthermore, in extrapolating from limited data there is often an exaggerated emphasis on cancer risk to humans. This can cause regulators to overlook non-negligible harms associated with sublethal stress. The EPA places a great emphasis on chemical carcinogens, but often for reasons related more to politics than to science, so that "current risk assessment practices do not adequately account for diseases other than cancers."[93] This is true despite the fact that new attention is being paid to emerging issues like endocrine disrupters.

The EPA has experienced similar pitfalls in meeting its mandate to oversee the manufacture of potentially harmful chemicals under the Toxic Substances Control Act (TSCA). Unable to test every one of the tens of thousands of new chemicals marketed, the EPA relies on a "structure activity relationships analysis" that depends on test data derived from chemicals of similar molecular structure. Yet the General Accounting Office notes that this methodology is unreliable and often inaccurate regarding the characteristics of new chemicals. When the EPA did begin chemical review testing in 1979, some 62,000 (86 percent) of roughly 72,000 chemicals in the TSCA inventory were already in commerce; therefore they have not been given priority review as new chemicals. EPA has since reviewed only about 1,200 (or 2 percent) of existing chemicals. The outcome is clearly a permissive regime in which the EPA has been able to issue regulations for only a handful of chemicals under the TSCA.[94]

These issues illuminate many of the problems faced in implementing the Clean Water Act. An early BAT mandate was replaced by weaker standards like best conventional pollutant control technology (BCT), which focuses on end-of-pipe controls without advancing to a rigorous BAT requirement.[95] Enforcement efforts thus continue to favor "what industry is prepared to give, rather than what the environment needs."[96] Because of such a backward drift, this law is largely devoid of the demanding technology-forcing language that achieves real progress.[97]

Finally, with its focus on human health rather than a broader concern with the total environment, the EPA still fails to protect freshwater and marine ecosystems from harms caused by nonpoint sources of pollution (for example, runoff from farms laden with pesticides or the oily runoff from roads). EPA's excessively narrow focus looks only to a few specified pollutants, rather than the actual diffuse causes of ecosystem degradation.[98] To satisfy the precautionary principle, then, both the CWA and EPA should again apply demanding technology-forcing standards, establish a system for broad ecosystems protection, and provide incentives for clean industrial production strategies.

THE OIL POLLUTION ACT

The Oil Pollution Act of 1990 (OPA) entails precautionary action in several ways. First, it envisions an eventual switch from single-hull to double-hull oil tankers. In this alone, OPA departs from the status quo ante.[99] Other precautionary elements include a broadened and more realistic regime that holds ship owners and operators liable in the event of an accident. These parties are now responsible for removing oil after a spill, as well as for damage to the environment. This goes a long way toward preventing contamination in the first place by instilling greater reason for caution. By internalizing what had been externalized costs to the earth from an oil spill, OPA has taken a genuinely precautionary step.

Many benefits are already easy to spot. Immediately following passage of OPA, "only" 55,000 gallons of oil and petroleum products were spilled by oil tankers in 1991—the lowest level in fourteen years.[100] An industry-sponsored study documented better procedures, improved safety provisions, and more inspection routines among tanker operators (raising the question of whether standards were adequate before). The law has also had global consequences: the International Maritime Organization has looked into a double-hull requirement for international routes. In general, the law, which has had positive global ramifications, represents a much-needed step in the right direction.[101]

THE MARINE PROTECTION, RESEARCH, AND SANCTUARIES ACT

Another first step toward precautionary ocean governance is the Marine Protection, Research, and Sanctuaries Act of 1972 (MPRSA), sometimes known as the Ocean Dumping Act.[102] A string of amendments have been added that reflect the ongoing need for regulatory action. For instance, MPRSA was amended in 1974 to bring the United States into conformity with international law as promulgated by the London Dumping Convention of 1972 (LDC). Although neither MPRSA nor its progeny have stopped all types of ocean dumping, their intent is to bring private and public dumping under a regulatory regime.

And regulation is clearly needed. In 1968 about 48 million tons of waste was dumped off the coasts of the United States. Eleven years later, and remarkably over a period when MPRSA was in force, the figure had grown to more than 100 million tons.[103] As the figures suggest, the law is not intended to ban all dumping at sea. Indeed, the economic rationale for dumping is hard to resist: it moves pollutants from land to sea where disposal is virtually cost-free.[104] It is arguably the moral responsibility of the United

States, as the world's leading ocean dumper, to take a lead in minimizing this harmful practice. (Between 1977 and 1982, over 400 million tons of wastes were dumped annually by parties to the London Dumping Convention.)[105] MPRSA does limit the dumping of radioactive materials, biological and chemical warfare agents, persistent plastics, toxic organics, and metals, yet the problem of dumping has not been solved.[106]

Dumping still continues in the United States, but under a regulatory regime like that administered by the Army Corps of Engineers (COE), and EPA. The Corps oversees the dumping of dredge spoils removed from river and harbor bottoms to maintain channels for navigation. Because of the need to keep navigational arteries open and the zest of the COE in this endeavor, by the 1980s dumping had grown fortyfold compared to fifteen years earlier.[107] Yet scientists are now finding that dumping the dredge spoils, even in deep ocean waters, may have far-reaching impacts on marine ecosystems.[108] Dumping sediments such as alluvial sand, clay, silt, or sludge can smother entire benthic communities. In more egregious cases there may be toxic contamination of the dredge spoils, which causes significant chemical or biological change and sublethal stress.[109]

A study of a dump site 115 miles off the New Jersey coast is illustrative. Contaminants dumped far offshore were discovered to be entering the marine food chain, beginning with bottom-dwelling organisms. Elevated levels of sewage sludge were found in worms, sea urchins, and sea cucumbers at a depth of 8,000 feet. Even organisms tested some forty-five miles away were found to be contaminated—although at lower levels than those nearer the dump site.[110]

Such pollution of the vasty depths by human activities has generally been ignored since it was assumed to be without consequence. But during the late 1980s many of the deleterious effects of dumping were unavoidably brought ashore when medical waste and fish washed up along the New York and New Jersey shores, costing taxpayers billions of dollars in cleanup and lost tourist revenues. In response to mounting political pressures, the Ocean Dumping Ban Act of 1988 strengthened the Marine Protection, Research, and Sanctuaries Act by giving renewed rigor to dumping deadlines.[111] Later, in an international setting, the so-called Yablokov report startled the world in 1993 when it revealed that the Soviet Union had clandestinely dumped 2.5 million curies of nuclear waste in violation of its obligations under the London Dumping Convention. The Clinton administration successfully pushed afterward for a worldwide ban on further dumping of radioactive wastes at sea.[112] Whether this latest obligation that exists on paper will actually be heeded remains to be seen.

Is the present U.S. regime on dumping as precautionary as it could be? To the extent that it has stemmed an earlier rush to dump at sea, it does satisfy a core element of precaution, but disturbing problems remain. The Corps of Engineers can issue a permit to dump once a proponent meets the (lenient) standard that their activity will not "unreasonably degrade" the marine environment.[113] The definition of *unreasonably* may be only weak protection when interpreted by an agency determined to view dumping permissively. The precautionary principle would instead shift the onus onto the produmping parties to show their actions would not adversely affect the environment.

A conflict of interest also hinders its implementation. Under the Marine Protection Act, the Army Corps of Engineers is responsible for issuing permits for dumping; meanwhile the Corps is also responsible for generating almost 90 percent of the dredged materials to be dumped at sea. This dual role of chief dumper and also regulator renders the decisions made by the Corps suspect—such as its finding that only 3 percent of the dredged material is highly contaminated. Last, the act is poorly enforced.[114] While some regulation of dumping is obviously preferable to what went on before, this regime can do more to prevent contamination of the seas.

If a key aim of ocean governance is to prevent further deterioration and maintain ecological integrity, then current regimes also reflect the sin of ignorance. In what should be a very significant finding, recent investigations by marine scientists have made it clearer than ever that land-based sources far outstrip dumping at sea as the chief source of marine pollution.[115] Yet environmental regimes still fail to recognize that most marine pollution comes from land-based sources. Listening to the sea largely requires action onshore.

It is now understood that roughly three-fourths of ocean pollution is caused by land-based human activities. This includes both point sources and nonpoint sources of pollution, as well as precipitation of contaminants from the atmosphere.[116] Ocean contamination that occurs at sea totals about 12 percent of marine pollution; this mainly consists of accidental spills and intentional operational discharges in transport activities, while another 10 percent of marine pollution comes from ocean dumping. These percentages are given by weight, which can be deceiving; measuring by weight, for instance, will mask the disastrous effects of only a few grams of plutonium. Nonetheless, the numbers reveal that most ocean pollution comes from activities on land.[117]

Wiser governance of the marine environment therefore requires a more holistic approach: land-based pollution sources must be addressed if the vexing problem of ocean pollution is to be solved. Current ocean dumping policies, like other regimes that make up ocean governance, have ignored the multiplicity of pathways by which pollution actually enters the marine environment. Thus the precautionary principle forces us to look upstream to minimize at the source many land-based sources of contamination.

UNITED NATIONS CONVENTION ON THE LAW OF THE SEA

The 1982 United Nations Convention on the Law of the Sea (UNCLOS III) has played a major role in establishing new norms and principles in international law. But given the great need for precautionary action, the near absence of that principle from UNCLOS III is troubling.[118] The evolution from the first UNCLOS regime to the third is instructive. As noted in chapter 3, UNCLOS I, signed in 1958, consisted of four parts. Only one, entitled Fishing and Conservation of Living Resources of the High Seas, imposed a responsibility to conserve marine life.[119] The breadth of the territorial sea was then a key focus of attention.

The conservation obligations of that agreement were put forth in simplistic terms. Management was not informed by holistic ecological factors such as complex and cascading human impacts; instead, its chief aim was to maximize the available catch for coastal nations. Fish were not distinguished from marine mammals, nor from desired migratory species, which left a real potential for overexploitation. From a conservationist perspective, the problems were legion: distant-water fishing nations like Japan and Russia never joined; scientific recommendations for desirable catch levels could be modified by political and economic considerations—usually toward overfishing; enforcement of its conservationist aims was lacking and international inspections were rare; the procedures for dispute settlement were seldom activated; and nations typically viewed the already weak conservation goals of UNCLOS I as a moral code they preferred to meet but were prepared to violate if the need was felt.[120] In sum, the chief aim of UNCLOS I and II was not genuine resource conservation.

UNCLOS III (1982) is the latest attempt at ocean resources management. The existence of UNCLOS III is a milestone, for the convention sets out norms that could bind the international community, including the United States.[121] But does it display robust precautionary thinking? No, for it still functions much like its predecessors. It was negotiated as a package deal, so its most thorny conservatory questions—those that were unlikely to achieve consensus—were finessed by the use of vague and ambiguous language. Instead of expressly allocating specific levels of total allowable catch, or agreeing on robust conservationist definitions for maximum sustainable yield, the convention left these matters to the discretion of individual nations or to be resolved in later treaties.[122]

The treaty contains no mechanisms to coordinate its assorted jurisdictional regimes. However, such coordination is essential to protect marine ecosystems and habitat (although Articles 61 and 94 go partway toward this goal). Linkages such as between Parts 5 and 7 on fisheries, and Part 12 on pollution can acknowledge the interrelationships between marine pollution and the long-term vitality of fish stocks.[123] Its many provisions on protecting marine environments are themselves hortatory and nonbinding, more aspirational than operational. It lacks the definitive standards that would limit toxic discharges and stress pollution prevention or clean production strategies.[124]

Yet UNCLOS III contains some elements of precaution. For instance, by creating 200-mile exclusive economic zones, the regime permits individual nations to take rigorous new steps toward conservation. They can protect their own domestic waters from overfishing by rigorous national laws and regulations. On the other hand, the poor record of achievement is disheartening. UNCLOS III can do more to foster precautionary action. Most critically, it should be implemented to require that catch efforts be reduced in proportion to uncertainty about a stock's status. That uncertainty is pervasive in the data used to guide fisheries management *ought* to be recognized in decision making.[125] Governments worldwide must begin to actually conserve stocks, regulate fishing gear and methods so as to minimize disturbances to essential habitat, and prevent bycatch.[126]

There is scope within UNCLOS III for precautionary implementation. And experience with the Magnuson-Stevens Act indicates that nations are just beginning to go down this path, as indicated by its 1996 amendments. But tensions will continue to flare and ecosystems will become yet more degraded before appropriately cooperative action is undertaken. Expect debates, for instance, between China and the Philippines over the oil near the Spratly "Islands" (no more than rocks, really);[127] Canada may clash again with Spain or the United States over valuable fisheries of the North Atlantic or North Pacific. The free-for-all aspect of the high seas exacerbates this problem. Nonetheless, as Sylvia Earle notes, "one thing is for sure: 'freedom of the seas' is no longer an acceptable doctrine."[128] Given a new political willpower, UNCLOS III is there as a vehicle for creating a conservationist stewardship of the seas.

THE STRADDLING STOCKS CONFERENCE AND OTHER MULTILATERAL AGREEMENTS

Many narrowly tailored international agreements have lately begun to supplement UNCLOS III as a global edifice of marine protection. These agreements not only exist in the context of UNCLOS III but also go beyond it.[129] Notable both for explicitly adopting precautionary action and for having U.S. support is the 1995 UN Agreement on Straddling and Highly Migratory Fish Stocks. By addressing straddling stocks, it is moving to manage stocks that can be found in both EEZs and ungoverned high seas. Already signed by more than forty nations, this treaty emphasizes (1) the precautionary principle, (2) conservation of marine biodiversity, and (3) sustainable use of fisheries. Its main elements include an ecosystems approach to governance that takes into account dependent or associated species, as well as robust enforcement of conservation measures through effective monitoring. This agreement on straddling stocks is designed to work closely with the FAO Code of Conduct for Responsible Fisheries, thus strengthening both.[130]

Among the significant events in creating multilateral protections for marine ecosystems was the 1946 International Convention for the Regulation of Whaling. That regime has evolved dramatically in the last few decades from resource extraction to conservation. A major treaty from the 1970s was the International Convention on the Prevention of Pollution from Ships. In 1987 there was a Montreal Protocol on Substances That Deplete the Ozone Layer. This is not an atmospheric issue only; depletion of the ozone layer poses large risks for the health of marine ecosystems as well.[131]

Another important milestone was Agenda 21, signed at a 1992 UN Conference on Environment and Development. Of special importance are chapters 13, chiding nations for their slowness to compensate for extraterritorial environmental damage, and 15, on the precautionary principle.[132] Also created in the 1990s was the UN General Assembly Drift-Net Resolution banning drift nets longer than 2.5 kilometers from the high seas, although this ban is reportedly being violated.[133] A United Nations Environment Program Conference was held in 1995 on protecting the marine environment from land-based activities. And talks that concluded in Kyoto, Japan, in 1997 have somewhat strengthened the Framework Convention on Climate Change. As with the impact of ozone depletion for marine environments, rising emissions of greenhouse gases can harm the integrity of marine ecosystems by fostering global changes that produce instability.[134]

THE INTERNATIONAL JOINT COMMISSION
ON THE GREAT LAKES

The above sampling makes it clear that comprehensive, multilateral undertakings like the UNCLOS III extravaganza are not the only avenues to action. Recently Canada and the United States have made the Great Lakes, on their common border, a topic of bilateral discussion through the International Joint Commission on Great Lakes Water Quality (IJC). Interestingly enough, the IJC explicitly adopts the precautionary principle.[135] A 1994 report states, "Persistent toxic substances are too dangerous to the biosphere and to humans to permit their release in any quantity," and "All persistent toxic substances are dangerous to the environment, deleterious to the human condition, and can no longer be tolerated in the ecosystem, whether or not unassailable scientific proof of acute or chronic damage is universally accepted."[136]

This is a bold response to the Great Lakes' dire situation.[137] It is also a major departure from traditional permissive policies toward the Great Lakes that permitted releasing a variety of pollutants.[138] As in the UN Straddling Stocks agreement, in this case the United States is now an advocate for precautionary action. While the IJC statement of principles has been criticized as lacking force, it should be recognized as a genuine vote of confidence and an endorsement of cooperative stewardship for the marine environment.

THE POLLUTION PREVENTION ACT

A major first step toward precaution and prevention in domestic environmental law is the Pollution Prevention Act of 1990 (PPA).[139] What is unusual is that the act was created in conference committee when enabling language was inserted in the Omnibus Budget Reconciliation Act of 1990. Thus the PPA did not appear in House or Senate budget bills.[140] The forward-looking PPA explicitly establishes a four-level ranking for preventing pollution. Source reduction (or pollution prevention) is clearly listed in the act as the most desirable option. Failing that, the PPA lists waste recycling as next best option. Waste treatment follows when recycling is unworkable. Finally, waste disposal is seen as a last resort.[141] And thus the environmentally popular option of recycling is also recognized as inferior to either eliminating or reducing waste at the source. The act intentionally leaves the initiative for pollution prevention with the states to take advantage of local knowledge. Indeed, "States have been at the forefront of the pollution prevention movement . . . [with] programs occasionally serving as a model for federal programs."[142]

Making prevention the number one priority is a novel idea. It is also common sense; it can be more economical than command-and-control methods that for decades mandated end-of-pipe thinking. Thus engineers and scientists are increasingly being asked to find clever means to avoid waste in the first place. An earlier attempt at source reduction was the Resource Conservation and Recovery Act of 1976, amended by the Hazardous and Solid Waste Amendments of 1984. However, it has been more narrowly interpreted than PPA and has generally had little success.[143] But times change. As reported in *Science*, a chemist at the Environmental Protection Agency was "tired of being an environmental cop." Rather than track the "hundreds of known toxic and carcinogenic substances released into the environment each year as they move from air to water to land and back again, he would rather replace his police uniform with a lab coat, and promote research into ways chemists can redesign existing compounds to render them harmless to humans and the environment."[144]

Engineering environmentally safer substitutes for current methods and products is clearly possible but too rarely tried. A new mind set can facilitate innovative thinking and enable the redesign of substances like dyes, paints, solvents, pesticides, weed killers, and other chemicals. In just this fashion, a safer way was found to manufacture quinoic acid, used in photographic agents and other chemicals; bacteria are incorporated in making the acid so that it releases sugars in place of benzene.[145] In another industrial setting, the commercially important polymer polytrimethylene terephthalate (3GT) is now being made without heavy metals, petroleum, or toxics. Instead it is produced using glucose from cornstarch, which is cheaper to boot. And all the liquid effluent in its production is now biodegradable. Further, this 3GT polymer can easily undergo methanolysis to reduce polyesters to original monomers, for indefinite recycling.

A strikingly different and yet ultimately similar strategy is seen in the Toxic Diet Project promoted by Save the Bay of Rhode Island.[146] Here the emerging aims of pollution prevention are being achieved by a combination of waste-water monitoring, together with education to encourage individuals to buy less toxic products for home use. It shows that a more sensible alternative to water contamination, and thus to costly sewage treatment, is to voluntarily reduce toxins at their source. Ideas like the Toxic Diet are an exciting, low-cost, and rational means to prevent pollution among the broad public.

Yet few federal dollars earmarked for the environment are being spent on prevention. In 1990, roughly $115 billion went toward all pollution control efforts in the United States, an immense figure that will rise to $170 billion by the year 2000. Yet, according to a GAO report, the EPA spends "less than 1 percent of the agency's annual budget for source reduction activities."[147] While hundreds of billions of dollars have initiated much eco-business for environmental cleanup or treatment, these dollars typically are directed to remediating damage after it has occurred.

Prevention has not been embraced more strongly in part because of problems in implementing the Pollution Prevention Act. According to a report from the General Accounting Office that evaluated PPA programs nation-wide, the primary goals of the act are not being met. While some state antipollution programs created by the PPA are properly focused on source reduction, many of them wrongly emphasize recycling, waste treatment, and even waste disposal. A curious result is that some state programs are awarded federal funds for pollution control but have neglected to ascertain if prevention is possible—an outcome inconsistent with the goals of the act.[148]

Another potential issue is that some 80 percent of the state PPA programs are nonregulatory, volunteer efforts. While this voluntary (nonmandatory) feature might be the smartest approach to prevention, without strong financial support the goals of PPA could be too easily overlooked. An information base for industry was created to disseminate knowledge on ways to prevent pollution at its source. The results included a Pollution Prevention Office and a Source Reduction Clearinghouse, and the GAO report notes that these should be expanded. Prevention must be strengthened by new outreach efforts if pollution prevention, reduction at the source, is to develop any momentum. And some way of assessing current PPA efforts will be necessary to ascertain which state prevention programs are working and which are not, and exactly why.[149] The EPA notes in its defense that stronger goals are not part of its mandate under PPA, which requires only that states "promote" reduction at the source.[150]

Realistically, preventing pollution is a daunting task. While the dollars are there for after-the-fact cleanup, no infrastructure or constituency truly supports pollution prevention. Moreover, for political reasons, PPA targets for voluntary action are deliberately vague to avoid entanglements with manufacturers who resist any limitation on their business decisions. Nonetheless, fiscal incentives and market tools to eliminate or reduce harms at the source ought to be considered. These include "green" subsidies and taxes. For instance, a levy on manufacturers that use virgin materials in making paper, plastics, glass, aluminum, and metal products can promote greater efficiency and recycling.[151] Carefully tailored "green" taxes can be incentives for prevention and reduce currently externalized environmental burdens. Revenues generated from "green" taxes should then be earmarked for new PPA action, creating a self-sustaining process.

Other attempts at source reduction should encourage industry to voluntarily reduce the use of problematic chemicals. The EPA's 33/50 program is one example. The program, begun during the Bush administration, sought to reduce releases of seventeen specified chemicals by 33 percent in 1992 and 50 percent in 1995. Generally speaking, the program has been a success as far as it attempted to go. But several issues still need to be solved. For example, because it relies on data from the toxics release inventory as the sole means to measure reductions, it is difficult to ascertain the true success rate because the inventory does not indicate specifically how reductions were made. While it shows changes in the total weight of chemicals released or transferred, it does not give good data on whether these were a result of closing a facility, of paperwork changes like new methods for calculating estimates, of transfers offsite such as for incineration or recycling, or of true source reduction.[152] Toxic release inventory data show that even though the reported release of certain chemicals into the environment has been dropping, the total amount of waste generated by industry continues to rise.[153] Nonetheless, the 33/50 program is a worthy first step.

During the 1990s the EPA began other new programs for incorporating pollution prevention into business, industrial, and consumer decision making. These include the Green Lights Project, which promotes the idea that more efficient practices can cut the use of electricity for lighting by 50–75 percent.[154] Other pollution prevention projects include the Energy Star Computers, which draw on less power when inactive, since 25–40 percent of computers are left on overnight, and the Water Alliances for Voluntary Efficiency, in which participants seek to reduce their water usage by some 2.25 billion gallons per year. This is a purposeful effort to move away from sector-specific, command-and-control regulations that had characterized earlier EPA actions.[155]

Looking Ahead: Industrial Ecology and Design for the Environment

The preceding discussion shows that the design phase is crucial to reducing waste and pollution in manufacturing. According to the National Research Council, roughly 70 percent of the costs associated with a product's development, manufacture, and use are determined at the outset—during the product's initial design stage.[156] More relevant here is that design decisions deeply influence a product's ecological impacts—from cradle to grave. At the design stage there is greatest flexibility to determine what materials to use, to choose benign manufacturing techniques, to consider ecological risks, and to determine the characteristics of waste streams.[157] The design phase is the best moment to apply new concepts of industrial ecology and design for the environment.[158]

In 1989 Robert Frosh and Nicholas Gallopoulos introduced the idea of industrial ecology to the public.[159] The aims of industrial ecology are to advance a more cyclical approach toward manufacturing design in which natural resources are used and reused as efficiently as possible. "This contrasts with the traditional linear model of manufacturing, in which materials are extracted, used in production, and then discarded."[160] Industrial ecology strives to emulate the cyclical processes found in ecosystems, since natural systems abhor waste. In nature one organism's waste is another's sustenance. In fact, many technological advances have been made by imitating patterns found in nature; dragonflies once served as a model for improving helicopter designs.[161]

The objective is to "network" industrial plants so that they work more like biological systems. A network of interrelationships could take the unwanted effluents from one plant, or "organism" (such as heat, waste water, surplus gas, steam, organic debris), and use them as input for other processes. By design, the by-products of metabolism (manufacturing) can be coordinated so that effluents support a much larger system. Although the biological metaphor is not perfect, the current state of industrial production could be compared to a stage of primitive life on earth when there was very little recycling of material and toxic wastes accumulated to the point where they presented problems for survival.[162] Microorganisms evolved over time to become consumers of other organisms' wastes. Once evolved from a primitive anaerobic to an aerobic metabolism, thus able to exploit what had been poisonous oxygen, the web of living systems grew more integrated and stronger because of its biological diversity.

A manifestation of the efficient ecosystems approach is design for the environment (DfE), an adaptation of the "Design for X" idea (DfX) in manufacturing. "In DfX, a desired product characteristic (such as safety or durability) is integrated as a goal into the design process. In DfE initiatives, environmental considerations become an integral part of the design of a product."[163] Like nature, DfE has many faces. In Germany, for instance, legislative initiatives have led to new product designs that incorporate ease of disassembly, recyclability, and pollution prevention into original specifications. More broadly, German law is beginning to require companies to check their production processes to identify by-products (waste) that may be used by other industries.[164] Such technology forcing is bound to improve ecological efficiency. Thus an enzymatic process was found to reduce wastes from one industrial process by about 90 percent while also making the remaining waste nontoxic.

On a larger scale, the DfE idea may be applied to the eco-industrial park. Here zoning is applied not only to set aside space for manufacturing but also to prevent pollution by initiating more sophisticated and interconnected business relationships. Industrial systems are viewed through a prism of biological systems using (where feasible) ecological ideas like materials flows, carrying capacity, resilience, and connectivity. Outputs from one plant are raw inputs for other plants in a process that both increases profits and minimizes wastes.[165]

There are many potential avenues for achieving environmental efficiency, materials recycling, and gaining ecological wisdom—all in a spirit of DfE. Possibilities include integrated pest management and aggressively designing houses and whole communities for greater energy conservation. In the fertile Salinas Valley of California, a smart new company has developed one such business that reflects DfE thinking.[166] A large agribusiness there had been processing several tons of lettuce daily for packaging, discarding unwanted vegetable pieces as waste. In an entrepreneurial fashion, this company now takes the excess and converts it into compost, which is then sold to farmers. This composting business supplants potentially harmful chemical fertilizers and reuses organic materials that otherwise would be wasted (by being thrown away in landfills). Any action that productively returns a product to the soil is the greatest recycling act of all.

Another example of the application of industrial symbiosis is a Danish biotech company named Novo Nordisk and the interrelationships among industrial plants in the small city of Kalundborg, Denmark. It cost an estimated $60 million to build this complex system, which has returned some $10–12 million per year, for a $120 million payback so far. The web of interrelationships works like this: a local oil refinery sells its waste— cooling water, waste water, and surplus gas and steam—to a local power plant. The power plant sells its waste, including heat, to some 5,000 homes; it sells gypsum to a plaster board factory; and it sells heated water to a fish farm. Waste in the form of steam is sold to the Novo Nordisk biotech company. At the same time, Novo Nordisk sells to farmers a nitrogen-rich biomass from its enzyme fermentation vats. Surplus yeast from Novo Nordisk's insulin production goes to farmers as fodder to feed animals.[167] This cooperation not only is commercially sound but also makes common sense.

Conclusion

In sum, present U.S. laws are just beginning to exhibit precautionary action. However, the government has started to play a needed catalytic role, as seen in the Design for the Environment program at the U.S. Environmental Protection Agency.[168] This voluntary DfE program offers selected industries information on ways to prevent pollution while also increasing profits by designing products and/or processes with an awareness of ecological consequences. That thinking is establishing cooperative government-industry partnerships for both precautionary action and pollution prevention. These are sophisticated, multifaceted approaches to solving the problem by going to the source of pollution.[169]

6

The Challenge of Integrating Science and Policy

> The symptoms of environmental deterioration are in the domain of the natural sciences, but the causes lie in the realm of the social sciences and humanities.
>
> *David Orr, "Ecological Literacy"*

HUMANITY HAS LONG BEEN profoundly ignorant of the natural linkages that exist across marine ecosystems, so for management purposes we have readily divided the ocean's waters. Centuries ago our categorizing intellect imposed simple demarcations like a three-mile limit that persist today. Such zones were once adequate to assign jurisdiction, but they never did describe reality. Now with ever increasing human pressures on the sea, it is time to move forward. Modern science has shown marine processes to be amazingly interdependent. With this in mind, we ought to approach the sea not as made up of isolated segments but as an integrated whole.[1]

To govern marine resources in more effective fashion will first mean listening to the sea. Rather than maintain politically derived jurisdictional boundaries it is time to adopt a complex, subtle, holistic, and organic view of nature. The goal, however, of joining the marine sciences with policy making is more difficult than commonly assumed. In part this is because the study of politics, social institutions, and the law were long ago separated from the natural sciences, with far-reaching consequences.

As a result, the physical sciences are usually regarded as far different disciplines from the social sciences and humanities.[2] "Hard" sciences like chemistry and physics seem to work in objectively useful ways; they rely on quantitative measurement, observation, and replication—in short, the scientific method. Technological advances brought by science have conferred great respect on these disciplines.[3] For example, that the atomic bomb works confers a particular authority on the study of physics.

But a particular world view accompanies the objective inquiry demanded of science. Scientists may investigate human-induced phenomena, but their concerns are purposefully devoid of attention to human values. Society's impact on nature may be studied, but no allowance is made there for subjective human feelings.[4] Scientists rightly approach in disinterested fashion the question as to whether consumption or conservation is preferable, and in doing so purposely remove thorny politicized issues of competing human desires from the analysis. Indeed, most scientists regard the conflict over the appropriate use of resources as subjective politics: that is a world they are understandably reluctant to enter.

By contrast, the social sciences pursue an understanding of human behavior and values. This is a subjective and inherently debatable world, dominated by shades of gray, in which they seek to interpret human experience.[5] There are no quantitative answers, as in the hard sciences. The gap between these two cultures poses subtle but thorny issues for ocean policy making. The sort of research expected from a social scientist exemplifies this gap. It might focus on the socioeconomic impacts of fishery restrictions for the human inhabitants of a fishing community. But a social science researcher typically pays scant attention to how these restrictions will also ecologically alter natural marine communities.

This divide is rarely questioned. Even if ecosystem perturbations stem from the very same human actions that are a focus of research, social scientists are usually not concerned with these environmental changes unless there is an immediate feedback affecting human beings. Yet in light of the failures in modern resource management, it is time now to reexamine this fictional division in how we approach the external world.

For their part, the social scientists should be called upon to improve public policy regarding resource governance, but certain criticisms should be heeded for their expertise to be better applied. At the outset, consider that many theoretical models produced by a small army of social scientists are too often jargon-laden, excessively long, and difficult to read, making them inaccessible to policy makers working in the field. In policy studies, as in other disciplines, often interesting theoretical material must be "translated" before it can be used by policy practitioners. As a result, useful academic work that could improve marine resources management is overlooked. Because of such a dependence on theory that is unknown outside a given field, potentially instructive insights may go unrecognized by scientists addressing related environmental issues but from a different angle. Yet policy studies need not be so inaccessible. Even complex policy theory could be put forward in a more understandable fashion. More can be done to demystify policy theory and broaden its applications.[6]

But social science can never state its conclusions with the certainty and confidence of the natural sciences. The physicist can observe that an electron has a certain mass of 9.1×10^{-28} grams, or that water changes to ice if the temperature drops to zero degrees Celsius. That confidence is made possible by consistent, measurable physical processes. In the tremendously subjective world of human actions, things are vastly different.[7] It is impossible to build models in the social sciences that are anywhere as predictive as phase change in water. Even in seemingly identical situations, no one behaves precisely the same way twice. This makes the integration of science and policy a thorny proposition because they go about their work in fundamentally different ways. In a hard science like physics, a hypothesis is put forth and then scientists attempt to find instances where the theory fails to fit all the facts. Thus a hypothesis is tested and a new level of scientific consensus is achieved.[8]

Take the theory of continuous creation offered by astronomers Hoyle, Bondi, and Gold to describe the origins of the universe. With that hypothesis there was new grist for research, investigation was stimulated, facts found, and theories composed. Once evidence was found refuting the theory, that older model was thrown out and a newer "big bang" hypothesis was formulated. That the earlier theory was later proved wrong does not detract from the benefits it provided.[9] The scientific method has worked exceptionally well because it enables scientists to build on the work of their intellectual ancestors. As Sir Isaac Newton remarked, "If I have seen farther, it is by standing on the shoulders of giants." Albert Einstein's theory of relativity moved beyond not only Euclidean geometry but also Newtonian physics. Einstein did not replace Newton, but went farther to see a quantum universe.[10]

On the other hand, many ideas in social science are not amenable to such objective disproof, for its theories can only approximate real-world events. Advances are commonly more akin to a networked knowledge—a path not inferior to the way in which information is built up in physics, merely different.[11] Despite the obstacles posed by lack of disproof, the social sciences should rank among the most meaningful of academic studies.

There is now a movement toward the ecologically cognizant integration of science and policy that is called for here—but tellingly it is coming from the hard sciences. Conservation biology is a new field devoted to understanding the means to preserve ecological integrity. This does not mean taking an ideological stance, for that runs counter to its great value as a rigorously objective scientific discipline.[12] Rather, it functions by furthering knowledge of how species and habitat richness can be conserved. While clearly rooted in objective scientific inquiry, many conservation biologists pay attention to policy making and the social environment in its genuinely broader sense.

Thus conservation biologists might ably assist regulators who seek to protect habitat diversity, species diversity, or genetic variety within a species. They can give policy makers guidance on robust biogeochemical cycling or provide insights into sustainable resource use. They might advise policy makers on how to best conserve the abiotic (nonliving) resources without which biological processes are unlikely to succeed.[13] While the closely related science of ecology is concerned with natural factors that affect diversity and abundance, conservation biologists may more readily apply their unique knowledge toward conservationist ends. Pioneering academics in this field have begun to bridge the gap that has long separated science from policy concerns.[14]

That interdisciplinary approach suggests the possibility for new subfields within the social sciences. If a subfield like policy studies gave more attention to the goals of improving environmental regimes, the results could be intellectually exciting. There is no reason why policy academics should not turn their efforts to the conservation of biodiversity. Indeed, such cross-pollination could improve environmental governance in bountiful ways. Political scientists might even point to ways in which management could better improve the health of ecosystems.[15] There is a growing awareness of environmental policy, but political science has long been concerned with social, not ecological issues, stressing the *processes* of decision making over their consequences. This is understandable, given the public's indifference to and unfamiliarity with ecology. Yet more than an uncomfortable fact, such a paucity of attention is a call to reexamine assumptions and discuss potential contributions for a wiser governance.[16]

Reductionist Thinking

Enhancing the role of science in forming environmental policy will require some effort. It means overcoming not only a division between science and policy, but also a reductionist paradigm that splinters our perspectives into countless disciplines. This reductionism is closely related to the basic segregation of policy from science already mentioned, but it is much older in origin. It can be traced to the ancient Greeks and the "atomist" Democritus, who taught that to best understand something, one should begin by breaking it into smaller parts. The idea is to first understand the basic building blocks, and from there to gain an understanding of the larger whole. This approach, formalized by scientists like Descartes, is now an axiom of the scientific study of nature.[17]

And yet the examination of parts has taken precedence over an appreciation of the whole. There is a penalty to be paid for the basic splintering of nature, which can obscure relational linkages between human activities and broad changes in the ecosystem. To witness this cubbyholing in action, one might visit a marine research institute. Scientists from varied disciplines could be studying the same ocean, yet they focus on very different things. For instance, a marine geologist might focus on the fault lines far beneath the seafloor, unconcerned with the dynamics of biota in the sea column such as fish populations. A marine biologist might focus on under-standing the optic nerves of a squid without attending to the larger-scale interchange of gases between atmosphere and ocean—a topic that would fill the entire career of a fellow scientist. Nothing is inherently wrong with such atomization of the sea into many parts. Only in this way can a scientist gaze deeper into one of the ocean's constituent components. What is lacking, however, is a concern with the broader perspective.

Gone are the romantic wide-ranging naturalists from an earlier era, the gentleman-scientist would be both botanist and chemist, the theologian who discovered oxygen, the lawyer who invented fuel cells, the discoverer of electricity who served as colonial ambassador to Britain and France. With an explosion of ever deepening knowledge, such multidisciplinary efforts are now a formidable proposition. Recognizing this, few scientists today study the land-sea interface in its entirety. Biology has some thirty subdisciplines.[18] Political science claims at least seven fields along with more subfields, each with its own theories, and specialists in one subfield may have little to say to those in another. Public funding bodies also in-tensify separations, since they have been slow to promote linkages across disciplines. To see natural systems as segregated into small pieces makes good sense for scientific advancement (of the reductionist type), but it im-pedes our ability to see the earth as a whole.

Most important, atomistic thinking carried into governance leads to bad policy.[19] To overlook the natural links in the environment, or to assume we can ignore ecological harm caused by human behavior, is folly. It can cause basic relational aspects of the web of life to be overlooked. Nonethe-less, we display what the Greeks called hubris in believing that the re-ductionist logic that is so powerful in physics can disarm the ecological consequences of our activities. A difficult lesson is that learned by the em-inent ecologist Aldo Leopold when he removed predators from game ranges. In a simplistic effort to improve hunting, Leopold discovered,

> the mountain and its vegetative cover can be made ill by atomistic manage-ment which manipulates populations without care for the impact of these manipulations on the larger, ecological system. Deer and wolf management must he concluded, be limited by concern for the larger system, the "moun-tain." . . . More formally, it is expressed as an endorsement of an essentially systematic approach to management.[20]

Human history is replete with attempts to transfigure the earth for human purposes; it is also rife with grave errors in predicting all of the environmental outcomes. Paul Sears, a pioneering ecological scientist, saw this dichotomy when he called ecology a "subversive science." His point was that "laws of human society and the laws of nature are at odds, at least in this civilization, and a reconciliation will require substantial revisions of government that some might consider downright revolutionary."[21] What is called for now may not be a revolution of law and policy, but a much gentler evolution.

Toward More Holistic Environmental Governance

For policy makers to recognize the interconnectedness of ecological processes means changing our perceptions. Words and their meanings matter. The phrase *holistic governance* should be scrutinized. The word *holistic* was coined only seventy years ago to convey the idea that a collection of organisms—or even a single one—is highly interconnected and that the whole is much more than the sum of its parts.[22] Regrettably, that new word has been hijacked in recent years to refer to a wide assortment of fuzzy new-age ideals. The trendy application of the concept was probably inevitable, since it expresses an enduring idea that life is to a degree interdependent, in opposition to the reductionist assumptions inherited from the Enlightenment. Lewis Thomas remarks,

> I wish holism could remain a respectable term for scientific usage, but alas, it has fallen in bad company. Science itself is really a holistic enterprise, and no other word would serve quite as well to describe it. Years ago, the mathematician Poincaré wrote, "Science is built up with facts as a house is with stones, but a collection of facts is no more a science than a heap of stones is a house." [But] the word is becoming trendy. . . . We need another word, a word to distinguish a system from the components of a system, and I cannot think of one.[23]

The great utility of the concept of holism is it encourages a comprehensive examination of entire ecosystems, rather than breaking them into component parts, as is typical of science. Yet it is notable for its absence in marine policy.[24]

The ostensibly neutral word *governance* also deserves reflection. It is defined as "to rule with authority, especially with the authority of a sovereign; to direct and control actions and affairs whether despotically or constitutionally." One etymological root, the thirteenth-century Old French *governer*, does not imply wise or beneficent rule.[25] Indeed, nothing in the modern definition suggests that a ruler should govern wisely or even knowledgeably. This sterile meaning is deeply unsatisfying, however, when one thinks about the proper way to govern the natural environment.

But an earlier root for *govern* is the Latin *gubernare*, to direct or to guide. This much earlier meaning implies a sense of stewardship for the ship of state, for the Greek root here is *kybernan*, meaning to steer wisely.[26] Centuries ago, then, the idea of governance meant "to attend to, care for, look after." These meanings embedded in the word more accurately reflect the wisdom and a sense of stewardship that are now required.

How then to act? The form and behavior of most marine life is vastly different from more familiar life in the terrestrial world.[27] This "unfathomable" character of the sea presents many obstacles to wise ocean management. The larvae of many fish are microscopic and planktonic (floating); thus in appearance and preferred habitat they are very unlike adults. A most curious result is that easily identifiable marine life like lobsters or urchins appear to just materialize as near-adults. And so the populations of well-known species seem to fluctuate wildly for no apparent reason.[28] Even to specialists, practically nothing is known about celebrated creatures like the great white shark (wrongly made out to be viciously evil in movies and on television). In our ignorance, we apply to the sea our own terrestrially formed ideas about boundaries and behavior—sorely inappropriate prerequisites for making good decisions about the marine environment.[29]

Perceptual hurdles also mean that we can scarcely grasp the tremendous scale of marine processes. Natural boundaries at sea are very different from those on land. A halocline that segregates out vertical layering of salinity in sea water, or a submerged mountain range, or continuously changing thermoclines are hidden to us, yet are very real boundaries. The typical range of a land animal may be a few dozen miles, but sea creatures do not observe such limits. Marine life frequently covers vast distances. Planktonic larvae carried at one knot for twenty-eight days will travel almost

600 nautical miles from their origin. A typical ocean life cycle relationship can occur over an area that is larger by a full order of magnitude than more familiar life on land. Reproductive strategies at sea are very different from what we are accustomed to.[30] The general failure to recognize this interconnectivity and range when managing marine systems is a grave problem. Surely, notions like a three-mile territorial sea have no ecological value.

Misunderstandings persist because of the difficulty of penetrating this alien environment. On land, observation of natural life can be done with comparatively little effort. In sharp contrast, even SCUBA will give an underwater diver only minutes of observation very near the surface, and the occluded nature of sea water limits long-range sensing.[31] To rectify common misperceptions about the sea, education must be the chief means to cultivate a greater appreciation and respect for this alien world.

Education is needed not only on the interconnected marine environment, but also on the long-term consequences of human activities. This requires attention to chronic ecological threats that will only be evident years or decades hence, which is practically speaking exceptionally hard to do. It is not easy to get politicians interested in drafting laws that address impacts that will be visible only in the distant future.

Moreover, cumulative harms are especially discordant with political time lines that drive legislative policy making. Politics often operates on a brief time scale: two years (for a House seat), four years (presidential term), or six years (for a Senate seat). Legislative responses are further constrained by a haphazard composition of various congressional committees, which themselves endlessly fight over turf issues. Constitutionally derived issues like length of terms in office and the composition of subcommittees do not mesh in any way with the management of marine processes—yet are relevant nonetheless.

Ecological Systems and Systems of Governance

Ecosystems by definition consist of interacting parts such that removal or failure of one part can incapacitate the whole. Like internal mechanisms of a watch, interconnected systems are sensitive to meddling. As in any system, some level of stability is essential for ensuring robust health. This can be a dynamic stability, such as with incremental change punctuated by significant shifts, yet it is stability nonetheless. The word *homeostasis* expresses the idea that ecosystems resist change by seeking to maintain a healthy equilibrium.[32] Stability has been shattered, as the geologic record shows. Five cataclysmic spasms of extinction occurred over the last 500 million years, but such moments were spaced out by millions of years, so in time a new form of stability was established. Although at least half all the marine fauna was lost in a mass extinction of the late Permian 225 million years ago, life reemerged and radiated outward with intense new speciation.[33] A mass extinction 65 million years ago in the Cretaceous-Tertiary period eventually gave way to new biological diversity. Stratified forests developed on land as many angiosperms replaced gymnosperms. In the seas, new marine species developed to fill the open ecological niches.[34]

The relevance for the present is that we may be living amid a new epoch of environmental change that is of geological-record proportions. Today the biosphere is subjected to massive forces released by human activities.[35] While we understand little about the large marine ecosystems within 200 miles of shore, the data indicate that overfishing and pollution are contributing to stock collapses in the northeast U.S. continental shelf, the Gulf of Thailand, and the Yellow Sea. Rapid declines in biomass as in the Baltic Sea are attributed to pollution. Human forces appear to be a chief cause for declining fisheries in the East Bering Sea, the Gulf of Alaska, the Antarctic, the Gulf of Mexico, the southeast U.S. continental shelf, and the North Sea.[36]

Some argue that species extinction is no cause for concern, since it has occurred before. Pointing to the past five spasms of extinction, they believe that the possibility of a sixth one should not be cause for alarm. It is true that mass extinctions are found in the geologic record, but they miss the fact that each time it took many millennia for perturbed ecosystems to readjust and for new speciation to arise. The threat is a rate of change so rapid that many ecosystems (fish, forests, farmland) could switch over to states we are unprepared for and would be harmed by. Were it not lost years ago in a sudden crash, a rich sardine fishery off the coast of Monterey could still be providing jobs, protein, and income.

Some biologists fear that a next extinction spasm may be already beginning that is the handiwork of our species.[37] We may be triggering drastic ecosystem changes, but given so little understanding of the marine environment, we can only catch glimpses of the synergistic mechanisms. A case in point is the unexpected impact of chlorofluorocarbons (CFCs) on the protective layer of stratospheric ozone in the earth's upper atmosphere. Changes threaten the earth's ability to shield most life from UV-B radiation and from the damage to DNA caused by solar radiation.[38]

A worrisome sign is the thinning of ozone in the atmosphere over the earth's poles. Some expected this "hole" to diminish once the effects of a volcanic explosion at Mount Pinatubo wore off. Yet it has not. Thus in the 1990s the ozone layer at the South Pole dipped to 102 DU (Dobson Units) —far less than in the late 1970s, when it was about 280 DU.[39] Only a 10 percent reduction in the ozone layer can result in a 28 percent increase in total UV-B radiation.[40] Thus, further significant increases in the size of this hole could potentially establish a feedback loop with nonlinear, cumulative environmental impacts that can only be guessed at. For instance, phytoplankton declines may trigger collapses in the krill that feed on phytoplankton, with cascading impacts throughout the food web stretching over polar waters and beyond. UV-B energy at these wavelengths may also harm plant leaves, suppress immune systems in mammals, and cause blindness.[41] If inert CFC gases released from air compressors far inland can harm krill in distant polar waters, than environmental policy should respond with greater foresight. Lewis Thomas writes, "In no other century of our brief existence have human beings learned so deeply, and so painfully, the extent and depth of their ignorance about nature."[42]

Preserving the stability of marine ecosystems is in our utilitarian self-interest.[43] Achieving that stability through laws that ensure evolutionary rather than revolutionary change in the environment is best: healthy adaptation is better than crisis and collapse.[44] Because the bulk of humanity lives near the coast, simply conserving marine biodiversity is forward-thinking and rational. And indeed we benefit from many marine processes.[45] Thus our concern should not be with change in itself, writes Joseph Sax, but rather "a rate of change so destabilizing as to promote crisis—social, biological, and economic. The disappearance of various species from the earth in the natural, evolutionary process is totally different from the disappearance of species over a short time. The key difference is not the fact of change, but the rate of change."[46]

An obstacle to improved governance is that ecosystems may now be deteriorating faster than regimes can respond. It is true that the industrialized nations are now giving more attention to recovering healthy and swimmable coastal seas. But in innumerable cases, the economic cost is proving far greater than anticipated. Even if a major cleanup effort were undertaken, the coastal seas may never rebound to their previous state. Newer, less robust, less biologically diverse equilibria could arise that are not adequate for increasing human needs.

Hence scientists and policy makers have diminishing room for error. An example is the debate over controlling the release of greenhouse gases into the atmosphere. We cannot know for certain whether they will unequivocally lead to climate change until it is too late, which makes policy making so vexing. When the next ecological catastrophe occurs (and it will), putting the pieces together again may be even more difficult. Recently new ecological dilemmas stemming from past changes have been coming to light. Typically these arise from what were thought to be benign activities. Examples include building dams that destroy ecosystems, such as the near-total loss of the Aral Sea; lack of safety precautions at the Chernobyl nuclear plant; and cavalier use of substances like DDT whose impact was not understood.[47] A legion of ecological errors show the harms caused by poor governance.

Consider more specifically the Chernobyl accident. This nuclear plant was regarded as a safe and beneficial substitute for the coal-fired power plants (which create pollution, including greenhouse gases) once necessary to generate electricity. But in the notoriously energy-inefficient Soviet Union, energy was priced far below its true cost through distortions built into the system. In retrospect, it is clear that scarce funds should have been spent instead on energy-efficiency upgrades of the existing distribution and use network. In a nation where copious supplies of oil and gas were lost from thousands of miles of leaky pipelines, where heat was wasted in crumbling infrastructure like uninsulated heating pipes exposed above Moscow streets, and where gasoline was priced far below cost and thus wasted, a more prudent goal would have been enhanced energy efficiency and conservation. Choices made in governance clearly matter.

Beginnings of a Shift in Attitudes

The case for a more holistic governance can be appreciated in the symbolic plight of Northwest salmon. Salmon are worth many millions of dollars. Yet human beings have caused their numbers to dwindle precipitously because the rights of landowners to exploit their property for their own economic benefit takes precedence over the impact of such exploitation on natural life.

This permissive paradigm has extended implications. For instance, it instructs that possibly damaging activities can be monitored and their ultimate effects predicted and held to acceptable limits. Oceans are portrayed as having near-boundless assimilative capacity. The traditional view is that exploiting the earth's resources in pursuit of maximizing one's economic self-interest is guided by a classic "invisible hand" and thus is rational.[48] Only where an ecosystem has already demonstrated that it cannot assimilate any more damage are expensive remediation efforts undertaken—even then only when there is an educated constitutency and adequate public funding to finance pollution control.

Yet a healthy ecosystem is becoming more important to increasingly "green" societies, and the implications are staggering. Profound changes in attitudes have occurred in the last few decades. Until the late 1960s, with a wink and a nod harm to the environment was dismissed as a price to be paid for economic gain. The law fueled this paradigm. The judicial system was clearly more friendly to industrialization than to pollution control, while prevention was all but ignored. Thus a court hearing a lawsuit brought upon the common law complaint of nuisance (until recently one of few remedies for harm from pollution) would take a limited view of the issues.

Such an approach is reflected in the classic 1970 case, *Boomer v. Atlantic Ce-*

ment Company (26 N.Y. 2d 219; 257 N.E. 2d 870 [1970]), which demonstrates the remedies available at law for a nuisance.[49] The court did find that dust, dirt, smoke, and vibrations from a cement plant damaged the plaintiff. The issue was: what award of damages would make the plaintiff "whole." The plaintiff, who lived nearby, sought an order for the plant either to install pollution control equipment or to be shut down. The court rejected that remedy, however, on grounds of public policy. Citing the loss of investment in the plant and of jobs, it awarded permanent damages of $12,500 based only on a decline in property value of the home. The plant did not reduce its pollution as a result of that decision. The court's decision was therefore neither technology-forcing nor an order to reduce pollutants (or be shut down). Instead, the dissenting opinion noted, it was a license for a continuing wrong. "It is the same as saying to the cement company, you may continue to do harm to your neighbors so long as you pay a fee for it."[50] Once the plant had paid the damages, there was no incentive to reduce pollution.

A sign of improvement is that the outcome in *Boomer* is inconceivable today. Will environmental laws continue toward pollution prevention? Recent history is instructive.[51] Following elections in the mid-1990s, a "wise-use" movement briefly popularized an agenda of regulatory "reform" —that is, scaling back regulation—and many "green" ideals were attacked in the House of Representatives. Yet that attack proved divisive and its strident advocates suffered at the polls.[52] The pendulum is now swinging toward moderation in both the Congress and the presidency.

In the near term we will likely continue to muddle through on the environment, with an emphasis on narrowly defined issues. Specialists will thus remain concerned with limited questions like making cost-benefit analysis more sophisticated. Improvement here is needed, given that "cost-benefit studies consistently undervalue the net benefits conferrable by species, since it is much easier to measure the costs of conservation than the ultimate gains, even in purely monetary terms."[53] But more important will be to tap a rising public desire to understand the seas around us. Aquariums are now being built in many cities. With them will come more accessible education about the seas. As the Senegalese ecologist Baba Dioum remarks, "In the end we will conserve only what we love; we will love only what we understand; and we will understand only what we are taught."[54] It is hard to overstate the importance of a public that seeks to understand the life of the sea and to hold it dear.

Shifts Toward a Science-Based Ocean Governance

Wide swaths of ocean coastline have been drastically transformed.[55] Those ecologically rich communities once called "swamplands" (but now more respectfully titled "estuaries") have been dredged as harbors, or drained and filled for development. We now know that maintaining estuaries is immensely important, for they are nursery grounds to the early life stages of many species of coastal and ocean fish. Estuaries form an ecotone —a species-rich transition zone with mixed properties of adjacent ecosystems. They are among the most fertile places on earth.[56]

An example of shifting values in governance is evident in changes seen in the San Francisco Bay area. Until gold was discovered in 1848, the ecologically lively San Francisco Bay once boasted robust flora and fauna. An influx of settlers and development led to rapid declines in coastal ecological health with no real appreciation by government officials for what was happening. During the early twentieth century, the San Francisco Bay area continued to see breathtakingly rapid, unregulated development. To provide new land space for industry and desirable sites for harbor facilities and other purposes, wetlands bordering the bay were reduced by an astonishing 90 percent. Of the 850 square miles of tidal marshlands in 1850, there is now only 6 percent of undiked marsh left.[57]

This deterioration came about in many hidden ways. Miners prospecting in the hills washed mud through their sluices and into rivers that drained into the bay system, reducing its depth by 10–39 inches. Cutting channels through marshes for navigation fragmented wetlands, while dredged materials smothered benthic communities. Saltwater intruded into what had been fresher areas of the bay, killing species with a low tolerance for salinity. Loss of salt-intolerant plants reduced sediment cohesion, bringing still more erosion.[58] It was a vicious cycle. The consequences of habitat destruction were not remotely understood and so were no cause for concern.

Later came the California agricultural dream built on cheap water and bargain-priced irrigation. In a monument to centralized planning by the state, subsidized diversions of water created a breadbasket out of the central California desert. A bounty of valuable and delicious produce was the welcome result, but it carried hidden ecological costs.[59] When the Sacramento and San Joaquin Rivers were diverted, no one fully appreciated that reducing their freshwater flow more than 60 percent would be severely destructive.[60] The bay's ecology has since been altered.

Following an elaborate system of subsidies, and under western water law, the uses for this vital resource have grown bizarre. Water for agriculture is now priced so cheaply that water-intensive, low-value crops like alfalfa are being planted, more appropriate for monsoon areas than California. Those crops consume as much water as three cities the size of Los Angeles.[61] Water to irrigate crops is priced so cheaply that much is wasted, such as through unlined ditches. Indeed, agriculture consumes over 80 percent of the state's water, while it accounts for under 10 percent of the economy. There is now a severe imbalance in the use of water. The impacts are not just confined to estuarine or inland environments. Sharp declines are found nearby among once abundant oceanic species. Upstream-running fish like salmon were long ago decimated by rapidly changing habitat. The numbers of returning adult winter-run salmon to the Sacramento River have declined from their historic runs of some 50,000 to a pitiful 191 in 1991.[62] Had the state persisted with conservation efforts, these salmon could now provide income and protein as an important renewable resource for the bay area. Instead, the salmon were senselessly lost because of diverted water, habitat destruction, and pollution.[63] (See figure 9.)

There is little reason to hope for a swift recovery of the area's salmon. That fish's unique life cycle encompasses a jurisdictional thicket of more than eleven government agencies. Each agency monitors only a portion of the salmon's path, so no one agency has an overview from which to protect the resource or to attempt to restore or even maintain stocks.[64] Recent efforts to list certain salmon as endangered species may help to slow their rapid slide toward oblivion, however. Meanwhile, problems mount for

Figure 9. Habitat destruction, pollution, and overfishing cause ecological declines and threaten harvesting as a way of life. *Artist: Jill Townsend*

other marine creatures. Reduced freshwater flows, together with pollution and other factors, also threaten the survival of the Delta smelt. In a saltwater analogy to the Northern Spotted Owl saga, pollution of the bay and reduced freshwater flows may also lead to a listing under the Endangered Species Act, if the Delta smelt declines further. Once-rich commercial ocean fisheries such as those for striped bass and Dungeness crab have been lost. At this point, only a hobbled commercial fleet remains for the small and fast-reproducing, low-value fish found in the disturbed marine habitats nearby.[65] Our ignorance here is not bliss. Traditionally fragmented, ad hoc approaches to managing marine resources are clearly not up to the task. Jurisdictional divisions based on archaic notions like a three-mile cannon shot have little to do with rational governance.[66] What is needed is a more rational mixture of science and political power.

The San Francisco Bay Estuary Program

An example of changing governance is the National Estuary Program created in 1987 by the federal Clean Water Act and administered by the Environmental Protection Agency.[67] The primary goals of the program are to protect and improve water quality and to enhance living resources. Its basic assumption, already demonstrated by the Great Lakes Program and the Chesapeake Bay Program, is that greater federal-state cooperation is essential.[68] The program both plays down artificial political borders and takes a holistic approach to natural processes.

Given the natural variability within marine ecosystems—their nonreducibility, interdependence, complexity, and diversity—the National Estuary Program is a beginning attempt at management that is flexible and has a capacity to adapt and learn.[69] It interprets effective governance as including interaction among scientists, politicians, and the public. Within each U.S. estuary covered by the program, a conference composed of federal, state, and local agencies, as well as affected industries and local residents, sets up a comprehensive conservation and management plan. Conferences may be aided by a scientific and technical advisory committee, a citizens' advisory committee, a local government committee, and a financial planning committee.[70]

The San Francisco Bay–Delta Estuary Project first identified the area's ecological resources in a baseline study, then set out to design a rational environmental policy.[71] Because financial resources were extremely limited, the goal was not further scientific research, but rather to draw on the large body of extant data on the contiguous San Francisco Bay and Sacramento–San Joaquin Delta regions of northern California. Scientific research was to be used as an "empirical base" but was only one consideration. In the words of one participant,

> An important goal was to transcend suspect documentation offered by "special interests" and arrive at more objective understandings of problems, [to provide] alternatives to the fierce interest group competition that often stalemated water and water-habitat policymaking for the Bay and Delta. Indeed the very creation of this estuary project reflected not only concern with degraded habitats and fish and wildlife populations, but dissatisfaction with [past] policies and estuary management.[72]

Driven by dissatisfaction with the perceived inadequacies of existing governance, the program aimed to "restore and maintain the chemical, physical, and biological integrity of the estuary."[73] That was an ambitious goal. The planning zone covered an immense contiguous area of some 4,142 square miles (of which 1,240 square miles was water), which also included a rapidly growing human population of over 7 million. Compiling an integrated assessment of resources was the task of a scientific and technical advisory committee made up of natural and social scientists. This group advised a decidedly politics-oriented management committee comprised of nonscientists.

The approach was an attempt to depart from politics as usual. While policy makers in the legislature may profess to rely on science, experience suggests otherwise. Too often advice from scientists is ignored during the rapid give-and-take and compromises of politics. In part this occurs because when decision makers turn to "environmental scientists for advice they usually receive only partial understandings of conditions, based on a preponderance of scientific opinion rather than certainty."[74] Faced with scientific uncertainty, legislators may be guided by a wide array of nonscientific, subjective factors, including their own overarching beliefs.

In the case of the San Francisco Estuary, one intent of the program was to substitute science-oriented analysis for politics mired in stalemate. It was only partially successful, yet the difficulties are instructive. First was lack of funding. While some federal funds went into preparation and planning, no money was available for implementation.[75] Also, the program's suggestions were not readily channeled into state policy.[76] Given the constraints on most states' financial resources, imagination, and political will to put environmentally oriented plans into action, lack of federal funding for implementation was a fatal defect.[77]

Other problems centered on culture. Members of the technical and scientific committee resisted policy questions, very possibly because as scientists they regarded them as too "politicized." Indeed, the policy-related tasks given to the committee created a "major tension felt by scientists in relation to the project."[78] The management committee, on the other hand, saw the scientists as unwilling to account for unsavory political realities. Despite an abundance of world-class academic scientists in research universities in the bay area, it is telling that those experts resisted involvement in the project. Academics tend not to identify with an applied local project out of fear that it might politicize their research.[79]

And academic scientists had reason for concern. State and federal agencies that employed nonacademic scientists were already regarded as politicized, and opinions from agency scientists were assumed to be suspect. Given the political importance of decisions regarding the bay, advisory committee scientists were ultimately not dominant players in this estuary project. Yet the committee did influence political discourse by providing education and by improving public understanding of complex ecological interactions. Prior to this process,

> developers typically had claimed that their projects did not harm the estuary. [But after the involvement of the technical and scientific advisory committee and] in face of growing public awareness of documented environmental damage, dialogues seem more candid. Developers now argue for trade-offs, and that economic benefits outweigh the environmental costs. While these calculations rarely are acceptable to environmentalists, the ensuing dialogues better reflect true interests and concerns, rather than posturing among allegedly scientific claims that scientists consider indefensible.[80]

An immediate benefit of the National Estuary Program was greater public understanding of ecological realities—for instance, that land-based development may have a serious impact on estuarine processes.[81] More needs to be done to educate the public about the interconnectedness of land and sea. In this effort, government bodies should call on a host of specialists ranging from hydrologists, chemists, biochemists, environmental engineers, geologists, toxicologists, agronomists, microbiologists, and ecologists—to geographers, economists, political scientists, and sociologists.[82]

Ecosystems Management: An Elusive Goal

Despite the practical difficulties of injecting scientists into marine policy making, science must play a key role in ocean resources decisions. But science alone is of little help in making subjective, value-laden judgments that are necessary for ocean governance. To achieve the needed synthesis of science and policy, we need to consider the emerging principle of ecosystems management, which looks beyond classic political boundaries.[83]

Ecosystems management seeks to conserve the integrity of healthy ecosystems by making natural processes more salient to decision making.[84]

As Edward Grumbine observes, this is a challenge to traditional thinking about resources policy, since it provides an innovative framework for moving away from resource extraction to ecosystems protection. A few core beliefs that have long guided the management of public lands in the United States, but that ecosystems management would now reconsider, are:

> Earth as a resource [solely] for human beings, competition over cooperation, control in place of adaptation, viewing all problems as soluble, and viewing nature as stable or balanced. Ecosystem management challenges all these assumptions, and that is why it is revolutionary. . . . Most people are so used to thinking about the public lands on a statute by statute, resource by resource, program by program basis, that it is difficult for them to adjust to . . . ecosystem management.[85]

Grumbine fleshes out the innovative themes that ecosystems management entails. These ideas, which should be basic to ocean governance, include: big-picture, systems thinking to conserve biodiversity; integrating science with policy across disciplines; recognizing the key role of ecological boundaries and realizing political boundaries are artificial and can constrain thinking; maintaining ecological integrity; closing data gaps and linking researchers and managers; monitoring to determine whether goals are being met; interagency cooperation; seeing humans as embedded within nature; adaptive management that rewards flexibility and openness; organizational change, since agencies are based on a linear and predictable image of nature while ecosystems are nonlinear and full of surprise; and finally, influencing what people want from nature.[86]

Such goals can never be fully met. Instead, they are intended as aspirational, guiding principles that point governance in a fresh direction.[87] For example, the idea of ecosystems management illuminates problems associated with the present system of arbitrary ocean management boundaries like the three-mile or twelve-mile limit. Rather than those concepts, new principles of governance would look beyond the reductionist views that have in the past emphasized parts over the whole.[88] (See figure 10.)

An attempt to apply ecosystems management is the 1980 Convention on Conservation of Antarctic Marine Living Resources (CCAMLR). This ambitious multinational regime covers the whole ecosystem of the Antarc-

Figure 10. Ecosystems management seeks to understand the complex and integrated mosaic of life and linkages across varied levels of biological diversity.
Artist: Jill Townsend

tic convergence—a management area defined by ecological relationships rather than manmade boundaries.[89] Hence the CCAMLR regulates fishing, but it aims to do so with an eye to the health of both targeted species and various other marine species that depend on them.[90]

On paper at least, the Antarctic resources convention seeks to ensure the greatest net recruitment of new year classes of fish and deemphasizes older extractive notions like maximum sustained yield. But implementation is difficult, as always. The regime is slow to set allowable fishing levels, for example. Meanwhile, extractive industries such as those that target krill are allowed to continue at current rates.[91] Because restrictions must be adopted through consensus while fishing efforts accelerate, the Arctic convention is still a permissive regime. The burden of proof remains on those who would protect the ecosystem, since they must show proof of harm before tighter restrictions can be imposed. Nonetheless, the CCAMLR is an important first step toward building ecosystems perspectives in marine governance.[92]

The surest start toward more holistic governance of the marine environment would be to adopt integrated coastal management.[93] This is still a nascent concept based on goals like regionalism and ecosystem management, which are only beginning to be fleshed out.[94] Nonetheless it can be useful in crossing the usual jurisdictional boundaries, and in the late 1990s there is growing interest in integrated coastal management.[95] One such integrated management program is now being tried at Australia's Great Barrier Reef Marine Park, an immense special planning area that covers more than 2,000 kilometers of valuable Australian coastline.[96] Other emerging programs include the Oregon Territorial Sea Plan and North Carolina's Areas of Environmental Concern.[97]

A New Yardstick: The Ecological Imperative

To earn the fruits of more effective ocean governance, wisdom is the key. This is not just the specialized knowledge or wisdom of scientific experts—although that is a necessary ingredient—but also greater wisdom among ordinary people. Jacques Cousteau was among the first to begin the requisite teaching of the mass public. For many, the environmental movement is becoming nearly a religion, so great is the devotion of its followers. By elevating a gospel of stewardship, along with the rights of nature, this movement proposes that government should adopt broadly different ways of looking at the world. Already these ideas bestride immense intellectual ground and have made many converts. Countless people and their cultures are recognizing the true interconnectedness of this planet.

This emerging environmental paradigm has struck such a responsive chord because of its clear respect for all living things, its concern for the quality of life of present and future generations, its demand for moving authority away from increasingly remote centers of power and toward local decision making; and its subtle vision of a greater harmony among all species. Countering the exploitative short-term view of nature for economic profit, this movement gives legitimacy to nonquantifiable values. Thus its core objectives are integrity, efficiency, conservative action, foresight, and prevention rather than cure. The aim is to alter past ways of consumerist thinking that unduly "cost the earth." Up to now, short-term exploitation has overshadowed calls for restraint, and the health of the earth's coastal seas has often been sacrificed to immediate goals. But humanity is now at a crossroads. With greater wisdom, we may move toward conservation and efficiency in the new millennium.

7

Solutions

Unless someone like you cares a whole awful lot,
nothing is going to get better. It's not.

Dr. Seuss, The Lorax

How WE GOVERN the sea as we approach the twenty-first century is still
disappointingly similar to eighteenth-century thinking. Maps still depict
the vibrant seas in featureless monotones with simple borderlines drawn
three, twelve, or two hundred miles offshore. Such limits are grossly misleading. They overlook the impact of land-based activities on the marine
environment and miss the complexity of ecosystems. A time has come for
better governance, incorporating an awareness of ecological dynamics in
decision making about marine resources. This wiser governance means listening to the sea.

Modern understanding of marine environments now demands an integrated perspective. The domestic three-mile limit that divides state from
federal authority offshore was never based on enlightened ecological thinking, but was a mere consequence of muddling through. Yet it persists today.

What began as a novel eighteenth century neutrality zone for warships is much harder to justify as a basis for ocean management.

The next decades will be critical. Despite some recent progress, we remain mired in first-generation ocean management. The most rational future path is integrated governance based on precautionary action, yet this is a challenging goal. It will require a degree of political discipline that is hard to achieve. The successes and failures of the last several decades point to the directions ahead. The Magnuson-Stevens Act is just beginning to move away from its long-standing reliance on the assimilative capacity of fish stocks and the sea. We are evolving toward the theme of prevention rather than cure. Rather than only treat the symptoms, regulatory regimes are starting to look upstream to address the causes of ecological stress. Yet such instances of holistic and multifaceted solutions still remain far too rare.

A notable example of ongoing failure is the case of offshore oil. Policy lurches from annual moratorium to moratorium, dragged down by perennial stalemate. The strict state-federal division that is a root cause of conflict must be replaced with cooperative governance. Further, the immoderate U.S. demand for oil ought to be given some thought. Rather than portraying the oil issue as a question of supply alone, we must consider how inefficiencies in our transportation system have accelerated demand. Instead of the internal combusion engine, alternative sources of energy like the fuel cell would reduce energy demand, while government subsidies for consumption of fossil fuels should be pared back.

The Pollution Prevention Act has begun in similarly innovative fashion to help eliminate pollution at the source, not just rely on classic after-the-fact treatment and disposal. Indeed, the old shell game whereby waste is created on land but later dumped into the sea should no longer be tolerated. Every pound of polluting waste eliminated upland is one pound less that finds its way to the sea—the ultimate receiving medium.

Looking ahead, exciting opportunities will be found to network manufacturing to function more like natural biological systems. By design, networked relationships can take the unwanted effluent from one manufacturing plant and use it as input for another plant. The hope is to emulate the evolution of primitive life on earth when early microorganisms developed in ways that made them consumers of the toxic wastes of other organisms. The web of living systems thus grew more integrated and stronger due to its new diversity.

Both pollution prevention and industrial ecology will gain adherents once their economic rewards are realized by pioneering companies. As thinking shifts from reliance on end-of-pipe control strategies to networked relationships, new environmental law and policy will reflect the "inventive genius of humankind," in the words of Franklin Roosevelt. It may be difficult to imagine, but our thinking one hundred years hence will be as different from current control strategies as these controls are from an absence of any environmental laws a century ago.

It is logical to assume that our thinking will evolve, including a new look at the ubiquitous materialism that characterizes the acquisitive American life style. Do extraordinary amounts of "stuff" bring happiness, as advertisements would have us believe? Calls for a simpler life may again receive a sympathetic ear. I have lived in places like the Fiji Islands, where people subsisted on far less income and with far fewer material goods than I was used to as an American—yet people there were family-oriented, spiritually rich, and joyful. Yet now that television has been introduced, even the Fijians are rapidly becoming Westernized. To move forward may mean relearning a past respect for a less materialist life, such as we in the United States once had; better governance of the seas may even encompass thinking anew about ourselves.

So before looking ahead, first look back. Over the millennia, homo sapiens has moved gradually through the Stone Age, the Iron Age, the Bronze Age, the Renaissance, the Enlightenment, and then an Industrial Age. Change now occurs at a blinding pace. We now inhabit the information age, characterized by electronically processed data. Yet whether it is current stock market prices or fluctuations in fish stocks, data alone will never provide all the answers. Information does not make decisions; that involves choices among competing values. Hence better than an age of information would be a coming age of knowledge. Superior still would be what lies ahead: an age of wisdom.[1]

Achieving such wisdom about the sea is far off. I once told an avid outdoorswoman that I studied the ocean. "What a narrow field!" she quickly replied. Although Diana has come around to accept the ocean's larger role on earth, since ours is more a water than land planet, her reply unwittingly gives some insight into human values. As land-based mammals, we rarely stop to think much about the sea. The oceans are very poorly understood and regarded as a foreign environment. The total land area in the United States being protected as national parks is itself quite limited; yet it is orders of magnitude larger than the areas of sea where fish are actually protected in marine sanctuaries.

Such benign neglect of the seas mattered little only a few decades ago; indeed, it could even have preserved a degree of marine ecological integrity. But signs of human life are now ubiquitous miles beyond the shore. For the first time in human history, much of our wastes flowing into the sea are toxic and persistent. We now have the power to fundamentally alter fish habitat. Thus, the twenty-first century will be a time when the values with which we approach nature will say much about whether the seas thrive or are degraded. Education must be the key to building wisdom about the hidden realm. In the words of Dr. Seuss's imaginary beast, the Lorax, who speaks for the earth, "Unless someone like you cares a whole awful lot, nothing is going to get better. It's not." What then can be done? I close with recommendations for a more refined kind of ocean governance, for moving toward what I call a Seastate.[2]

1. It should be cross-sectoral, embracing all categories of marine ecosystems and species, types of human use, and sources of threats to ecological integrity.

2. It should manage actions on land as well as at sea, since much of the pollution that damages marine ecosystems originates on land.

3. It should decentralize authority toward levels of government that are closest to an issue.

4. It should require policies to be flexible, efficient, compatible with market-based strategies wherever possible, and capable of maintaining different priorities in different locations.

5. It should adopt the precautionary principle by promoting pollution prevention and industrial ecology.

6. It should emphasize the use of scientific knowledge to inform policy making at all levels.[3]

More specifically, a future framework of ocean governance, worthy of human advances yet to come, should:[4]

1. expand public understanding of marine environments;
2. apply the precautionary principle in policy making;
3. build marine ecosystems management;
4. foster cooperative state-federal governance of marine resources;
5. advance pollution prevention, rather than end-of-pipe controls;
6. recognize that the sea is not infinitely capable of assimilating harm;
7. promote industrial ecology and clean production strategies;
8. adopt "green" taxes to encourage efficiency and conservation;
9. diminish subsidies for petroleum-based transportation;
10. create incentives for manufacturing hybrid-fuel and alternative-fuel vehicles;
11. increase our capacity to learn in marine resources management;
12. prevent overcapitalization of a fishery;
13. bring down bycatch wherever possible to levels approaching zero;
14. protect spawning habitat by creating marine reserves and harvest refugia;
15. curtail subsidies to the fishing industry that lead to unsustainable fishing practices;
16. apply more local knowledge in resources management;
17. police and enforce fishery restrictions;
18. promote transparency and public participation in fisheries management;
19. lessen the dominance of the fishing industry in fishery management;
20. move off maximum sustainable yield in relation to scientific uncertainty;
21. add a substantive element to the National Environmental Policy Act;
22. strengthen technology-forcing standards in the Clean Water Act;
23. begin to address nonpoint sources of pollution;
24. implement the Pollution Prevention Act;
25. support a conservationist III UN Convention on the Law of the Sea;
26. better coordinate United Nations agencies that consider coasts and oceans;

27. integrate conservation as a goal in free-trade agreements like NAFTA and GATT;

28. monitor local status and trends in marine ecosystems;

29. coordinate global activity for integrated coastal management; and

30. expand funding for basic scientific marine research.

Notes

References

Index

Notes

Chapter 1. New Light on an Old Limit

1. Swarztrauber, *The Three-Mile Limit*, 7.
2. Ibid., 10; on piracy, see Hendrickson, *Ocean Almanac*, 200–32.
3. Fulton, *The Sovereignty of the Sea*, 5.
4. Jessup, *The Law of Territorial Waters*, 4.
5. See Fulton, *The Sovereignty of the Sea*, 3.
6. See Swarztrauber, *The Three-Mile Limit*, 11.
7. See Fulton, *The Sovereignty of the Sea*, 3–4.
8. Ibid., 4, n. 1.
9. Swarztrauber, *The Three-Mile Limit*, 11.
10. Ibid. See also Crocker, ed., *The Extent of the Marginal Sea*, 424–26. See also Swarztrauber, *The Three-Mile Limit*, 7, 60; Jessup, *The Law of Territorial Waters*, xxxvii–viii. For the Romans and early Italians, a mile was a distance of roughly 1,478 meters. Thus Bartolus's "hundred-mile limit" measured roughly 150 kilometers, or 90 English statute miles.
11. See Schachte, "The History of the Territorial Sea from a National Security Perspective," 143, 145.
12. Swarztrauber, *The Three-Mile Limit*, 11.
13. Ibid. See also Fulton, *The Sovereignty of the Sea*, 539–41.
14. Fulton, *The Sovereignty of the Sea*, 539, 542–49.
15. Prescott, *The Political Geography of the Oceans*, 34–36.
16. Swarztrauber, *The Three-Mile Limit*, 11–12.
17. Ibid., 12.
18. Ibid., 12–13.
19. Ibid.
20. Jessup, *The Law of Territorial Waters*, xxxviii.
21. Swarztrauber, *The Three-Mile Limit*, 12–13.

22. Ibid.

23. See Fulton, *The Sovereignty of the Sea*, 4–5.

24. Swarztrauber, *The Three-Mile Limit*, 13.

25. Jessup, *The Law of Territorial Waters*, xxxiv; see also Fenn, *The Origin of the Right of Fishery in Territorial Waters*, 101–08. Cf. Fulton, *The Sovereignty of the Sea*, 540–41.

26. Fulton, *The Sovereignty of the Sea*, 541.

27. Swarztrauber, *The Three-Mile Limit*, 15.

28. Bartley, *The Tidelands Oil Controversy*, 8–9.

29. Swarztrauber, *The Three-Mile Limit*, 18.

30. Bartley, *The Tidelands Oil Controversy*, 8. See also Fulton, *The Sovereignty of the Sea*, 9–12.

31. Swarztrauber, *The Three-Mile Limit*, 18, 20.

32. Oudendjik, *Status and Extent of Adjacent Waters*.

33. Swarztrauber, *The Three-Mile Limit*, 15–16, 19–20.

34. Ibid., 19, 272, emphasis added.

35. Grotius, cited in ibid., 19.

36. Ibid.

37. Bartley, *The Tidelands Oil Controversy*, 8.

38. Swarztrauber, *The Three-Mile Limit*, 20, 271.

39. Ibid., 25.

40. See Crocker, ed., *The Extent of the Marginal Sea*, 64.

41. Swarztrauber, *The Three-Mile Limit*, 20.

42. Ibid., 21–22.

43. Ibid., 24. The Scandinavian league (roughly four nautical miles) should not be confused with the league (or marine league), about three nautical miles.

44. Ibid., 46–48.

45. Kent, "The Historical Origins of the Three-Mile Limit," 537–39.

46. Swarztrauber, *The Three-Mile Limit*, 44.

47. Kent, "The Historical Origins of the Three-Mile Limit," 539, 552–53.

48. Swarztrauber, *The Three-Mile Limit*, 48–49.

49. Crocker, ed., *The Extent of the Marginal Sea*, 608; Swarztrauber, *The Three-Mile Limit*, 46–49.

50. Swarztrauber, *The Three-Mile Limit*, 39–43.

51. Ibid., 38–43.

52. Crocker, ed., *The Extent of the Marginal Sea*, 631.

53. See Swarztrauber, *The Three-Mile Limit*, 40.

54. Ibid., 36, 62.

55. Ibid., 25–30; see also Fulton, *The Sovereignty of the Sea*, 549–50.

56. Kent, "The Historical Origins of the Three-Mile Limit," 537 (emphasis added).

57. Swarztrauber, *The Three-Mile Limit*, 35.

58. Ibid., 23–30, 35, 269; see also Crocker, ed., *The Extent of the Marginal Sea*, 15.

59. Kent, "The Historical Origins of the Three-Mile Limit," 548, n. 66, 550.

60. Swarztrauber, *The Three-Mile Limit*, 54.

61. Kent, "The Historical Origins of the Three-Mile Limit," 548, n. 66.

62. See Swarztrauber, *The Three-Mile Limit*, 54–56.

63. Ibid., 55–56.

64. Crocker, ed., *The Extent of the Marginal Sea*, 630–32.

65. Swarztrauber, *The Three-Mile Limit*, 58.

66. Ibid., 56–57.

67. See Crocker, ed., *The Extent of the Marginal Sea*, 632–36.

68. Swarztrauber, *The Three-Mile Limit*, 56.

69. Kmiec, "Legal Issues Raised by the Proposed Presidential Proclamation to Extend the Territorial Sea."

70. Crocker, ed., *The Extent of the Marginal Sea*, 636. See also Swarztrauber, *The Three-Mile Limit*, 57.

71. See Swarztrauber, *The Three-Mile Limit*, 58–59.

72. Ibid., 59–60.

73. Ibid., 60, 63.

74. Ibid., 60–61.

75. Ibid., 65–66.

76. Ibid., 69.

77. Ibid., 51, 70.

78. Ibid., 70–71.

79. Ibid.

80. Ibid., 71.

81. Ibid., 97.

82. Ibid., 97–98.

83. See Norse, *Global Marine Biological Diversity*.

84. Swarztrauber, *The Three-Mile Limit*, 95–97.

85. Ibid., 87.

86. See Bean, *The Evolution of National Wildlife Law*.

87. Swarztrauber, *The Three-Mile Limit*, 86–87.

88. Ibid., 86.

89. Ibid.

90. Ibid., 87–88.

91. Ibid., 88.

92. See Bean, *The Evolution of National Wildlife Law*, 255–57.

93. See Norse, *Global Marine Biological Diversity*, 30.

94. See generally Crocker, ed., *The Extent of the Marginal Sea*, 630–64.

95. Adams, quoted in ibid., 641–42.

96. See Swarztrauber, *The Three-Mile Limit*, 58–59.

97. Ibid., 58.

Chapter 2. The Tidelands Debate

1. See Bartley, *The Tidelands Oil Controversy*.

2. See Mangone, *Marine Policy for America*, 127–36.

3. Sollen, "An Ocean of Oil," 8.

4. Ibid., 15. See also Lima, "The Politics of Offshore Oil Development," 144, n. 2.

5. Lima, "The Politics of Offshore Oil Development," 144.

6. Sollen, "An Ocean of Oil," 18–28.

7. See Lima, "The Politics of Offshore Oil Development," 144–45.

8. This paragraph is is based on ibid., 144–46; Sollen, "An Ocean of Oil," 10.

9. Sollen, "An Ocean of Oil," 13.

10. Report from the California Coastal Commission, *California Offshore Oil and Gas Development* (1992), cited in ibid., 18.

11. Cited in Sollen, "An Ocean of Oil," 19.

12. Ibid.

13. See Molotch and Freudenburg, *Santa Barbara County*, 24–27; see also Lima, "The Politics of Offshore Oil Development," 146.

14. Lima, "The Politics of Offshore Oil Development," 141–42.

15. Sollen, "An Ocean of Oil," 17.

16. Cited in Bartley, *The Tidelands Oil Controversy*, 67.

17. Ibid.

18. Ibid. See also Sollen, "An Ocean of Oil," 12.

19. See Bartley, *The Tidelands Oil Controversy*, 67–69.

20. Lima, "The Politics of Offshore Oil Development," 156.

21. *Boone v. Kingsbury*, 206 Cal. 148 (1928), ibid., 170. See also *Workman v. Boone*, 280 U.S. 517 (1929), cited in Bartley, *The Tidelands Oil Controversy*, 68–69.

22. See Bartley, *The Tidelands Oil Controversy*, 67–69.

23. Calif. Stats. 1929, p. 944, cited in Bartley, *The Tidelands Oil Controversy*, 69.

24. See Bartley, *The Tidelands Oil Controversy*, 69–71.

25. Ibid., 70.

26. Armstrong and Ryner, *Ocean Management*, 12.

27. Bartley, *The Tidelands Oil Controversy*, 72.

28. See ibid., 70–73.

28. Armstrong and Ryner, *Ocean Management*, 12.

29. See references to this letter in Hearings on S. J. Res. 83 and 92 (1939), 23–24; Hearings on H. J. Res. 176 and 181 (1939), 172–73; and Hearings on H. J. Res. 118 et al. (1945) (Bartley, *The Tidelands Oil Controversy*, 129).

30. See answer of the State of California, "Pleadings Before the U.S. Supreme Court in the Case of *United States v. California* (1945)," 461–63; Bartley, *The Tidelands Oil Controversy*, 129.

31. Bartley, *The Tidelands Oil Controversy*, 133.

32. See Engler, *The Politics of Oil*, 88.

33. See Bartley, *The Tidelands Oil Controversy*, 74, 243.

34. Ibid., 131, n. 25.

35. Ibid., 132–33, 136–37.

36. Letter from Harold Ickes to Ernest Bartley, 29 November 1947, in ibid., 134; see also Ickes, *Secret Diary*, 2:127.

37. This argument was presented in a series of articles in the *Dallas Morning News*. See also Joint Hearings on S. 1988 (1948), 1118–24, 1128, 1132–34; Hearings on S. J. Res. 20 (1951) 235 (Bartley, *The Tidelands Oil Controversy*, 242).

38. Armstrong and Ryner, *Ocean Management*, 14.

39. Ibid., 134–35.

40. See Christie, "Making Waves."

41. See Eisenhower, *Mandate for Change*, 203; Juda, *Ocean Space Rights*, 12–13.

42. Bartley, *The Tidelands Oil Controversy*, 101–02.

43. Ibid., 102.

44. Armstrong and Ryner, *Ocean Management*, 14.

45. See Nash, *United States Oil Policy*, 15–19.

46. Mangone, *Marine Policy for America*, 180–81.

47. Bartley, *The Tidelands Oil Controversy*, 102.

48. Ickes, 330–31; see also Bartley, *The Tidelands Oil Controversy*, 137, n. 43.

49. See Bartley, *The Tidelands Oil Controversy*, 104.

50. See Ickes, *Autobiography of a Curmudgeon*, 299–311.

51. Bartley, *The Tidelands Oil Controversy*, 104–05.

52. Ibid., 106–07.

53. See Hollick, *U.S. Foreign Policy and the Law of the Sea*, 28.

54. Juda, *Ocean Space Rights*, 12–13.

55. See Swarztrauber, *The Three-Mile Limit*, 131–77.

56. See U.S. Department of Defense, *Annotated Supplement to the Commander's Handbook on the Law of Naval Operations*.

57. Juda, *Ocean Space Rights*, 13.

58. Ibid., 29.

59. See Hollick, *U.S. Foreign Policy and the Law of the Sea*, 29–30.

60. Ibid., 29.

61. Ibid., 29–30.

62. Ibid., 30.

63. Ibid.

64. Ibid., 31.

65. Memorandum from Secretary of State Cordell Hull to Joseph Grew, U.S. ambassador to Japan, 5 June 1937.

66. Ibid., 743.

67. Scheiber, "Origins of the Abstention Doctrine in International Law."

68. Memorandum from Hull to Grew, 5 June 1937, 743–44.

69. Ibid., 743, 745; Hollick, *U.S. Foreign Policy and the Law of the Sea*, 22–23. But cf. Hull, telegram to Grew, 20 November 1937.

70. See Hollick, *U.S. Foreign Policy and the Law of the Sea*, 22–23.

71. See Hull, telegrams to Grew, 22–24 March 1937, 734–36.

72. Hollick, *U.S. Foreign Policy and the Law of the Sea*, 23.

73. Hull, letter to Copeland, 4 August 1937, 754–56.

74. Ibid., 756.

75. Ibid., 757.

76. Juda, *Ocean Space Rights*, 12.

77. Hollick, *U.S. Foreign Policy and the Law of the Sea*, 24.

78. Roosevelt, memorandum to Moore, 21 November 1937, 768–69.

79. Memorandum dated 20 November 1937 from Secretary of State Hull, to American Ambassador in Japan Grew, ibid., 763, 765 (emphasis added).

80. Roosevelt, memorandum to Moore, 22 November 1937, 771.

81. H. R. 8344, 75th Cong., 3rd sess., reprinted in Juda, *Ocean Space Rights*, 12.

82. Moore, memorandum to Roosevelt, 24 November 1937, 772–73.

83. Ickes, *Secret Diary*, 2:296–97.

84. See Juda, *Ocean Space Rights*, 12.

85. Grew, letter to Hull, 31 March 1938, 190.

86. Hollick, *U.S. Foreign Policy and the Law of the Sea*, 31–32.

87. See ibid., 33.

88. Ibid.

89. Ickes, letter to Roosevelt, 5 June 1943.

90. Armstrong and Ryner, *Ocean Management*, 20.

91. Ibid., 13, 19.

92. See Juda, *Ocean Space Rights*, 14–18; see also Hull, memorandum to Roosevelt, 10 June 1943 from Secretary of State Hull, to President Roosevelt, 1482; Hollick, *U.S. Foreign Policy and the Law of the Sea*, 34.

93. See Hollick, *U.S. Foreign Policy and the Law of the Sea*, 34.

94. Roosevelt, memorandum to Hull, 9 June 1943, 1482.

95. Hollick, *U.S. Foreign Policy and the Law of the Sea*, 36.

96. Straus, memorandum to Harold Ickes, 22 May 1944; see also Hollick, *U.S. Foreign Policy and the Law of the Sea*, 36.

97. Hollick, *U.S. Foreign Policy and the Law of the Sea*, 31, 38.

98. See "Tidelands Men Opposing U.S. Oil Suit Made Big Gifts"; see also Bartley, *The Tidelands Oil Controversy*, 138–41; Armstrong and Ryner, *Ocean Management*, 25.

99. Bartley, *The Tidelands Oil Controversy*, 138–41.

100. Straus, memorandum to Harold Ickes, 14 July 1944.

101. Armstrong and Ryner, *Ocean Management*, 21–22.

102. See Juda, *Ocean Space Rights*, 16, 22–24.

103. Hollick, *U.S. Foreign Policy and the Law of the Sea*, 39.

104. Ibid., 40–41.

105. Stettinius, memorandum to Harold Ickes, 19 December 1944, 1488–90.

106. Hollick, *U.S. Foreign Policy and the Law of the Sea*, 41.

107. Ibid., 42–43.

108. Straus, memorandum to Harold Ickes, 12 August 1944.

109. Hollick, *U.S. Foreign Policy and the Law of the Sea*, 43–44.

110. Grew and Ickes, memorandum to Franklin Roosevelt, 22 January 1945, 1490–91.

111. Swarztrauber, *The Three-Mile Limit*, 160–61.

112. Juda, *Ocean Space Rights*, 17.

113. Hollick, *U.S. Foreign Policy and the Law of the Sea*, 45.

114. Executive Order 9633, of 28 September 1945.

115. See Lee, memorandum to Michael Straus, 2 May 1945.

116. Nash, *United States Oil Policy*, 191–92.

117. Truman, *Memoirs*, 2:480–82.

118. Nash, *United States Oil Policy*, 183; also reported in the *New York Times*, 8, 14–17, 19 February 1946 (ibid). See also Bartley, *The Tidelands Oil Controversy*, 138–41.

119. Nash, *United States Oil Policy*, 182–83.

120. Bartley, *The Tidelands Oil Controversy*, 145–48.

121. See Grew and Ickes, memorandum to Harry Truman, 30 April 1945, 1503, 1504, n. 45.

122. See Bartley, *The Tidelands Oil Controversy*, 138, 161.

123. But see "Joint Memorandum in Support of Rehearing in United States v. Texas."

124. Bartley, *The Tidelands Oil Controversy*, 163.

125. Ibid., 166.

126. Bartley, *The Tidelands Oil Controversy*, 166.

127. Ibid., 167.

128. Ibid., 173.

129. Armstrong and Ryner, *Ocean Management*, 26.

130. See Bartley, *The Tidelands Oil Controversy*, 190–94.

131. 332 U.S. 19, 44.

132. See Bartley, *The Tidelands Oil Controversy*, 180.

133. Ibid., 186–87.

134. Hollick, *U.S. Foreign Policy and the Law of the Sea*, 106.

135. See Ickes, "The Court Proposes, Interior Disposes," 18.

136. Hollick, *U.S. Foreign Policy and the Law of the Sea*, 106.

137. See, e.g., S. 1988; H.J. Res. 51, 52, 67, 157, 263, 286, and 299; H.R. 5010, 5099, 5105, 5121, 5128, 5132, 5136, 5162, 5167, 5238, 5273, 5281, 5288, 5297, 5308, 5320, 5349, 5372, 5380, 5443, and 5461, cited in Bartley, *The Tidelands Oil Controversy*, 195, n. 3. See also Hollick, *U.S. Foreign Policy and the Law of the Sea*, 107.

138. Hollick, *U.S. Foreign Policy and the Law of the Sea*, 107.

139. Christie, "State Historic Interests in the Marginal Seas." See also Bartley, *The Tidelands Oil Controversy*, 79–94; Armstrong and Ryner, *Ocean Management*, 27–28.

140. Hollick, *U.S. Foreign Policy and the Law of the Sea*, 109.

141. Ibid., 109, 429, n. 21. See also Truman, *Memoirs*, 2:480–87.

142. Bartley, *The Tidelands Oil Controversy*, 213–46.

143. Armstrong and Ryner, *Ocean Management*, 28.

144. Unidentified newspaper clipping in the National Archives, RG 48, Straus files.

145. Truman, *Memoirs*, 2:485.

146. Eisenhower, *Mandate for Change*, 206. Hollick, *U.S. Foreign Policy and the Law of the Sea*, 110.

147. Bartley, *The Tidelands Oil Controversy*, 229–30.

148. Ibid., 258.

149. See Hollick, *U.S. Foreign Policy and the Law of the Sea*, 115.

150. See Eisenhower, *Mandate for Change*, 206.

151. Fitzgerald, "The Tidelands Controversy, Revisited"; see also Christie, "State Historic Interests in the Marginal Seas."

152. See Juda, *Ocean Space Rights*, 30–31.

153. See Hollick, U.S. Foreign Policy and the Law of the Sea, 116.

154. See Eisenhower, Mandate for Change, 206.

155. See Hollick, U.S. Foreign Policy and the Law of the Sea, 111.

156. Eisenhower, Mandate for Change, 206.

157. See Hollick, U.S. Foreign Policy and the Law of the Sea, 114.

158. Ibid., 114–15.

159. See Christie, "State Historic Interests in the Marginal Seas," 81, 91; see also Bartley, The Tidelands Oil Controversy; Fitzgerald, "The Tidelands Controversy, Revisited"; Juda, Ocean Space Rights.

160. See Armstrong and Ryner, Ocean Management, 29–31.

Chapter 3. Is This Holistic Ecology?

1. See Ray, "Coastal-Marine Discontinuities," 1095–96.

2. Ibid., 1104; Ray, "Biodiversity Is Biogeography."

3. See, e.g., Norse, Global Marine Biological Diversity, 281–306; Holing, Coastal Alert, 13–46.

4. See Swarztrauber, The Three-Mile Limit, 178–92; Hollick, U.S. Foreign Policy and the Law of the Sea, 117–22.

5. See Swarztrauber, The Three-Mile Limit, 180–81.

6. See Garcia Amador and Rodríguez, The Exploitation and Conservation of the Resources of the Sea, Swarztrauber, The Three-Mile Limit, 181–83.

7. Swarztrauber, The Three-Mile Limit, 181.

8. Ibid., 192.

9. See ibid., 193, 211.

10. See ibid., 197–98.

11. See ibid., 198, 188.

12. See Hollick, U.S. Foreign Policy and the Law of the Sea, 135; Swarztrauber, The Three-Mile Limit, 204.

13. See Hollick, U.S. Foreign Policy and the Law of the Sea, 137–38; Swarztrauber, The Three-Mile Limit, 211.

14. See Hollick, U.S. Foreign Policy and the Law of the Sea, 135–36.

15. Swarztrauber, The Three-Mile Limit, 209.

16. Hollick, U.S. Foreign Policy and the Law of the Sea, 140–153; Swarztrauber, The Three-Mile Limit, 204–14.

17. McDougal and Burke, The Public Order of the Oceans, 467.

18. Swarztrauber, The Three-Mile Limit, 184.

19. Ibid., 229.

20. Hollick, U.S. Foreign Policy and the Law of the Sea, 162, 442, n. 8.

21. Swarztrauber, The Three-Mile Limit, 230–32.

22. Ibid., 232–33.

23. Ibid., 244.

24. Ibid., 245.

25. U.S. Department of Defense, Memorandum to Office of the Secretary of Defense/Joint Chiefs of Staff Representative for Ocean Policy Affairs.

26. Swarztrauber, *The Three-Mile Limit*, 246.

27. See ibid., 246–47.

28. See Hollick, *U.S. Foreign Policy and the Law of the Sea*, 196–97. See also Payoyo, *Ocean Governance*, xli.

29. See Hollick, *U.S. Foreign Policy and the Law of the Sea*, 198–216.

30. See ibid., 250–52.

31. Ibid., 196–349.

32. Ibid., 353.

33. See ibid.; see also Scheiber and Carr, "Constitutionalism and the Historical Sea."

34. See IUCN, *The Law of the Sea*, 13.

35. Briscoe, "The Effect of President Reagan's 12-Mile Territorial Sea Proclamation," 225, 285.

36. Broad, *The Universe Below*, 262–63.

37. See Bledsoe and Boczek, *The International Law Dictionary*, 27–28, 200–02.

38. See IUCN, *The Law of the Sea*, 5, 13–14.

39. Swarztrauber, *The Three-Mile Limit*, 130.

40. See *Annotated Supplement to the Commander's Handbook on the Law of Naval Operations*, table ST1-6.

41. Ibid.

42. Anonymous interviews, March–April 1990; see also Robert J. Wilder, "Cooperative Governance."

43. Presidential Proclamation no. 5928, *Fed. Reg.* 54 (1989): 777.

44. Article 3 of the 1982 UNCLOS, *Annotated Supplement to the Commander's Handbook on the Law of Naval Operations*, 1–14.

45. U.S. Department of Defense, Memorandum to Office of the Secretary of Defense/Joint Chiefs of Staff Representative for Ocean Policy Affairs.

46. Carlucci, letter to George Shultz, 6 May 1988.

47. Kmiec, "Legal Issues Raised by the Proposed Presidential Proclamation"; but see Saurenman, "The Effects of a Twelve-Mile Territorial Sea"; see also Archer, "Evolution of Major 1990 CZMA Amendments," 191.

48. See Archer, "Evolution of Major 1990 CZMA Amendments," 219.

49. See Kmiec, "Legal Issues Raised by the Proposed Presidential Proclamation."

50. Carlucci, letter to Donald Hodel, 30 September 1988.

51. Van Dyke, "Reauthorization of the Coastal Zone Management Act," 33.

52. Ray, "Ecology, Law, and the 'Marine Revolution,'" 7, 13. See also IUCN, *The Law of the Sea*.

53. MacKenzie, "The Cod That Disappeared," 24–25. The following discussion is based on this source.

54. Ibid., 25–26.

55. Ibid., 25–28.

56. Ibid.

57. Ibid., 27.

58. Ibid., 27–28.

59. Ibid., 26.

60. Ibid., 27–28.

61. Ibid., 28.

62. Ibid., 29.

63. Norse, *Global Marine Biological Diversity*, 232.

64. Ibid., 264.

65. See Canfield, "More Heartache Ahead," 30, 32.

66. Ibid., 33.

67. Ibid., 32.

68. Ibid., 33.

69. Ibid., 37.

70. See National Research Council, *Science, Policy, and the Coast*, 41.

71. See Norse, *Global Marine Biological Diversity*, 264–66.

72. Ibid., 264.

73. Ibid.

74. Ibid., 90.

75. Norse, *Global Marine Biological Diversity*, 91.

76. Ibid., 282.

77. Ibid., 206.

78. Ibid., 282. This list closely follows four suggestions found in Norse.

79. Letter from President George Washington to Governor [of Maryland] Thomas Sim Lee, October 16, 1793, quoted in Kmiec, "Legal Issues Raised by the Proposed Presidential Proclamation," 9, n. 24 (emphasis in original).

80. Swarztrauber, *The Three-Mile Limit*, 56–59, 64–71.

81. See Robert J. Wilder, "Is This Holistic Ecology?" 209, 211–19.

82. See Forester, "Bounded Rationality," 23–24.

83. Ibid.

84. See March and Simon, *Organizations*. See also Forester, "Bounded Rationality," 24.

85. Crocker, *The Extent of the Marginal Sea*, 636.

86. Ibid.; but see Swarztrauber, *The Three-Mile Limit*, 54–57; see also Robert J. Wilder, "The Three-Mile Territorial Sea," 681.

87. Perrow, *Complex Organizations*, 149. See also Forester, "Bounded Rationality," 24.

88. See Lindblom, "The Science of Muddling Through," 79.

89. Ibid., 83–85; Swarztrauber, *The Three-Mile Limit*, 58.

90. See Knudson and Vogel, "Pacific Blues," 2.

91. Ibid., 2–3.

92. Ibid., 2–4.

93. Ibid., 2.

94. Ibid., 1–12.

95. Ibid., 4.

96. Ibid., 2–3.

97. Ibid., 9.

98. Ibid., 3.

99. Ibid.

100. See Jacobs, "Boom in Holdings Puts Wildlife Agency to the Test."

101. See Knudson and Vogel, "Pacific Blues," 7.

102. See Norse, *Global Marine Biological Diversity*, 9.

103. Ibid., 10, 14.

104. Ibid., 14.

105. Ibid.

106. Ibid. See also Hendrickson, *Ocean Almanac*, 14.

107. National Research Council, *Understanding Marine Biodiversity*, 27.

108. Ray, "Coastal-Marine Discontinuities," 1100.

109. National Research Council, *Understanding Marine Biodiversity*, 6.

110. Ibid.

111. Hollick, U.S. *Foreign Policy and the Law of the Sea*, 16.

112. Ray, "Coastal-Marine Discontinuities," 1101–05. The seascape idea is a valuable means to overcome the usual emphasis on dividing the governance of land, versus that of the sea.

Chapter 4. Fine-Tuning the Governance of Offshore Oil

1. See Van de Kamp and Saurenman, "Outer Continental Shelf Oil and Gas Leasing," 73.

2. Hildreth, "Ocean Resources and Intergovernmental Relations in the 1980s," 155, 189; see also Freudenburg and Gramling, *Oil in Troubled Waters*.

3. Paul Stang, Minerals Management Service, cited in *Coastal Zone Management Newsletter* 25 (15 Sept. 1994): 4; see also Babbitt, reply to Robert Jordan, 22 March 1994; Cicin-Sain and Knecht, "Federalism Under Stress," 149, 159.

4. See Minerals Management Service, "Moving Beyond Conflict to Consensus," 49.

5. See Daniel S. Miller, "Offshore Federalism."

6. See Knecht, "The Exclusive Economic Zone," 263.

7. Van de Kamp and Saurenman, "Outer Continental Shelf Oil and Gas Leasing," 130, n. 210; Oregon Ocean Policy Advisory Council, State of Oregon, Territorial Sea Plan 211 (1994); see also Daniel S. Miller, "Offshore Federalism," 404–05; Cicin-Sain and Knecht, "Federalism Under Stress," 166–67.

8. Hershman, "Building a Federal-State Partnership"; see also Western Legislative Conference of the Council of State Governments, Resolution No. 91-14, Extension of the Territorial Sea (1991).

9. Minerals Management Service, "Moving Beyond Conflict to Consensus," 41.

10. Farrow, *Managing the Outer Continental Shelf Lands*, 4–7; quote from p. 4.

11. See Minerals Management Service, "Moving Beyond Conflict to Consensus," 36.

12. Swenson, "A Stitch in Time."

13. LePage, "Oil Study Cites Area Economic Benefits."

14. Douros, "Where Is Oil Industry Today?"

15. Sollen, "An Ocean of Oil," 176.

16. National Research Council, *Science, Policy and the Coast*, 41; but see Sollen, "An Ocean of Oil," 175–95.

17. Sollen, "An Ocean of Oil," 176.

18. Holing, *Coastal Alert*, 13–38.

19. See Cicin-Sain and Knecht, "Federalism Under Stress."

20. See Hildreth, "Ocean Resources and Intergovernmental Relations in the 1980s," 189.

21. See Lester, "The Search for Dialogue in the Administrative State."

22. See Cicin-Sain and Knecht, "Federalism Under Stress."

23. See Douros, "Where Is Oil Industry Today?"

24. See Daniel S. Miller, "Offshore Federalism," 404–05.

25. Cicin-Sain and Knecht, "Federalism Under Stress," 166.

26. Minerals Management Service, "Moving Beyond Conflict to Consensus," 23.

27. See ibid., 45.

28. "The Great Transport Cop-Out."

29. See Holing, *Coastal Alert*, 13–38.

30. See "The Great Transport Cop-Out," 18.

31. See Lovins, "The Role of Energy Efficiency," 193.

32. Holing, *Coastal Alert*, 67 (emphasis added).

33. Ibid., 68–69.

34. Babbitt, "Will America Join the Waste Watchers?"

35. See Fiore, "Balanced Budget Plan Linked to Gas Tax"; but see Weber and Gradwohl, *The Wealth of Oceans*, 109.

36. "Much Heat, Little Light," 73.

37. Van de Kamp and Saurenman, "Outer Continental Shelf Oil and Gas Leasing," 128, n. 206. See also "Car Industry Survey," 15–16.

38. "At Last, the Fuel Cell," 89.

39. Farrow, *Managing the Continental Shelf Lands*, 136.

40. Lester, "The Search for Dialogue in the Administrative State," 75–76.

41. See Knecht and Westermeyer, "State vs. National Interests in an Expanded Territorial Sea," 317; Shapiro and Rosella Shapiro," Opportunities for a State-Federal Partnership," 335; Littleton, "Coastal States," 539; Cook, "Federalism at Sea?"

42. Cicin-Sain and Knecht, "Federalism Under Stress," 168.

43. See Fairfax, "Old Recipes for New Federalism."

44. See Ball, *The Law of the Sea*.

45. See Cicin-Sain, "Ocean Resources and Intergovernmental Relations," 241, 243, 246, 258–59; see also Fairfax, "Old Recipes for New Federalism," 947–49, 959.

46. See Ball, *The Law of the Sea*, 59–61; Ball, "Good Old American Permits."

47. Ball, *The Law of the Sea*, 61.

48. Ibid., 66.

49. Ball, "Good Old American Permits," 642; Ball, *The Law of the Sea*, 66.

50. See Cicin-Sain, "Essay: A National Ocean Governance Strategy for the United States Is Needed Now," 171, 175.

51. See Lester, "The Search for Dialogue in the Administrative State," 226–57.

52. Ibid.

53. See Hildreth, "Ocean Resources and Intergovernmental Relations in the 1980s," 155, 161–82.

54. Farrow, *Managing the Continental Shelf Lands*, 35; see also U.S. House of Representatives, *Improving the OCS Lands Act*; Van de Kamp and Saurenman, "Outer Continental Shelf Oil and Gas Leasing," 134.

55. See Fairfax, "Old Recipes for New Federalism," 960.

56. Ibid., 978–80. See also Hershman, "Building a Federal-State Partnership," 221, 224.

57. See Fairfax, "Old Recipes for New Federalism," 965, 969.

58. W. Riker, cited in Fairfax, "Old Recipes for New Federalism," 955.

59. Fairfax, "Old Recipes for New Federalism," 965.

60. Cicin-Sain and Knecht, "Federalism Under Stress," 172.

61. See Koester, "State-Federal Jurisdictional Conflicts," 195, 204.

62. Pub. L. No. 92-583, 86 Stat. 1280 [1972]; 16 U.S.C.A. Secs. 1451–64, substantially amended in 1990 to restore some authority over federally permitted oil activities to states. Archer, "Evolution of Major 1990 CZMA Amendments"; Rieser and Milliken, "A Review of Developments in U.S. Ocean and Coastal Law," 291, 297.

63. See, for example, Saurenman, "The Effects of a Twelve-Mile Territorial Sea"; but see Kmiec, "Legal Issues Raised."

64. Koester, "State-Federal Jurisdictional Conflicts," 204.

65. See Van de Kamp and Saurenman, "Outer Continental Shelf Oil and Gas Leasing," 130–34.

66. See *Santa Barbara News-Press*, 22 February 1991.

67. U.S. House of Representatives, *Outer Continental Shelf Lands Act Amendments of 1978*.

68. U.S. House of Representatives, *Outer Continental Shelf Lands Act Amendments of 1977*, 50, 53, 101.

69. See U.S. House of Representatives, *Improving the OCS Lands Act*.

70. See Cicin-Sain, "Ocean Resources and Intergovernmental Relations," 255–56; Farrow, *Managing the Continental Shelf Lands*, 35.

71. Statement of Leon Panetta, in U.S. House of Representatives, *Improving the OCS Lands Act*, 10.

72. See Ingram and Mann, "Policy Failure," 12, 17, 22, 30.

73. Cicin-Sain and Knecht, "Federalism Under Stress," 169.

74. U.S. House of Representatives, *Improving the OCS Lands Act*, 2.

75. See Hildreth, "Ocean Resources and Intergovernmental Relations in the 1980s," 161–75.

76. Statement of Leon Panetta (D-Calif.), in U.S. House of Representatives, *Improving the OCS Lands Act*, 8; statement of Chester Atkins (D-Mass.), ibid., 13; statement of Ralph Regula (R-Ohio), ibid., 15.

77. Daniel S. Miller, "Offshore Federalism," 440.

78. See Hershman, "Building a Federal-State Partnership," 225–26.

79. See, for example, H.R. 536, 102nd Cong., 1st sess. (1991).

80. Charles Bennett, member of House Committee on Merchant Marine and Fisheries, telephone interview, 2 December 1991.

81. See Cicin-Sain and Knecht, "Federalism Under Stress," 149, 154.

82. Sabatier and Mazmanian, *Can Regulation Work?*, 7. This analysis borrows from Sabatier and Mazmanian's list.

83. See Mazmanian and Sabatier, "The Role of Attitudes and Perceptions," 107–08; Sabatier and Mazmanian, *Can Regulation Work?*, 5, 9.

84. Farrow, *Managing the Continental Shelf Lands*, 26.

85. 43 U.S.C.A. 1332 (1989 Supp.). See also U.S. House of Representatives, *Outer Continental Shelf Lands Act Amendments of 1977*, 3.

86. See Sabatier and Mazmanian, *Can Regulation Work?*, 48.

87. Ibid., 7.

88. These are adopted from the Sabatier and Mazmanian model (ibid., 10).

89. Ibid., 50.

90. "House Panel Investigates DOI's Restructured Budget."

91. Farrow, *Managing the Continental Shelf Lands*, 27.

92. Ibid.

93. Simon, *Administrative Behavior*, xvi; James Q. Wilson, *Bureaucracy*, 24.

94. Farrow, *Managing the Continental Shelf Lands*, 27–28.

95. Ibid., 28.

96. Ibid., 27.

97. Cicin-Sain, "Ocean Resources and Intergovernmental Relations," 257.

98. See Kaufman, *The Forest Ranger*, 198.

99. Kaufman, *The Limits of Organizational Change*, 17.

100. Sabatier and Mazmanian, *Can Regulation Work?*, 10, 50.

101. U.S. House of Representatives, *Outer Continental Shelf Lands Act Amendments of 1977*, 50; see Daniel S. Miller, "Offshore Federalism," 436.

102. See Daniel S. Miller, "Offshore Federalism," 438.

103. H.R. Conf. Rep. No. 1474, 95th. Cong., 2d sess. 106 (1978), in ibid., 438. See also U.S. House of Representatives, *Outer Continental Shelf Lands Act Amendments of 1977*.

104. See Hildreth, "Ocean Resources and Intergovernmental Relations in the 1980s," 166.

105. See Sabatier and Mazmanian, *Can Regulation Work?*, 10, 24, n. 42.

106. See Daniel S. Miller, "Offshore Federalism," 440–49.

107. See Van de Kamp and Saurenman, "Outer Continental Shelf Oil and Gas Leasing," 79–100.

108. Hildreth, "Ocean Resources and Intergovernmental Relations in the 1980s," 164.

109. Van de Kamp and Saurenman, "Outer Continental Shelf Oil and Gas Leasing," 131.

110. Ibid.

111. Ibid.

112. See ibid., 131–32.

113. Ibid., 129–30.

114. Minerals Management Service, "Moving Beyond Conflict to Consensus," 32.

115. Ibid., 11–12.

116. Ibid., 9, 12.

117. Minerals Management Service, "Moving Beyond Conflict to Consensus," 9.

118. See ibid., 50–65.

119. See Speer, "Comments of the Natural Resources Defense Council."

120. Ibid., 1.

121. Ibid., 2–3.

122. Ibid.

123. Ibid., 3–4.

124. See Minerals Management Service, "Moving Beyond Conflict to Consensus," 45–46.

125. Speer, "Comments of the Natural Resources Defense Council," 45.

126. Commoner, *Making Peace with the Planet*, 197–98.

127. "Car Industry Survey," 5.

128. Van de Kamp and Saurenman, "Outer Continental Shelf Oil and Gas Leasing," 130, n. 211.

129. "Warm Words," 89.

130. Ibid., 89–90.

131. Ibid., 90.

132. Ibid.

Chapter 5. Prevention Rather Than Cure

1. See O'Riordan and Cameron, *Interpreting the Precautionary Principle*. See also Robert J. Wilder, "Prevention Rather Than Cure."

2. See United Nations, Food and Agriculture Organization, *The Precautionary Approach to Fisheries*, 2.

3. See Thorne-Miller, "The Precautionary Principle/Approach."

4. See Dethlefsen, Jackson, and Taylor, "The Precautionary Principle," 41, 54–62; Gaba and Stever, *Law of Solid Waste*.

5. See Diana Wilder, "Save the Bay's 'Toxic Diet' Project."

6. See Commoner, *Making Peace with the Planet*, 41–55.

7. Ibid.

8. See Lovins, "The Role of Energy Efficiency," 193–223.

9. See "Energy Efficiency: Feeling the Pinch."

10. See Manik, "Pollution Prevention, Organizational Culture, and Social Learning."

11. See Roush, "When Rigor Meets Reality"; Stone, "Taking a New Look at Life."

12. Culotta, "The Case of the Missing Mussel"; see also MacGarvin, "Precaution, Science and the Sin of Hubris."

13. Commoner, *Making Peace with the Planet*, 41–42.

14. See Jackson, "Principles of Clean Production," 143, 155–64; International Joint Commission (United States–Canada), "Seventh Biennial Report on Great Lakes Water Quality," 13–14.

15. See Murphy and Noon, "Coping With Uncertainty in Wildlife Biology," 773–76.

16. See Robert J. Wilder, "Is This Holistic Ecology?" 209, 212–13.

17. "Toxic Use Reduction Case Study." The Dydee Diaper Company has since gone out of business.

18. See Percival, *Environmental Regulation*, 199–200. Two federal statutes that may potentially encourage greater pollution prevention—the Resource Conservation and Management Act (RCRA)—and the Comprehensive Environmental Response, Compensation, and Liability Act (Superfund, or CERCLA) are not yet very effective. See ibid., 201–424.

19. See Weintraub, "Science, International Regulation, and the Precautionary Principle."

20. See Haigh, "The Introduction of the Precautionary Principle into the U.K.," 229–51; Cameron and Aboucher, "The Precautionary Principle." On Germany and the Nordic nations, see Garvin, "Implementation of the Second North Sea Conference."

21. See De Fontaubert, Downes, and Agardy, *Biodiversity in the Seas*, 58–65; Cameron, "The Status of the Precautionary Principle in International Law," 262–89; Weintraub, "Science, International Regulation, and the Precautionary Principle," 184–91. See also Costanza and Cornwell, "The 4P Approach," 12, 20–21.

22. See Baender, "Pesticides and Precaution," 557, 594. See also Thorne-Miller, "The Precautionary Principle/Approach," 27–28.

23. See Birnie and Boyle, *International Law and the Environment*, 98–102, 406.

24. See Burke, "Unregulated High Seas Fishing," 235–71, 257; but see Floit, "Reconsidering Freedom of the Seas," 310–26.

25. See MacGarvin, "Implementation of the Second North Sea Conference," 1–4. See also Stairs and Taylor, "Non-Governmental Organizations and the Legal Protection of the Oceans," 110, 134–41.

26. See Bodansky, "Scientific Uncertainty and the Precautionary Principle," 4–5; see also Haas, "Protecting the Baltic and North Seas," 133, 151–81.

27. See Weintraub, "Science, International Regulation, and the Precautionary Principle," 173–223; Burke, "Unregulated High Seas Fishing," 256–65.

28. "Secretary Baker Addresses the National Governor's Association," *Federal News Service*, 26 February 1990, quoted in Weintraub, "Science, International Regulation, and the Precautionary Principle," 188.

29. See Thorne-Miller, "The Precautionary Principle/Approach," 25.

30. See Broadus, "Creature Feature Too," 6–7.

31. See Bodansky, "Scientific Uncertainty and the Precautionary Principle," 4–5; but see Thorne-Miller, "The Precautionary Principle/Approach," 26.

32. Thorne-Miller, "The Precautionary Principle/Approach," 25–26.

33. See Young, *For Our Children's Children*.

34. For definitions, see Greenpeace International, "The Principle of Precautionary Action."

35. See Dethlefsen, Jackson and Taylor, "The Precautionary Principle," 41–62.

36. See Bean, *The Evolution of National Wildlife Law*, 195–202; Caldwell, "Implementing NEPA."

37. See Percival, *Environmental Regulation*, 1024.

38. *Calvert Cliffs Coordinating Committee v. United States Atomic Energy Commission*, 449 F.2d 1109 (D.C. Cir. 1971), cited in Percival, *Environmental Regulation*, 1029.

39. 42 U.S.C. Sec. 4331 (1976) (italics added), cited in Caldwell, "Implementing NEPA"; see also Bean, *The Evolution of National Wildlife Law*, 196.

40. Percival, *Environmental Regulation*, 1024–84.

41. Ibid., 1061–62.

42. See Bean, *The Evolution of National Wildlife Law*, 201–02.

43. See Percival, *Environmental Regulation*, 1081.

44. Lynton K. Caldwell, personal communication, 21 February 1995.

45. Ibid.

46. See Bean, *The Evolution of National Wildlife Law*, 384–408.

47. See Robert J. Wilder, "The Three-Mile Territorial Sea."

48. Buck, *Congressional Research Service Issue Brief*.

49. Holmes, "Biologists Sort the Lessons of Fisheries' Collapse," 1252–53. See also Finch, "Fishery Management under the Magnuson Act," 174–79. For international aspects of overfishing, see, e.g., Hayashi, "United Nations Conference on Straddling and Highly Migratory Fish Stocks."

50. See Norse, *Global Marine Biological Diversity*; Weiner, *The Beak of the Finch*.

51. See Marc L. Miller, "Regional Fishery Management Councils," 309–17.

52. Earle, *Sea Change*.

53. Meier, "Fight in Congress Looms on Fishing."

54. See Marc L. Miller, "Regional Fishery Management Councils."

55. See "The Catch About Fish."

56. See Van Dyke, "International Governance and Stewardship of the High Seas," 18–19.

57. Marine Mammal Commission, *Annual Report to Congress, 1994*. See also Percival, *Environmental Regulation*, 60–64.

58. Ray, "Coastal-Marine Discontinuities and Synergisms"; see also Marine Mammal Commission, *Annual Report to Congress, 1994*, 12; Percival, *Environmental Regulation*, 60.

59. See Percival, *Environmental Regulation*, 61.

60. Cooke, "The Precautionary Approach to Fisheries."

61. See United Nations, *The Precautionary Approach to Fisheries*, 5.

62. Cooke, "The Precautionary Approach to Fisheries," 7.

63. See ibid., 1.

64. See ibid., 7.

65. See "A New Deal for the Northeast."

66. Knudson and Vogel, "Pacific Blues," 11; see also Kelley, "The Marine Fish Conservation Network," 56–57.

67. See Knudson and Vogel, "Pacific Blues," 11–12.

68. See Drumm, "When Scientists Become Advocates"; but see Grimes, "Scientist Responds to Advocacy Charge," 4–5.

69. See Cooke, "The Precautionary Approach to Fisheries," 1.

70. See Robert J. Wilder, "Sea Change from Bush to Clinton."

71. See ibid.

72. Van de Kamp and Saurenman, "Outer Continental Shelf Oil and Gas Leasing," 73, 131.

73. See Robert J. Wilder, "Sea Change from Bush to Clinton," 168.

74. See Lovins, "The Role of Energy Efficiency," 193–223.

75. See "Japan, U.S. Differ on Science."

76. See Gordon, *Steering a New Course*.

77. See Robert J. Wilder, "Sea Change from Bush to Clinton," 169–70.

78. See Gordon, *Steering a New Course*.

79. Percival, *Environmental Regulation*, 1096.

80. *TVA v. Hill*, 437 U.S. 153 (1978), cited in Percival, *Environmental Regulation*, 1092–99.

81. See Percival, *Environmental Regulation*, 1090–98.

82. See ibid., 1099.

83. Ibid., 1103.

84. See Bean, *The Evolution of National Wildlife Law*, 335.

85. See Adler, Landman and Cameron, *The Clean Water Act Twenty Years Later*.

86. See Percival, *Environmental Regulation*, 879–80.

87. U.S. General Accounting Office, *Water Pollution: EPA Needs to Set Priorities for Water Quality Criteria Issues* (hereinafter GAO Report on Water Pollution).

88. See Percival, *Environmental Regulation*, 895. 330, 912.

89. 32 ERC (BNA) 1969, 1972 n. 25 (D.D.C. 1991), cited in ibid.

90. GAO Report on Water Pollution, 2–3.

91. See Locke, "Reorienting Risk Assessment," 28–33.

92. See U.S. General Accounting Office, *Toxic Substances Control Act* (hereinafter GAO Report on TSCA).

93. Locke, "Reorienting Risk Assessment," 29. See also Silbergeld and Tonat, "Investing in Prevention."

94. See generally, GAO Report on TSCA, 3–6.

95. BCT differs from BAT, in that a focus under BCT is "cost-effective" reasonableness. See *Chemical Manufacturers Assn. v. United States E.P.A.*, 870 F. 2d 177 (5th Cir. 1989), cited in Percival, *Environmental Regulation*, 913.

96. MacGarvin, "0–2000: The Future, Clean Production."

97. Houck, "The Regulation of Toxic Pollutants," cited in Percival, *Environmental Regulation*, 915.

98. See generally, GAO Report on Water Pollution.

99. See Wilkinson, Pittman, and Dye, "Slick Work."

100. Solomon, "U.S. Oil Spills Have Declined Sharply," cited in supplement to Percival, *Environmental Regulation*, 31–32.

101. See generally, Wilkinson, Pittman and Dye, "Slick Work."

102. Pub. L. No. 92-532, 85 Stat. 1052 (1972) (codified as amended at 33 U.S.C. secs. 1401–45 and 16 U.S.C. secs. 1431–34 [1988]).

103. Steven J. Moore, "Troubles in the High Seas."

104. Ibid., 915; see also Percival, *Environmental Regulation*, 876.

105. See Steven J. Moore, "Troubles in the High Seas," 917.

106. See De Fontaubert, Downes, and Agardy, *Biodiversity in the Seas*, 62–63.

107. See Steven J. Moore, "Troubles in the High Seas," 917, n. 25.

108. Ibid., 920. See also Broad, *The Universe Below*.

109. See Steven J. Moore, "Troubles in the High Seas," 921–24.

110. See Naj, "Sewage Dumped Offshore Is Found Within Tiny Animals"; Sullivan, "Sewage Bacteria in Food Chain."

111. Pub. L. No. 100-688, Sec. 1001, 102 Stat. 4139 (1988) (codified at scattered sections of 33 U.S.C. [1988]).

112. Broad, *The Universe Below*, 301–03.

113. Percival, *Environmental Regulation*, 876.

114. Steven J. Moore, "Troubles in the High Seas," 937–38, 941–48.

115. See Norse, *Global Marine Biological Diversity*, 121.

116. Weber, *Abandoned Seas*, see also Norse, *Global Marine Biological Diversity*, 121.

117. See Norse, *Global Marine Biological Diversity*, 121; Weber, *Abandoned Seas*, 17.

118. See Robert J. Wilder, "The Precautionary Principle."

119. Birnie and Boyle, *International Law and the Environment*, 504.

120. Ibid., 506.

121. See Caron, "The Law of the Sea Treaty," 14.

122. Birnie and Boyle, *International Law and the Environment*, 516.

123. Ibid., 516–17.

124. Friedheim, *Negotiating the New Ocean Regime*, 287–88.

125. Cooke, "The Precautionary Approach to Fisheries," 1, 7.

126. Kelley, "The Marine Fish Conservation Network," 56–57.

127. See "The Turtle Soup Factor."

128. Earle, *Sea Change*, 163.

129. See De Fontaubert, Downes, and Agardy, *Biodiversity in the Seas*, 59; see also, generally, IUCN/World Conservation Union, *The Law of the Sea*.

130. See De Fontaubert, Downes, and Agardy, *Biodiversity in the Seas*, 59, 25–26.

131. Ibid., 60–64.

132. See ibid., 59; see also Van Dyke, "The Rio Principles," 1, 9–10.

133. See De Fontaubert, Downes, and Agardy, *Biodiversity in the Sea*, 60.

134. See ibid., 59–64.

135. See Beatley, Brower, and Schwab, *An Introduction to Coastal Zone Management*, 139–42.

136. International Joint Commission, *Seventh Biennial Report on Great Lakes Water Quality*.

137. See Beatley, Brower, and Schwab, *An Introduction to Coastal Zone Management*, 140; "Stuck in the Mud: Great Lakes Pollution."

138. See International Joint Commission, *Seventh Biennial Report on Great Lakes Water Quality*, 9–15.

139. See U.S. General Accounting Office, *Pollution Prevention* (hereinafter GAO Report on the PPA); see MacGarvin, 4–6.

140. Percival, *Environmental Regulation*, 213–14.

141. Pollution Prevention Act of 1990, Section 6602(b), 42 U.S.C. 13101(b), as cited in GAO Report on the PPA, 12.

142. GAO Report on the PPA, 13, citing U.S. Environmental Protection Agency, *Pollution Prevention 1991*.

143. An example is Freeman, *Industrial Pollution Prevention Handbook*.

144. Flam, "EPA Campaigns for Safer Chemicals," 1519.

145. Ibid.

146. See "The Pew Charitable Trusts Funds Toxic Diet Project."

147. GAO Report on the PPA, 11.

148. Ibid., 3, 39, 53.

149. Ibid., 2–4.

150. Ibid., 53–54.

151. Percival, *Environmental Regulation*, 420.

152. Environmental Defense Fund, "Pollution Prevention Alliance."

153. See U.S. Environmental Protection Agency, "1993 TRI Data Show Past Trends Continuing."

154. U.S. Environmental Protection Agency, EPA *Pollution Prevention Accomplishments: 1994*, 15; U.S. Environmental Protection Agency, *Green Lights; Pollution Prevention 1991*.

155. See U.S. Environmental Protection Agency, EPA *Pollution Prevention Accomplishments: 1994*, 10–26.

156. See Parker and Boyd, "An Introduction to EPA's Design for the Environment Program," citing National Research Council, *Improving Engineering Design*.

157. Ibid., 1.

158. See Graedel and Allenby, *Industrial Ecology*; Freeman, *Industrial Pollution Prevention Handbook*.

159. Frosch and Gallopoulos, "Strategies for Manufacturing," cited in Parker and Boyd, "An Introduction to EPA's Design for the Environment Program," 1; see also Edgington, "Industrial Ecology."

160. Parker and Boyd, "An Introduction to EPA's Design for the Environment Program," 1.

161. Ibid., 1–2.

162. Edgington, "Industrial Ecology," 31.

163. Parker and Boyd, "An Introduction to EPA's Design for the Environment Program," 1.

164. Edgington, "Industrial Ecology," 33. See also Enquete Commission of the German Bundestag, *Shaping Industrial Society*.

165. See Kirschner, "Eco-Industrial Plants Find Growing Acceptance."

166. See Grobe, "Composter Links Up with Food Processor." This "Good Humus Man" was started by my stepfather.

167. See Edgington, "Industrial Ecology," 32–33.

168. Hart, Boger, and Kerr, "Design for the Environment."

169. See U.S. Environmental Protection Agency, *Design for the Environment*.

Chapter 6. The Challenge of Integrating Science and Policy

1. This paraphrases the message presented in a dissimilar context in Capra, *The Tao of Physics*.

2. A classic treatment of this distinction is found in the works of C. P. Snow. See also Caldwell, *Between Two Worlds*; Hardin, *Filters Against Folly*, 16–25; Lovelock, *The Ages of Gaia*.

3. See Tuohy, "Characterizing the San Francisco Estuary," 113–14.

4. Hardin, *Filters Against Folly*, 12.

5. Ibid.

6. See Robert J. Wilder, "Is This Holistic Ecology?" 209, 211–13.

7. "74.6% of Sociology Is Bunk."

8. See Murphy and Noon, "Coping with Uncertainty in Wildlife Biology," 773–82.

9. Lovelock, *The Ages of Gaia*, 42.

10. See Rosovsky, *The University: An Owner's Manual*, 103.

11. See Capra, *The Tao of Physics*, 331–33.

12. See Barry and Oelschlaeger, "A Science for Survival"; see also Noss, "Whither Conservation Biology?" 215; Shrader-Frechette, "Throwing out the Bathwater of Positivism"; Lovejoy, "The Obligations of a Biologist," 329.

13. Allaby, *The Concise Oxford Dictionary of Ecology*, 50.

14. For a sampling, see Wilson, *The Diversity of Life*; Woodwell, "How Does the World Work?"; Ray, "Establishing Biosphere Reserves for Coastal Barrier Systems"; Davis, "The Need for a New Global Ocean Governance System."

15. Exceptions include Fiorino, *Making Environmental Policy*; Lee, *Compass and Gyrscope*.

16. See Thomas, *Late Night Thoughts*, 23–24.

17. See Capra, *The Tao of Physics*, 21, 328.

18. See Thomas, *Late Night Thoughts*, 11–13.

19. Editorial, "Multidisciplinary Research," *Science* 266 (11 November 1994): 951.

20. Norton, "Ecological Health and Sustainable Resource Management," 102–04.

21. Woodwell, "How Does the World Work?" 31.

22. Thomas, *The Fragile Species*, 72–73.

23. Ibid.

24. See generally, Robert J. Wilder, "Is This Holistic Ecology?"

25. Barnhart, ed., *The Barnhart Dictionary of Etymology*, 443.

26. Ibid.

27. Kenchington, *Managing Marine Environments*, 37.

28. Ibid., 37–38.

29. Ibid., 28, 37.

30. Ibid., 28–39, 33.

31. Ibid., 37.

32. Allaby, *The Concise Oxford Dictionary of Ecology*, 196, 378.

33. See Thomas, *The Fragile Species* 120.

34. Ibid., 120–21; see also Allaby, *The Concise Oxford Dictionary of Ecology*, 100, 383; Culotta, "Ninety Ways to Be a Mammal," 1161.

35. See Norse, *Global Marine Biological Diversity*.

36. Sherman, "Productivity, Perturbations, and Options for Biomass Yields."

37. Wilson, *The Diversity of Life*, 311–42; Thomas, *The Fragile Species*, 121.

38. Percival et al., *Environmental Regulation*, 1152–59.

39. Kerr, "Antarctic Ozone Hole Fails to Recover," 217.

40. See Norse, *Global Marine Biological Diversity*, 136–37.

41. See Thomas, *The Fragile Species*, 125.

42. Thomas, *The Medusa and the Snail*.

43. "Random Jottings."

44. See Thomas, *The Fragile Species*, 176.

45. Flam, "Chemical Prospectors Scour the Seas," 1324.

46. See Sax, "Liberating the Public Trust Doctrine," 185.

47. See, for example, Bulloch, *The Wasted Ocean*, 9; Reisner, *Cadillac Desert*, 487; Feshbach and Friendly, *Ecocide in the USSR*; Carson, *Silent Spring*.

48. See Daly and Cobb, *For the Common Good*.

49. The *Boomer* case is discussed in Plater, Abrams, and Goldfarb, *Environmental Law and Policy*, 103, 150.

50. Ibid., 107.

51. See Holt and Talbot, "New Principles for the Conservation of Wild Living Resources," 43.

52. See Paarlberg, "A Domestic Dispute," 16.

53. Wilson, *The Diversity of Life*, 310; Percival et al., *Environmental Regulation*, 535.

54. Norse, *Global Marine Biological Diversity*, 193.

55. See Woodwell, "How Does the World Work?"; Nash, *Wilderness and the American Mind*.

56. Allaby, *The Concise Oxford Dictionary of Ecology*, 132.

57. Norse, *Global Marine Biological Diversity*, 85, 148–49.

58. Ibid., 109.

59. See Reisner, *Cadillac Desert*.

60. Norse, *Global Marine Biological Diversity*, 149.

61. See Cairncross, *Costing the Earth*.

62. See DesJardins, "Restoration Wars," 8.

63. Norse, *Global Marine Biological Diversity*, 149.

64. See Committee for the National Institute for the Environment, *A Proposal for a National Institute for the Environment*, 21–22.

65. Norse, *Global Marine Biological Diversity*, 149.

66. See Robert J. Wilder, "Is This Holistic Ecology?"

67. See Beatley, Brower, and Schwab, *An Introduction to Coastal Zone Management*, 134–36.

68. Ibid., 134.

69. Imperial, Hennessey, and Robadue, "The Evolution of Adaptive Management," 147–48. See also Hennessey, "Governance and Adaptive Management for Estuarine Ecosystems," 147–48.

70. Imperial, Hennessey, and Robadue, "The Evolution of Adaptive Management," 150–51, 160, 163.

71. See Tuohy, "Characterizing the San Francisco Estuary," 115.

72. Ibid., 113.

73. Sec. 320(b) of the Clean Water Act; see ibid., 117.

74. See Tuohy, "Characterizing the San Francisco Estuary," 114.

75. See Imperial, Hennessey, and Robadue, "The Evolution of Adaptive Management," 173; Beatley, Brower, and Schwab, An Introduction to Coastal Zone Management, 136.

76. See Beatley, Brower, and Schwab, An Introduction to Coastal Zone Management, 136.

77. See Imperial, Hennessey, and Robadue, "The Evolution of Adaptive Management," 169–70.

78. Tuohy, "Characterizing the San Francisco Estuary," 118.

79. Ibid., 120.

80. Ibid., 127.

81. Ibid.

82. See Committee for National Institute for the Environment, 20–21.

83. See Congressional Research Service, Marine Ecosystem Management; Vig and Kraft, Environmental Policy, 369–88; U.S. Office of Technology Assessment, "OTA Technologies to Maintain Biological Diversity," cited in Percival et al., Environmental Regulation, 1084.

84. National Research Council, Conserving Biodiversity, 13; Birnie and Boyle, International Law and the Environment, 438–39, 445.

85. Grumbine, "Reflections on 'What Is Ecosystem Management?'" 41–42.

86. Ibid.

87. See Hennessey, "Governance and Adaptive Management for Estuarine Ecosystems," 40; Van Dyke et al., "Freedom for the Seas in the 21st Century."

88. Ray, "Coastal-Marine Discontinuities and synergisms," 1095; see also Capra, The Tao of Physics, 285–86.

89. See Birnie and Boyle, International Law and the Environment, 438–39.

90. Norse, Global Marine Biological Diversity, 229.

91. See Birnie and Boyle, International Law and the Environment, 439.

92. See Norse, Global Marine Biological Diversity, 229; De Fontaubert, Downes, and Agardy, Biodiversity in the Seas, 57.

93. See Thia-Eng, "Essential Elements of Integrated Coastal Zone Management," 81.

94. See De Fontaubert, Downes, and Agardy, Biodiversity in the Seas, 1–4.

95. This list paraphrases material in Kenchington and Crawford, "On the Meaning of Integration in Coastal Zone Management," 109, 112.

96. See Kenchington, Managing Marine Environments.

97. See Beatley, Brower, and Schwab, An Introduction to Coastal Zone Management, 142–43.

Chapter 7. Solutions

1. See "In Praise of Knowledge," 20. In the words of T. S. Eliot ("The Rock," part 1):

> Where is the Life we have lost in living?
> Where is the wisdom we have lost in knowledge?
> Where is the knowledge we have lost in information?

2. Norse, ed., *Global Marine Biological Diversity*, 282.

3. See National Research Council, *Science, Policy, and the Coast*, 63–76.

4. Some of the recommendations here are from "Sinking Fast: How Factory Trawlers Are Destroying U.S. Fisheries and Marine Ecosystems: A Greenpeace Report." See also Norse, ed., *Global Marine Biological Diversity*, 281–306.

References

Books

Adler, Robert, Jessica Landman, and Diane Cameron. *The Clean Water Act Twenty Years Later*. Washington, D.C.: Island Press, 1993.

Allaby, Michael. *The Concise Oxford Dictionary of Ecology*. New York: Oxford University Press, 1994.

Alliance to Save Energy et al. *America's Energy Choices: Investing in a Strong Economy and a Clean Environment*. Cambridge, Mass.: Union of Concerned Scientists, 1991.

Altshuler, Alan. *The Politics of the Federal Bureaucracy*. New York: Dodd, Mead and Company, 1968.

Andersen, Svein. *The Struggle over North Sea Oil and Gas: Government Strategies in Denmark, Britain and Norway*. New York: Oxford University Press, 1993.

Archer, Jack, Donald Connors, Kenneth Laurence, Sarah Columbia, and Robert Bowen. *The Public Trust Doctrine and Management of America's Coasts*. Amherst: University of Massachusetts Press, 1994.

Armstrong, John, and Peter Ryner. *Ocean Management: A New Perspective*. Ann Arbor: Ann Arbor Science Publishers, 1982.

"At Last, the Fuel Cell." *Economist*, 25 October 1997, 89.

Ball, Milner. *The Law of the Sea, Federal-State Relations and the Extension of the Territorial Sea*. Athens: Dean Rusk Center, University of Georgia, 1978.

Barnhart, Robert K., ed. *The Barnhart Dictionary of Etymology*. New York: H. W. Wilson, 1988.

Bartley, Ernest. *The Tidelands Oil Controversy*. Austin: University of Texas Press, 1953.

Bean, Michael J. *The Evolution of National Wildlife Law*. New York: Praeger, 1983.

Beatley, Timothy, David J. Brower, and Anna Schwab. *An Introduction To Coastal Zone Management*. Washington, D.C: Island Press, 1994.

Berger, Raoul. *Federalism, the Founders' Design*. Norman: University of Oklahoma Press, 1987.

Berrill, Michael. *The Plundered Seas: Can the World's Fish Be Saved?* San Francisco: Sierra Club, 1997.

Birnie, Patricia W., and Boyle, Allen E. *Basic Documents on International Law and the Environment*. Oxford: Clarendon Press, 1995.

Birnie, Patricia W., and Allen E. Boyle. *International Law and the Environment*. New York: Oxford University Press, 1992.

Bledsoe, Robert, and Boleslaw Boczek. *The International Law Dictionary*. Santa Barbara, Calif.: ABC-CLIO, 1987.

Broad, William. *The Universe Below: Discovering the Secrets of the Deep Sea*. New York: Simon and Schuster, 1997.

Brooks, L. Anathea, and Stacey D. VanDeveer. *Saving the Seas: Values, Scientists, and International Governance*. College Park: University of Maryland Sea Grant, 1997.

Buck, Eugene. *Congressional Research Service Issue Brief: Marine Fisheries Issues*, CRS-5. Energy and Natural Resources Policy Division, Code #IB93004, March 17, 1993.

Bulloch, David. *The Wasted Ocean*. New York: Lyons and Burford Press, 1989.

Cairncross, Frances. *Costing the Earth: The Challenge for Governments, the Opportunities for Business*. Boston: Harvard Business School Press, 1992.

Caldwell, Lynton Keith. *Between Two Worlds: Science, the Environmental Movement, and Policy Choice*. Cambridge: Cambridge University Press, 1990.

———. *International Environment Policy: Emergence and Dimensions*. Durham: Duke University Press, 1990.

California Coastal Commission. *California Offshore Oil and Gas Development*. San Francisco, July 1992.

California State Lands Commission. *California Comprehensive Offshore Resource Study*. Draft. Sacramento: California State Lands Commission, 1991.

Capra, Fritjof. *The Tao of Physics*. Shambhala: Boston, 1991.

———. *The Web of Life: A New Scientific Understanding of Living Systems*. New York: Anchor, 1996.

Carson, Rachel. *Silent Spring*. Houghton Mifflin: Boston, 1962.

Center for Ocean Management Studies. *Comparative Marine Policy*. New York: Praeger, 1981.

Chasis, Sarah, et al. *Upstream Solutions to Downstream Pollution: A Citizens' Guide to Protecting Seacoasts and the Great Lakes by Cleaning Up Polluted Runoff*. New York: Natural Resources Defense Council, and the Coast Alliance, 1993.

Cicin-Sain, Biliana, and Lori Denno, eds. *Moving Ahead on Ocean Governance*. Ocean Governance Study Group 26. Center for the Study of Marine Policy, University of Delaware, 1994.

Cicin-Sain, Biliana, and Katherine Leccese, eds. *Implications of Entry Into Force of the Law of the Sea Convention for U.S. Ocean Governance.* Newark: University of Delaware, 1995.

Colombos, John C. *International Law of the Sea.* New York: MacKay, 1967.

Commission on Marine Science, Engineering and Resources (Stratton Commission). *Our Nation and the Sea.* Washington, D.C.: GPO, 1969.

Committee for the National Institute for the Environment. *A Proposal for a National Institute for the Environment: Need, Rationale, and Structure.* 1993.

Commoner, Barry. *Making Peace with the Planet.* New York: New Press, 1992.

Congressional Research Service, Report for Congress. *Marine Ecosystem Management.* Washington, D.C.: Library of Congress, 1993.

Costanza, Robert, ed. *Ecological Economics: The Science and Management of Sustainability.* New York: Columbia University Press, 1991.

Council of State Governments. *State Management of Ocean Resources.* Louisville: Merrick, 1988.

Crocker, Henry, ed. *The Extent of the Marginal Sea: A Collection of Official Documents and Views of Representative Publicists.* Washington, D.C.: GPO, 1919.

Daly, Herman E., and John B. Cobb. *For the Common Good: Redirecting the Economy Toward Community, the Environment, and a Sustainable Future.* Boston: Beacon Press, 1989.

De Fontaubert, Charlotte, David R. Downes, and Tundi S. Agardy. *Biodiversity in the Seas.* Washington, D.C.: IUCN/CIEL/WWF, 1996.

Ditton, Robert, John Seymour, and Gerald Swanson. *Coastal Resources Management.* Lexington: D.C. Heath, 1977.

Downs, Anthony. *Inside Bureaucracy.* Boston: Little, Brown, 1967.

Earle, Sylvia. *Sea Change: A Message of the Oceans.* New York: Putnam, 1995.

Eisenhower, Dwight David. *Mandate for Change.* New York: New American Publishing, 1963.

Elazar, Daniel, ed. *Federalism as Grand Design: Political Philosophers and the Federal Principle.* Lanham, Md.: University Press of America, 1987.

Engler, Robert. *The Politics of Oil: Private Power and Democratic Directions.* Chicago: University of Chicago Press, 1961.

Enquete Commission of the German Bundestag on the Protection of Humanity and the Environment. *Shaping Industrial Society: Prospects for Sustainable Management of Substance Chains and Material Flows.* Bonn: Economica Verlag, 1995.

Fabbri, Paolo, ed. *Ocean Management in Global Change.* London: Elsevier, 1992.

Farrow, Scott. *Managing the Outer Continental Shelf Lands: Oceans of Controversy.* New York: Taylor and Francis, 1990.

Fenn, Percy T. *The Origin of the Right of Fishery in Territorial Waters.* Cambridge: Harvard University Press, 1926.

Feshbach, Murray, and Alfred Friendly Jr. *Ecocide in the USSR.* New York: Basic Books, 1992.

Findley, Roger W., and Daniel A. Farber. *Environmental Law in a Nutshell.* St. Paul: West Publishing, 1992.

Fiorino, Daniel J. *Making Environmental Policy.* Berkeley: University of California Press, 1995.

Flavin, Christopher, and Alan Durning. *Building on Success: The Age of Energy Efficiency.* Worldwatch Paper no. 82. Washington, D.C.: Worldwatch Institute, 1988.

Freeman, Harry M. *Industrial Pollution Prevention Handbook.* New York: MacGraw-Hill, 1995.

Freidheim, Robert. *Managing Ocean Resources.* Boulder: Westview, 1979.

Freudenburg, William R., and Robert Gramling. *Oil in Troubled Waters: Perceptions, Politics, and the Battle over Offshore Drilling.* Albany: State University of New York Press, 1994.

Friedheim, Robert L. *Negotiating the New Ocean Regime.* Columbia: University of South Carolina Press, 1993.

Fulton, Thomas. *The Sovereignty of the Sea.* London: William Blackwood and Sons, 1911.

Gaba, Jeffrey, and Donald Stever. *Law of Solid Waste, Pollution Prevention, and Recycling.* New York: Clark, Boardman and Callaghan, 1992.

Gamble, John. *Marine Policy.* Lexington: Heath, 1977.

Garcia, Amador, and F. V. Rodriguez. *The Exploitation and Conservation of the Resources of the Sea.* Leyden: A. W. Sythoff, 1959.

Goldstein, Joan, ed. *The Politics of Offshore Oil.* New York: Praeger Publishers, 1982.

Gordon, Deborah. *Steering A New Course: Transportation, Energy, and the Environment.* Washington, D.C.: Island Press, 1991.

Gore, Al. *Earth in the Balance: Ecology and the Human Spirit.* New York: Houghton Mifflin, 1990.

Gottlieb, Robert, ed. *Reducing Toxics: A New Approach to Policy and Industrial Decisionmaking.* Washington, D.C.: Island Press, 1995.

Graedel, T. E., and B. R. Allenby, *Industrial Ecology.* Englewood Cliffs, N.J.: Prentice-Hall, 1995.

Greene, William. *Strategies of the Major Oil Companies.* Ann Arbor: UMI Research Press, 1985.

Haas, Peter M. *Saving the Mediterranean: The Politics of International Environmental Cooperation.* New York: Columbia University Press, 1990.

Haas, Peter, Robert Keohane, and Marc Levy, eds. *Institutions for the Earth: Sources of Effective International Environmental Protection.* Cambridge, Mass.: MIT Press, 1993.

Handl, Gunther, et al. *Yearbook of International Law.* Boston: Graham and Trotman/Martinus Nijhoff (1994).

Hardin, Garrett. *Filters Against Folly: How to Survive Despite Economists, Ecologists, and the Merely Eloquent.* Binghamton, N.Y.: Maple Press Company, 1985.

Harris, Richard A., and Sidney M. Milkis. *The Politics of Regulatory Change*. New York: Oxford University Press, 1989.

Heikoff, Joseph. *Coastal Resources Management*. Ann Arbor: Ann Arbor Science Publishers, 1977.

Hendrickson, Robert. *Ocean Almanac*. New York: Doubleday, 1984.

Hennessey, Timothy. *Formulating Marine Policy: Limitations to Rational Decision-Making*. Proceedings of Second Annual Conference, Center for Ocean Management Studies. Kingston: University of Rhode Island, 1978.

Holing, Dwight. *Coastal Alert: Ecosystems, Energy, and Offshore Oil Drilling*. Washington, D.C.: Island Press, 1990.

Hollick, Ann. *U.S. Foreign Policy and the Law of the Sea*. Princeton: Princeton University Press, 1981.

Hoole, Francis, Robert Friedheim, and Timothy Hennessey, eds. *Making Ocean Policy*. Boulder: Westview, 1981.

Hurrell, Andrew, and Benedict Kingsbury, eds. *The International Politics of the Environment*. New York: Oxford University Press, 1992.

Ickes, Harold. *Autobiography of a Curmudgeon*. New York: Reynal and Hitchcock Press, 1943.

———. *The Secret Diary of Harold L. Ickes*. Vols. 1–3. New York: Simon and Schuster, 1954.

Ingram, Helen, and Dean Mann, eds. *Why Policies Succeed or Fail*. Beverly Hills, Calif.: Sage Publications, 1980.

International Joint Commission (United States–Canada). *Seventh Biennial Report on Great Lakes Water Quality*, 1994.

IUCN/World Conservation Union. *The Law of the Sea: Priorities and Responsibilities in Implementing the Convention*. International Union for the Conservation of Nature. Gland, Switzerland, 1995.

Jackson, Tim. *Clean Production Strategies: Developing Preventive Environmental Management in the Industrial Economy*, ed. Jackson. Boca Raton, Fla.: Lewis Publishers, 1993.

Jasanoff, Sheila. *The Fifth Branch: Science Advisors as Policy Makers*. Cambridge: Harvard University Press, 1990.

Jessup, Philip. *The Law of Territorial Waters and Maritime Jurisdiction*. New York: G. A. Jennings Co., 1927.

Juda, Lawrence. *Ocean Space Rights*. New York: Praeger Publishers, 1975.

Kaufman, Herbert. *The Forest Ranger: A Study in Administrative Behavior*. Washington, D.C.: Resources for the Future, 1986.

———. *The Limits of Organizational Change*. Tuscaloosa: University of Alabama Press, 1971.

———. *Time, Chance, and Organizations*. Chatham, N.J.: Chatham House, 1985.

Kenchington, Richard A. *Managing Marine Environments*. New York: Taylor and Francis, 1990.

King, Lauriston R., and Amy Broussard. *Proceedings of the National Conference on the States and an Extended Territorial Sea*. Texas A and M Sea Grant Publication no. AMU-SG-87-114. December 1985.

Kingdon, John. *Agendas, Alternatives, and Public Policies*. Boston: Little, Brown, 1984.

Leach, Richard, ed. *Intergovernmental Relations in the 1980s*. New York: Marcel Dekker, 1983.

Lee, Kai. *Compass and Gyroscope: Integrating Science and Policy for the Environment*. Washington, D.C.: Island Press, 1993.

Legget, Jeremy., ed. *Global Warming: The Greenpeace Report*. Oxford: Oxford University Press, 1990.

Lehman, John, Jr. *The Command of the Seas*. New York: Charles Scribner's Sons, 1988.

Lichtblau, John, and Dillard Spriggs. *The Oil Depletion Issue*. New York: Petroleum Industry Research Foundation, 1959.

Lovelock, James. *The Ages of Gaia: A Biography of Our Living Earth*. New York: Norton, 1988.

Mangone, Gerard. *Marine Policy for America*. New York: Taylor and Francis, 1988.

Mann, Dean, ed. *Environmental Policy Formation*. Lexington, Mass.: Heath, 1981.

March, James, and Herbert Simon. *Organizations*. New York: Wiley, 1958.

Marine Mammal Commission. *Annual Report to Congress, 1994*. Washington, D.C.: MMC, 31 January 1995.

Marx, Wesley. *The Frail Ocean: A Blueprint for Change in the 1990's and Beyond*. Chester, Conn.: Globe Pequot Press, 1991.

Masterson, William. *Jurisdiction in Marginal Seas*. Port Washington, N.Y.: Kennikat Press, 1929.

McDougal, Myres, and William Burke. *The Public Order of the Oceans*. New Haven: Yale University Press, 1962.

Minerals Management Service. U.S. Department of the Interior. *Moving Beyond Conflict to Consensus: Report of the OCS Policy Committee's Subcommittee on OCS Legislation 49*. Washington, D.C.: GPO, 1993.

———. *Outer Continental Shelf Natural Gas and Oil Resource Management: Comprehensive Program, 1992–1997*. Washington, D.C.: GPO, 1993.

———. *Proposed Final Comprehensive Program, 1992–1997*. Washington, D.C.: GPO, 1992.

Mitchell, Edward, ed. *The Question of Offshore Oil*. Washington, D.C.: American Enterprise Institute for Public Policy Research, 1976

Molotch, Harvey, and William Freudenburg, eds. *Santa Barbara County: Two Paths*. Final Report to the Minerals Management Service, OCS Study MMS 96-0036. Camarillo, Calif.: MMS, July 1996.

Mulvaney, Kieran. "A Sea of Troubles." *E Magazine*, January 1998, 28.

Nash, Gerald. *United States Oil Policy, 1890–1964: Business and Government in Twentieth Century America*. Pittsburgh: University of Pittsburgh Press, 1968.

Nash, Roderick. *Wilderness and the American Mind.* New Haven: Yale University Press, 1982.

National Research Council. *Improving Engineering Design: Designing for Competitive Advantage.* Washington, D.C.: National Academy Press, 1991.

———. *Conserving Biodiversity: A Research Agenda for Development Agencies.* Washington, D.C.: National Academy Press, 1992.

———. *Science, Policy, and the Coast: Improving Decisionmaking.* Washington, D.C.: National Academy Press, 1995.

———. *Understanding Marine Biodiversity: A Research Agenda for the Nation.* Washington, D.C.: National Academy Press, 1995.

Nelsen, Brent. *The State Offshore: Petroleum, Politics, and State Intervention on the British and Norwegian Continental Shelves.* New York: Praeger, 1991.

Norse, Elliott, ed. *Global Marine Biological Diversity: A Strategy for Building Conservation into Decision Making.* Washington, D.C.: Island Press, 1993.

Odum, Eugene. *Ecology and Our Endangered Life-Support System.* Sunderland: Sinauer Associates, 1993.

Oregon Ocean Policy Advisory Council. *Territorial Sea Plan: Second Draft.* State of Oregon, 1994.

O'Riordan, Timothy, and James Cameron, eds. *Interpreting the Precautionary Principle.* London: Earthscan Publications, 1994.

Orr, David. *Ecological Literacy.* Albany: State University of New York Press, 1992.

Oudendijk, J. K. *Status and Extent of Adjacent Waters.* Leyden: A. W. Sitjhoff, 1970.

Payoyo, Peter, ed. *Ocean Governance: Sustainable Development of the Seas.* New York: United Nations University Press, 1994.

Percival, Robert, et al., eds. *Environmental Regulation: Law, Science, and Policy.* Boston: Little, Brown, 1992.

———. Supplement to *Environmental Regulation: Law, Science, and Policy.* Boston: Little, Brown, 1993.

Perrow, Charles. *Complex Organizations.* Glenview, Ill.: Scott, Foresman, 1972.

Peters, Robert, and Thomas Lovejoy, eds. *Global Warming and Biological Diversity.* New Haven: Yale University Press, 1992.

Plater, Zygmunt, Robert Abrams, and William Goldfarb. *Environmental Law and Policy: Nature, Law, and Society.* St. Paul: West Publishing, 1992.

Poen, Monte, ed. *Strictly Personal and Confidential: The Letters Harry Truman Never Mailed.* Boston: Little, Brown, 1982.

Pound, Roscoe, Charles McIlwain, and Roy Nichols. *Federalism as a Democratic Process.* New Brunswick, N.J.: Rutgers University Press, 1942.

Prescott, J. R. V. *The Political Geography of the Oceans.* New York: John Wiley, 1975.

Reisner, Marc. *Cadillac Desert: The American West and Its Disappearing Water.* New York: Penguin, 1986.

Rosovsky, Henry. *The University: An Owner's Manual.* New York: Norton, 1990.

Ross, David. *Opportunities and Uses of the Ocean*. New York: Springer-Verlag, 1978.

Rourke, Francis, ed. *Bureaucratic Power in National Politics*. Boston: Little, Brown, 1978.

Sabatier, Paul, and Daniel Mazmanian. *Can Regulation Work? The Implementation of the 1972 California Coastal Initiative*. New York: Plenum Press, 1983.

Safina, Carl. *Song for the Blue Ocean*. New York: Henry Holt, 1998.

Sands, Philippe, ed. *Greening International Law*. New York: New Press, 1994.

Scheiber, Harry, ed. *Perspectives on Federalism: Papers of the First Berkeley Seminar on Federalism*. Institute of Governmental Studies, University of California at Berkeley, 1987.

Seidman, Harold. *Politics, Position, and Power*. New York: Oxford University Press (1970).

Seneca, Joseph, and Michael Taussig. *Environmental Economics*. Englewood Cliffs, N.J.: Prentice-Hall, 1984.

Sherman, Kenneth, Lewis Alexander, and Barry Gold, eds. *Large Marine Ecosystems: Patterns, Processes and Yields*. Washington, D.C.: American Association for the Advancement of Science Press, 1990.

Silva, Maynard, ed. *Ocean Resources and U.S. Intergovernmental Resources in the 1980's*. Westview Press, 1986.

Simon, Herbert. *Administrative Behavior*. New York: Free Press, 1976.

Sitarz, Daniel, ed. *Agenda 21: The Earth Summit Strategy To Save Our Planet*. Boulder, Colo.: Earth Press, 1993.

Smith, Zachery A. *The Environmental Policy Paradox*. Englewood Cliffs, N.J.: Prentice-Hall, 1995.

Sollen, Robert. *An Ocean of Oil*. Juneau: Denali Press, 1998.

Straus files. *Office Files of Assistant Secretary of Interior Michael Straus, 1943–1945*. U.S. National Archives. RG 48, Stack 12E-3, Entry 779, Box 8.

Swarztrauber, Sayre. *The Three-Mile Limit of Territorial Seas*. Annapolis: Naval Institute Press, 1972.

Thia-Eng, Chua, and Louise Fallon-Scura, eds. *Integrative Framework and Methods for Coastal Area Management*. Manila: International Center for Living Aquatics Resources Management, 1992.

Thomas, Lewis. *The Fragile Species*. New York: Macmillan, 1993.

———. *Late Night Thoughts on Listening to Mahler's Ninth Symphony*. New York: Bantam Books, 1991.

———. *The Lives of a Cell: Notes of a Biology Watcher*. New York: Viking, 1974.

———. *Medusa and the Snail: More Notes of a Biology Watcher*. New York: Viking, 1979.

Thorne-Miller, Boyce, and John Catena. *The Living Ocean: Understanding and Protecting Marine Biodiversity*. Washington, D.C.: Island Press, 1991.

Truman, Harry. *Memoirs*. 2 vols. Garden City, N.Y.: Doubleday, 1956.

United Nations. Food and Agriculture Organization. *The Precautionary Approach to Fisheries with Reference to Straddling Fish Stocks and Highly Migratory Fish Stocks*. Report

A/CONF.164/INF/8 26 January 1994. Presented at the UN Conference on Straddling Fish Stocks and Highly Migratory Fish Stocks, New York, 14–31 March 1994.

U.S. Department of State. *Foreign Relations of the United States, Diplomatic Papers.* Washington, D.C.: GPO, 1954 (for years 1937, 1939, 1945). *[FRUS]*

U.S. Environmental Protection Agency. Office of Pollution Prevention and Toxics. *Design for the Environment.* EPA 774-F-94-003. Washington, D.C.: EPA, 1994.

———. *EPA Pollution Prevention Accomplishments, 1994: Incorporating Pollution Prevention into Business Decisions.* EPA 100-R-95-001. Washington, D.C.: EPA, 1995.

———. *Green Lights: An Enlightened Approach to Energy Efficiency and Pollution Prevention.* EPA 430-K-93-001. Washington, D.C.: EPA, 1993.

———. *Pollution Prevention 1991: Progress on Reducing Industrial Pollutants.* EPA 21P-3003. Washington, D.C.: EPA, 1991.

U.S. General Accounting Office. *Pollution Prevention: EPA Should Reexamine the Objectives and Sustainability of State Programs.* Report to the Chairman, Subcommittee on Environment, Energy, and Natural Resources, of the Committee on Government Operations, U.S. House of Representatives, January 1994. [GAO Report on the PPA]

———. *Toxic Substances Control Act: Preliminary Observations on Legislative Changes to Make TSCA More Effective.* GAO/T-RCED-94-263, 13 July 1994. [GAO Report on TSCA]

———. *Water Pollution: EPA Needs to Set Priorities for Water Quality Criteria Issues.* GAO/RCED-94-117 (1994). [GAO Report on Water Pollution]

U.S. House of Representatives. *Improving the OCS Lands Act, Hearing Before the Subcommittee on Panama Canal/Outer Continental Shelf of the House Committee on Merchant Marine and Fisheries.* 101st Cong., 1st sess., August 1, 1989.

———. *Outer Continental Shelf Lands Act Amendments of 1977: Report by the Ad Hoc Select Committee on the Outer Continental Shelf.* H.R. Rep. No. 590, 95th Cong., 1st sess., 29 August 1977.

———. *Outer Continental Shelf Lands Act Amendments of 1978,* Pub. L. No. 95-372, 92 Stat. 629 (1978) (codified at 43 U.S.C.A. Secs. 1331 et seq. [1986 and 1989 Supp.]).

———. *Reauthorization of the Coastal Zone Management Act, Hard Mineral Resources in the Exclusive Economic Zone, Fisheries Issues, and Extension of the Territorial Sea.* Hearings Before the House Committee on Merchant Marine and Fisheries. 101st Cong., 2nd sess. (1990).

———. *Territorial Sea and Contiguous Zone Extension Act of 1988. Hearing before the Subcommittee on Oceanography of the House Committee on Merchant Marine and Fisheries.* 100th Cong., 2nd sess., 10 August 1988.

———. *Territorial Sea and Contiguous Zone Extension and Enforcement Act of 1991. Hearing before the Committee on Merchant Marine and Fisheries.* 103rd Cong., 2nd sess., 4 February 1992.

———. *Territorial Sea Extension. Hearing before the Subcommittee on Oceanography and Great Lakes of the House Committee on Merchant Marine and Fisheries.* 101st Cong., 1st sess., 21 March 1989.

U.S. Navy. *Annotated Supplement to the Commander's Handbook on the Law of Naval Operations,* U.S. Navy JAGC. NWP 9 (REV. A)/FMFM 1-10. Washington, D.C., 1989.

U.S. Senate. *Submerged Lands, Hearings Before the Committee on Interior and Insular Affairs,* 83rd Cong., 2nd sess., 16 February–4 March 1953.

Van Dyke, Jon, Durwood Zaelke, and Grant Hewison, eds. *Freedom for the Seas in the 21st Century: Ocean Governance and Environmental Harmony.* Washington, D.C.: Island Press, 1993.

Vig, Norman, and Michael Kraft, eds. *Environmental Policy in the 1990s: Toward A New Agenda.* Washington, D.C.: Congressional Quarterly Press, 1994.

Weber, Michael, and Judith Gradwohl. *The Wealth of Oceans.* New York: Norton, 1995.

Weber, Peter. *Abandoned Seas: Reversing the Decline of the Ocean.* Worldwatch Paper no. 116. Washington, D.C.: Worldwatch Institute, 1993.

Weiner, Jonathan. *The Beak of the Finch: A Story of Evolution in Our Time.* New York: Vintage Books, 1995.

Wenk, Edward. *The Politics of the Ocean.* Seattle: University of Washington Press, 1972.

Wilson, Edward O. *The Diversity of Life.* New York: Norton, 1993.

Wilson, Edward O., ed. *Biodiversity.* Washington, D.C.: National Academy Press, 1988.

Wilson, James Q. *Bureaucracy: What Government Agencies Do and Why They Do It.* New York: Basic Books, 1989.

Young, Michael. *For Our Children's Children: Some Practical Implications of Inter-Generational Equity and the Precautionary Principle.* Occasional Paper no. 6. Australia: CSIRO Division of Wildlife and Ecology, 1993.

Zuckerman, Alan. *Doing Political Science.* Boulder, Colo.: Westview, 1991.

Articles

Alexander, Bruce. "The Territorial Sea of the United States: Is It Twelve Miles or Not?" *Journal of Maritime Law and Commerce* 20 (1989): 449.

Archer, Jack. "Evolution of Major 1990 CZMA Amendments: Restoring Federal Consistency and Protecting Coastal Water Quality." *Territorial Sea Journal* 1 (1991): 191.

———. "Resolving Intergovernmental Conflicts in Marine Resource Management: The U.S. Experience." *Ocean and Shoreline Management* 12 (1989): 253.

"At Last, the Fuel Cell." *Economist* 25 October 1997, 89.

Babbitt, Bruce. "Federalism and the Environment: An Intergovernmental Perspective of the Sagebrush Rebellion." *Environmental Law* 12 (1982): 847.

———. Reply to Robert Jordan, chairman of Minerals Management Service, OCS Policy Committee, 22 March 1994.

———. "Will America Join the Waste Watchers?" *World Monitor*, June 1991, 59.

Baender, Margo. "Pesticides and Precaution: The Bamako Convention as a Model for an International Convention on Pesticides Regulation." *New York University Journal of International Law and Politics* 24 (1991): 557.

Ball, Milner. "Good Old American Permits: Madisonian Federalism on the Territorial Sea and Continental Shelf." *Environmental Law* 12 (1982), 623.

Barry, Dwight, and Max Oelschlaeger. "A Science for Survival: Values and Conservation Biology." *Conservation Biology* 10 (1996): 905.

Bennett, Charles. Member of House Committee on Merchant Marine and Fisheries, telephone interview, 2 December 1991.

Bodansky, Daniel. "Scientific Uncertainty and the Precautionary Principle." *Environment* 33 (1991): 4.

Botsford, Louis, Juan Carlos Castilla, and Charles Peterson. "The Management of Fisheries and Marine Ecosystems." *Science* 277 (25 July 1997): 509.

Briscoe, John. "The Division of American Offshore Zones as Between Nation and State." Paper presented at the Western Legislative Conference, Monterey, California, 11 November 1989.

———. "The Effect of President Reagan's 12-Mile Territorial Sea Proclamation on the Boundaries and Extraterritorial Powers of the Coastal States." *Territorial Sea Journal* 2 1992): 225.

Broadus, James. "Creature Feature Too: Principium Precautionarium." *Oceanus* 35 (1992): 6.

Burke, William. "Unregulated High Seas Fishing and Ocean Governance." In *Freedom for the Seas in the 21st Century: Ocean Governance and Environmental Harmony*, ed. Van Dyke, Zaelke, and Hewison.

Caldwell, Lynton Keith. "Implementing NEPA: A Non-Technical Political Task." Unpublished paper, Department of Public and Environmental Affairs, Indiana University, 23 January 1995.

Cameron, James. "The Status of the Precautionary Principle in International Law." In *Interpreting the Precautionary Principle*, ed. O'Riordan and Cameron.

Cameron, James, and Juli Aboucher. "The Precautionary Principle: A Fundamental Principle of Law and Policy for the Protection of the Global Environment." *Boston College International and Comparative Law Review* 14 (1991): 1.

Canfield, Clarke. "More Heartache Ahead: New England's Groundfish Stocks Aren't Recovering Fast Enough, Neither Are Its Fishermen." *National Fisherman* 77 (1997): 30.

"Car Industry Survey." *Economist*, 17 October 1992.

Carlton, James. "Understanding Marine Biodiversity: A Research Agenda for the Nation." *Oceanus* 38 (1995): 4.

Carlucci, Frank. Letter to Donald Hodel, 30 September 1988. Obtained by author under U.S. Freedom of Information Act, Request #90-FOI-0810, April 1990.

———. Letter to George Shultz, 6 May 1988. Obtained by author under U.S. Freedom of Information Act, Request #90-FOI-0810, April 1990.

Caron, David. "The Law of the Sea Treaty and the United States: Reflections Given the Small Likelihood of Ratification in 1995." In *Implications of Entry into Force of the Law of the Sea Convention for U.S. Ocean Governance*, ed. Cicin-Sain and Leccese.

"A Caspian Gamble." *Economist*, 7 February 1998, 57.

"The Catch About Fish." *Economist*, 19 March 1994.

Chandler, Melinda. "The Biodiversity Convention: Selected Issues of Interest to the International Lawyer." *Colorado Journal of International Law and Policy* 4 (1993): 141.

Christie, Donna. "Making Waves: Florida's Experience with Extended Territorial Sea Jurisdiction." *Territorial Sea Journal* 1 (1990).

———. "State Historic Interests in the Marginal Seas." *Territorial Sea Journal* 2 (1992): 151, 158–81.

Cicin-Sain, Biliana. "Essay: A National Ocean Governance Strategy for the United States Is Needed Now." *Coastal Management* 22 (1994): 171.

———. "Ocean Resources and Intergovernmental Relations: An Analysis of the Patterns." In *Ocean Resources and U.S. Intergovernmental Relations in the 1980s*, ed. Silva.

———. "Offshore Oil Development in California: Challenges to Government and to the Public Interest." *Public Affairs Report* 1–2 (1986)

Cicin-Sain, Biliana, and Robert Knecht. "Federalism Under Stress: The Case of Offshore Oil and California" in *Ocean Resources and U.S. Intergovernmental Relations in the 1980s*, ed. Silva.

Cicin-Sain, Biliana, and Robert Knecht. "The Problem of Governance of U.S. Ocean Resources and the New Exclusive Economic Zone." *Ocean Development and International Law* 15 (1985): 289.

Clausen, Ely. "The Delaney Clause: An Obscure EPA Policy Is to Blame." *EPA Journal*, January–March 1993.

"Coastal Zone Management and Resource Protection, Hearings Before the Subcommittee on Fisheries and Wildlife Conservation and the Environment, House Committee on Merchant Marine and Fisheries. 100th Congress, 28 September 1988.

"Conflicting State and Federal Claims of Title in Submerged Lands of the Continental Shelf." *Yale Law Journal* 56 (1947): 356.

Cook, Edward. "Federalism at Sea? State-Federal Relations in an Extended Territorial Sea." *Journal of Law and Politics* 5 (1989): 429.

Cooke, Justin G. "The Precautionary Approach to Fisheries and Reference Points for Fishery Management." Report submitted by IUCN/World Conservation

Union to the UN Conference on Straddling Fish Stocks and Highly Migratory Fish Stocks, New York, 14–31 March 1994.

Costanza, Robert, and Laura Cornwell. "The 4P Approach to Dealing with Scientific Uncertainty." *Environment* 34 (1992): 12.

Culotta, Elizabeth. "The Case of the Missing Mussel." *Science* 267 (20 January 1995): 331.

———. "Ninety Ways to Be a Mammal." *Science* 266 (18 November 1994): 1161.

Davis, W. Jackson. "The Need for a New Global Ocean Governance System." In *Freedom for the Seas in the 21st Century*, ed. Van Dyke, Zaelke, and Hewison.

Derthick, Martha. "American Federalism: Madison's Middle Ground in the 1980's." *Public Administration Review* 66 (January–February 1987).

DesJardins, Marc. "Restoration Wars." *National Fisherman* 74 (March 1994): 8.

Dethlefsen, Volkert, Tim Jackson, and Peter Taylor. "The Precautionary Principle— Towards Anticipatory Environmental Management." In *Clean Production Strategies: Developing Preventive Environmental Management in the Industrial Economy*, ed. Jackson.

Douros, William. "Where Is Oil Industry Today, Where Is It Heading?" *Santa Barbara News-Press*, 29 December 1996, G1.

Drumm, Russell. "When Scientists Become Advocates." *National Fisherman* 74 (April 1994): 46.

Edgington, Stephen M. "Industrial Ecology: Biotech's Role in Sustainable Development." *Bio/Technology* 13 (13 January 1995): 31.

Environmental Defense Fund. "Pollution Prevention Alliance." *Network News*, 5 (March 1995): 4–5.

Eichenberg, Tim, and Jack Archer. "The Federal Consistency Doctrine: Coastal Zone Management and 'New Federalism.'" *Ecology Law Quarterly* 14 (1987): 9.

"Energy Efficiency: Feeling the Pinch." *Economist*, 20 August 1994, 66.

Esler, Eric. "CZMA Consistency Review: The Supreme Court's Attitude Toward Administrative Rulemaking and Legislative History in 'Secretary of the Interior v. California.'" *Ecology Law Quarterly* 13 (1986): 687.

Evans, Nathan, and John Bailey. "Creating Symmetry Between the Commonwealth and States by Sharing Benefits and Avoiding Costs." *Ocean and Coastal Management* 34 (1997): 173.

Fairfax, Sally. "Old Recipes for New Federalism." *Environmental Law* 12 (1982): 945.

Finch, Roland. "Fishery Management Under the Magnuson Act." *Marine Policy* 9 (1985): 170.

Fiore, Faye. "Balanced Budget Plan Linked to Gas Tax." *Los Angeles Times*, 10 May 1997, A15.

Fitzgerald, Edward. "Natural Resources Defense Council v. Hodel: The Evolution of Interior's Five Year Outer Continental Shelf Oil and Gas Leasing Program." *Temple Environmental Law and Technology Journal* 12 (1993): 1.

———. "Outer Continental Shelf Revenue Sharing: A Proposal to End the Seaward Rebellion." *UCLA Journal of Environmental Law* 5 (1985): 1.

———. "The Tidelands Controversy Revisited." *Environmental Law* 19 (1988): 209.

Flam, Faye. "Chemical Prospectors Scour the Seas for Promising Drugs." *Science* 266 (25 November 1994): 1324.

———. "EPA Campaigns for Safer Chemicals." *Science* 265 (9 September 1994): 1519.

Floit, Catherine. "Reconsidering Freedom of the Seas: Protection of Living Marine Resources on the High Seas." In *Freedom for the Seas in the 21st Century: Ocean Governance and Environmental Harmony*, ed. Van Dyke, Zaelke, and Hewison.

Forester, John. "Bounded Rationality and the Politics of Muddling Through." *Public Administration Review* 44 (January–February 1984): 23.

Frohnmayer, Dave. "A New Look at Federalism: The Theory and Implications of 'Dual Sovereignty'" *Environmental Law* 12 (1982): 903.

Frosch, Robert, and Nicholas Gallopoulos. "Strategies for Manufacturing." *Scientific American* 261 (1989): 144.

Geiser, Kenneth. "The Unfinished Business of Pollution Prevention." *Georgia Law Review* 29 (1995): 473.

"The Great Transport Cop-Out: A Sensible Transport Policy Must Include Road Pricing." *Economist*, 17 June 1995, 18.

Greenpeace International. "The Principle of Precautionary Action: Definition and Implementation." Report to the Fourteenth Consultative Meeting of the London Dumping Convention, London, 25–29 November 1991.

———. "Sinking Fast: How Factory Trawlers Are Destroying U.S. Fisheries and Marine Ecosystems: A Greenpeace Report." 1997.

Grew, Joseph. Letter to Cordell Hull, 31 March 1938. U.S. Department of State. *FRUS* 1939.

Grew, Joseph, and Harold Ickes. Memorandum to Franklin Roosevelt, 22 January 1945. *FRUS* 1945.

Grew, Joseph, and Harold Ickes. Memorandum to Harry Truman, 30 April 1945. *FRUS* 1945.

Grimes, Charles. "Scientist Responds to Advocacy Charge." *National Fisherman* 75 (July 1994).

Grobe, Karin. "Composter Links up with Food Processor." *Biocycle* 35 (July 1994): 40.

Grotius, Hugo. "The Freedom of the Seas, or the Right Which Belongs to the Dutch to Take Part in the East Indian Trade (Mare Liberum)." In *Classics of International Law*, ed. J. B. Scott. New York: Oxford University Press, 1916.

Grumbine, Edward. "Reflections on 'What Is Ecosystem Management?'" *Conservation Biology* 11 (1997): 41.

Gündling, Lothar. "The Status in International Law of the Precautionary Principle." *International Journal of Estuarine and Coastal Law* 5 (1990): 23.

Haas, Peter. "Protecting the Baltic and North Seas." In *Institutions for the Earth: Sources of Effective International Environmental Protection*, ed. Haas, Keohane, and Levy.

Haigh, Nigel. "The Introduction of the Precautionary Principle into the U.K." In *Interpreting the Precautionary Principle*, ed. O'Riordan and Cameron.

Hart, Katherine M., Deborah L. Boger, and Michael A. Kerr, "Design for the Environment: A Partnership for a Cleaner Future." *Printed Circuit Fabrication* 18 (April 1995): 16.

Hayashi, Moritaki. "United Nations Conference on Straddling and Highly Migratory Fish Stocks: An Analysis of the 1993 Sessions." Presented at the Pacem in Maribus XXI Conference, Takaoka City, Japan, 6–9 September 1993.

Hennessey, Timothy. "Governance and Adaptive Management for Estuarine Ecosystems: The Case of Chesapeake Bay." *Coastal Management* 22 (1994): 119.

Hershman, Marc. "Building a Federal-State Partnership for U.S. Ocean Resource Management." In *Ocean Resources and U.S. Intergovernmental Relations in the 1980s*, ed. Silva.

Hildreth, Richard. "Federal-State Revenue Sharing and Resource Management Under the Outer Continental Shelf Lands Act Section 8 (g)." Coastal Management 17 (1989): 171.

———. "Marine Use Conflicts Arising from Development of Seabed Hydrocarbons and Minerals: Some Approaches from the United States West Coast." *Ocean and Shoreline Management* 12 (1989): 271.

———. "Ocean Resources and Intergovernmental Relations in the 1980s: Outer Continental Shelf Hydrocarbons and Minerals." in *Ocean Resources and U.S. Intergovernmental Relations in the 1980s*, ed. Silva.

Holmes, Barry. "Biologists Sort the Lessons of Fisheries' Collapse." *Science* 264 (27 May 1994).

Holt, Sidney, and Lee Talbot. "New Principles of the Conservation of Wild Living Resources." *Journal of Wildlife Management* 7 (Supplemental Monograph no. 59) (1978): 43.

Houck, Oliver. "The Regulation of Toxic Pollutants Under the Clean Water Act." *Environmental Law Reporter* 21 (September 1991): 10528–39.

"House Panel Investigates DOI's Restructured Budget." *EESI Weekly Bulletin* (3 April 1995), 9–10.

Huffman, James. "Governing America's Resources: Federalism in the 1980's." *Environmental Law* 12 (1982): 863.

Hull, Cordell. Letter to Senator Copeland, chairman of Senate Committee on Commerce, 4 August 1937. U.S. Department of State, FRUS 1937.

———. Memorandum to Joseph Grew, U.S. ambassador to Japan, 5 June 1937. U.S. Department of State, FRUS 1937.

———. Memorandum to Franklin Roosevelt, 10 June 1943. U.S. Department of State, FRUS 1945.

————. Telegrams to Joseph Grew, 22–24 March 1937. U.S. Department of State, *FRUS 1937*.

————. Telegram to Joseph Grew, 20 November 1937. U.S. Department of State, *FRUS 1937*.

Ickes, Harold. "The Court Proposes, Interior Disposes." *New Republic*, 27 March 1950.

————. Letter to Franklin Roosevelt, 5 June 1943. National Archives, RG 48, Straus files.

Imperial, Mark, Timothy Hennessey, and Donald Robadue Jr. "The Evolution of Adaptive Management for Estuarine Ecosystems: The National Estuary Program and Its Precursors." *Ocean and Coastal Management* 20 (1993): 147.

Ingram, Helen, and Dean Mann. "Policy Failure: An Issue Deserving Analysis." In *Why Policies Succeed or Fail*, ed. Ingram and Mann.

"In Praise of Knowledge." *Economist*, 27 May 1995, 22.

International Joint Commission (United States–Canada). "Seventh Biennial Report on Great Lakes Water Quality." 1994.

Jackson, Tim. "Principles of Clean Production: Developing an Operational Approach to the Preventive Paradigm." In *Clean Production Strategies: Developing Preventive Environmental Management in the Industrial Economy*, ed. Jackson.

Jacobs, Paul. "Boom in Holdings Puts Wildlife Agency to the Test." *Los Angeles Times*, 28 April 1997, A1.

Jacobson, Jon. "U. S. Coastal States and the International Law of the Sea." *Ocean Development and International Law* 24 (1993): 393.

"Japan, U.S. Differ on Science." *Science* 269 (21 July 1995).

"Joint Memorandum in Support of Rehearing in United States v. Texas." *Baylor Law Review* 3 (1951): 115, 319–35.

Kamienicki, Sheldon, and Eliz Sanasarian. "Conducting Comparative Research in Environmental Policy." *Natural Resources Journal* 30 (1990): 321.

Kelley, Ken. "The Marine Fish Conservation Network: Pressing for Basic Changes in How Fisheries Are Managed." *National Fisherman* 74 (April 1994): 56.

Kenchington, Richard, and David Crawford. "On the Meaning of Integration in Coastal Zone Management." *Ocean and Coastal Management* 21 (1993): 109.

Kent, H. S. K. "The Historical Origins of the Three-Mile Limit." *American Journal of International Law* 48 (1954): 537.

Kerr, Richard A. "Antarctic Ozone Hole Fails to Recover." *Science* 266 (14 October 1994): 217.

Kindt, John. "International Environmental Law and Policy, An Overview of Transboundary Pollution." *San Diego Law Review*, 23 (1986): 583.

Kirschner, Elisabeth. "Eco-Industrial Plants Find Growing Acceptance." *Chemical and Engineering News* 73 (20 February 1995): 15.

Kistos, Thomas. "Remarks at the 16th Annual Seminar of the Center for Oceans Law Review." *Ocean Science News* 2 (24 January 1992).

Kmiec, Douglas. "Legal Issues Raised by the Proposed Proclamation to Extend the Territorial Sea." *Territorial Sea Journal* 1 (1990): 1.

Knecht, Robert. "The Exclusive Economic Zone: A New Opportunity in Federal-State Ocean Relations." In *Ocean Resources and U.S. Intergovernmental Relations in the 1980s*, ed. Silva.

Knecht, Robert, Biliana Cicin-Sain, and Jack Archer. "National Ocean Policy: A Window of Opportunity." *Ocean Development and International Law* 19 (1988): 113.

Knecht, Robert, and William Westermeyer. "State v. National Interests in an Expanded Territorial Sea." *Coastal Zone Management Journal* 11 (1984).

Knudson, Tom, and Nancy Vogel. "Pacific Blues: Californians Are Squandering Their Coastal Heritage." *Sacramento Bee*, special report, 22–26 December 1996.

Koester, Thomas. "State-Federal Jurisdictional Conflicts in the U.S. 12-Mile Territorial Sea: An Opportunity to End the Seaweed Rebellion." *Coastal Management* 18 (1990): 195.

Lee, F. W. Memorandum to Michael Straus, 2 May 1945. National Archives, RG 48, Straus files.

Leman, Christopher, and Robert Nelson. "The Rise of Managerial Federalism: An Assessment of Benefits and Costs." *Environmental Law* 12 (1982): 981.

LePage, Andrew. "Oil Study Cites Area Economic Benefits." *Santa Barbara News-Press*, 22 March 1997.

Lester, Charles. "Reforming the Offshore Oil and Gas Program: Rediscovering the Public's Interests in the Outer Continental Shelf Lands." *Ocean and Coastal Management* 30 (1996): 1.

———. "The Search for Dialogue in the Administrative State: The Politics, Policy and Law of Offshore Oil Development." Ph.D. diss., University of California at Berkeley, 1991.

Lima, James. "The Politics of Offshore Oil Development." Ph.D. diss., University of California at Santa Barbara, 1994.

Lindblom, Charles. "The Science of 'Muddling Through.'" *Public Administration Review* 19 (1959): 79.

Littleton, Richard. "Coastal States, Inland States, and a 12-Mile Territorial Sea." *Journal of Maritime Law and Commerce* 17 (1986): 530.

Locke, Paul A. "Reorienting Risk Assessment." *Environmental Forum* 11 (1992): 28.

Lovejoy, Thomas. "The Obligations of a Biologist." *Conservation Biology* 3 (1989): 329.

Lovins, Amory. "The Role of Energy Efficiency." In *Global Warming: The Greenpeace Report*, ed. Jeremy Leggett. New York: Oxford University Press, 1990.

Lyons, William. "Federalism and Resource Development: A New Role for States?" *Environmental Law* 12 (1982): 931.

MacGarvin, Malcolm. "Implementation of the Second North Sea Conference: An Overview." Greenpeace Paper 32. Report prepared for the Third International North Sea Conference, Greenpeace International.

———. "Precaution, Science and the Sin of Hubris." In *Interpreting the Precautionary Principle*, ed. O'Riordan and Cameron, 69–101.

———. "0-2000: The Future, Clean Production." Greenpeace Paper 30. Report prepared for Third International North Sea Conference, Greenpeace International.

MacKenzie, Debora. "The Cod That Disappeared." *New Scientist*, 16 September 1995.

Malakoff, David. "Extinction on the High Seas." *Science* 277 (25 July 1997): 486.

Manik, Roy. "Pollution Prevention, Organizational Culture, and Social Learning." *Environmental Law* 22 (1991): 189.

Marshall, Tyler. "U.S. Dives into a Sea of Major Rewards and Risks." *Los Angeles Times*, 23 February 1998.

Mazmanian, Daniel, and Paul Sabatier. "The Role of Attitudes and Perceptions in Policy Evaluation by Attentive Elites: The California Coastal Commissions." In *Why Policies Succeed or Fail*, ed. Ingram and Mann.

McKibben, Bill. "Hello, I Must Be Going." *Outside* 22 (1997): 58.

Meier, Barry. "Fight in Congress Looms on Fishing: Concerns Raised on Ethics of Regulatory Councils." *New York Times*, 19 September 1994.

Meyerhoff, Al. "The Delaney Clause: Let's Reform a Failed Food Safety Regime." *EPA Journal*, January–March 1993.

Miller, Daniel S. "Offshore Federalism: Evolving Federal-State Relations in Offshore Oil and Gas Development." *Ecology Law Quarterly* 11 (1984): 401.

Miller, Marc L. "Regional Fishery Management Councils and the Display of Scientific Authority." *Coastal Management* 15 (1987): 309.

Moore [U.S. Department Legal Counselor]. Memorandum to Franklin Roosevelt, 24 November 1937. *FRUS 1937*.

Moore, Steven J. "Troubles in the High Seas: A New Era in the Regulation of U.S. Ocean Dumping." *Environmental Law* 22 (1992): 913.

Morgan, Joseph. "Marine Regions: Myth or Reality?" *Ocean and Shoreline Management* 12 (1989): 1.

Morris, Richard. "The Forging of the Union Reconsidered: A Historical Refutation of State Sovereignty Over Seabeds." *Columbia Law Review* 74 (1974): 1056.

"Much Heat, Little Light." *Economist*, 12 June 1993, 73.

Mulvaney, Kieran. "A Sea of Troubles: In the International Year of the Ocean, Are We Reaching the Limits?" *E Magazine* 9 (1998): 28.

Murphy, Dennis, and Barry Noon. "Coping with Uncertainty in Wildlife Biology." *Journal of Wildlife Management* 54 (1991): 773.

Naj, A. K. "Sewage Dumped Offshore Is Found Within Tiny Animals." *Wall Street Journal*, 12 November 1992.

"A New Deal for the Northeast." Editorial, *National Fisherman* 74 (March 1994), 6.

Norton, Bryan G. "Ecological Economics: The Science and Management of Sustainability." In *Ecological Economics*, ed. Costanza.

Noss, Reed. "Whither Conservation Biology?" *Conservation Biology* 7 (1993): 215.

Ocean Resources Program of the Western Legislative Conference. Materials for Participants. Monterey, California, November 1989.

Paarlberg, Robert. "A Domestic Dispute: Clinton, Congress, and International Environmental Policy." *Environment* 38 (1996): 16.

Parker, Jean E., and Beverly L. Boyd. "An Introduction to EPA's Design for the Environment Program." Washington, D.C.: U.S. Environmental Protection Agency, n.d.

"The Pew Charitable Trusts Funds Toxic Diet Project." [Rhode Island] *Bay Bulletin* 6 (1994): 25.

Pickering, Helen. "Artificial Reefs of Bulk Waste Materials: A Scientific and Legal Review of the Suitability of Using the Cement Stabilised By-Products of Coal-Fired Power Stations." *Marine Policy* 20 (1996): 483.

"Random Jottings." *Economist*, 19 November 1994.

Raustiala, Kal, and David Victor. "The Future of the Convention on Biological Diversity." *Environment* 38 (1996): 17.

Ray, G. Carleton. "Biodiversity Is Biogeography: Implications for Conservation." *Oceanography* 9 (1996): 50.

———. "Coastal-Marine Discontinuities and Synergisms: Implications for Biodiversity Conservation." *Biodiversity and Conservation* 5 (1996): 1095.

———. "Ecology, Law, and the 'Marine Revolution.'" *Biological Conservation* 3 (1970): 7.

———. "Establishing Biosphere Reserves for Coastal Barrier Systems." *Bioscience* 41 (1991): 301.

Rieser, Alison. "International Fisheries Law, Overfishing and Marine Biodiversity." *Georgetown International Environmental Law Review* 9 (1977): 251.

Roosevelt, Franklin D. Memorandum to Cordell Hull, 9 June 1943. FRUS 1945.

———. Memorandums to Moore, State Department counselor, 21–22 November 1937. FRUS 1937.

Roush, Wade. "When Rigor Meets Reality." *Science* 269 (21 July 1995): 313.

Sabatier, Paul. "An Advocacy Coalition Framework of Policy Change and the Role of Policy-Oriented Learning Therein." *Policy Sciences* 21 (1988): 129.

———. "Top-Down and Bottom-Up Approaches to Implementation Research: A Critical Analysis and Suggested Synthesis." *Journal of Public Policy* 6 (1987): 21.

Saurenman, John. "The Effects of a Twelve-Mile Territorial Sea on Coastal State Jurisdiction: Where Do Matters Stand?" *Territorial Sea Journal* 1 (1990): 39.

Sax, Joseph. "Liberating the Public Trust Doctrine from Its Historical Shackles." *University of California Davis Law Review* 14 (1980): 185.

Schachte, William. "The History of the Territorial Sea from a National Security Perspective." *Territorial Sea Journal* 1 (1990): 143.

74.6% of Sociology Is Bunk: An Uppity Biologist Has an Important Message for the Social Sciences." *Economist* 15 (13 May 1995).

Sheiber, Harry. "Origins of the Abstention Doctrine in International Law: Japanese-U.S. Relations and the Pacific Fisheries, 1937–1958." *Ecology Law Quarterly* 16 (1989): 29–36.

Scheiber, Harry, and Chris Carr. "Constitutionalism and the Historical Sea: An Historical Study." *Territorial Sea Journal* 2 (1992): 67, 77–85.

Shapiro, Michael. "Sagebrush and Seaweed Robbery: State Revenue Losses from Onshore and Offshore Federal Land." *Ecology Law Quarterly* 12 (1985): 481.

Shapiro, Michael, and Rosella Shapiro. "Opportunities for a State-Federal Partnership in an Expanded Territorial Sea." *Coastal Zone Management Journal* 11 (1984).

Sherman, Kenneth. "Productivity, Perturbations, and Options for Biomass Yields in Large Marine Ecosystems." In *Large Marine Ecosystems*, ed. Sherman, Alexander, and Gold.

Shrader-Frechette, Kristen. "Throwing Out the Bathwater of Positivism, Keeping the Baby of Objectivity: Relativism and Advocacy in Conservation Biology." *Conservation Biology* 10 (1996): 912.

Silbergeld, Ellen, and Kevin Tonat. "Investing in Prevention: Opportunities to Prevent Disease and Reduce Health Care Costs by Identifying Environmental and Occupational Causes of Noncancer Disease." *Toxicology and Industrial Health* 10, no. 6, special issue (1994).

Sollen, Robert. "An Ocean of Oil." Manuscript, Special Collections, Library of the University of California at Santa Barbara, n.d.

Solomon, Caleb. "U.S. Oil Spills Have Declined Sharply, Study Says: Stiffer Federal Law Is Cited." *Wall Street Journal*, 24 August 1992.

Speer, Lisa. "Comments of the Natural Resources Defense Council [NRDC], on the Report of the OCS Policy Committee's Subcommittee on Legislation, 'Moving Beyond Conflict to Consensus.'" N.d.

Stairs, Kevin, and Peter Taylor. "Non-Governmental Organizations and the Legal Protection of the Oceans: A Case Study." In *The International Politics of the Environment*, ed. Hurrell and Kingsbury.

Stettinius. Memorandum to Harold Ickes, 19 December 1944. FRUS 1945.

Stone, Richard. "Taking a New Look at Life Through a Functional Lens." *Science* 269 (21 July 1995).

Straus, Michael. Memorandum to Harold Ickes, 22 May 1944. National Archives, RG 48, Straus files.

———. Memorandum to Harold Ickes, 14 July 1994. National Archives, RG 48, Straus files.

———. Memorandum to Harold Ickes, 12 August 1944. National Archives, RG 48, Straus files.

"Stuck in the Mud: Great Lakes Pollution." *Economist*, 6 August 1994, 24.

Sullivan, Walter. "Sewage Bacteria in Food Chain." *New York Times*, 17 November 1992.

Swenson, Kenneth. "A Stitch in Time: The Continental Shelf, Environmental Ethics, and Federalism." *Southern California Law Review* 60 (1987): 851.

"Symposium on Submerged Lands." *Baylor Law Review* 3 (1951).

Thia-Eng, Chua. "Essential Elements of Integrated Coastal Zone Management." *Ocean and Coastal Management* 21 (1993): 81.

Thorne-Miller, Boyce. "The Precautionary Principle/Approach in International Agreements on the Marine Environment." In *Moving Ahead on Ocean Governance*, ed. Cicin-Sain and Denno.

"Tidelands Men Opposing U.S. Oil Suit Made Big Gifts to Democratic Campaign." *St. Louis Post-Dispatch*, 23 October 1945.

"Toxic Use Reduction Case Study: Customer Education and Zinc Use Reduction at Dydee Diaper Service, Inc." Office of Technical Assistance, Executive Office of Environmental Affairs, Commonwealth of Massachusetts, n.d.

Tuohy, William. "Characterizing the San Francisco Estuary: A Case Study of Science Management in the National Estuary Program." *Coastal Management* 21 (1993): 113.

"The Turtle Soup Factor." *Economist*, 8 July 1995.

U.S. Department of Defense. *Annotated Supplement to the Commander's Handbook on the Law of Naval Operations*, NWP 9 (REV. A) FM FM 1-10, I-22 (1989).

———. Formerly classified internal documentation acquired by the author under the Freedom of Information Act, via request no. 9-FOI-0810 (1990–1995).

———. Memorandum to Office of the Secretary of Defense/Joint Chiefs of Staff Representative for Ocean Policy Affairs, n.d. Obtained by author under U.S. Freedom of Information Act, Request #90-FOI-0810, April 1990.

U.S. Environmental Protection Agency. "1993 TRI Data Show Past Trends Continuing." EPA 742-N-95-002. *Pollution Prevention News*, March–April 1995, 3.

Van de Kamp, John, and John Saurenman. "Outer Continental Shelf Oil and Gas Leasing: What Role for the States?" *Harvard Environmental Law Review* 14 (1990): 73.

Van Dyke, Jon. "International Governance and Stewardship of the High Seas and Its Resources." In *Freedom for the Seas in the 21st Century: Ocean Governance and Environmental Harmony*, ed. Van Dyke, Zaelke, and Hewison.

———. "The Rio Principles and Our Responsibilities of Ocean Stewardship." *Ocean and Coastal Management* 31 (1996): 1.

"Warm Words." *Economist*, 14 June 1997.

Weintraub, Bernard. "Science, International Regulation, and the Precautionary Principle: Setting Standards and Defining Terms." N.Y.U. *Environmental Law Journal* 1 (1992): 173.

Wilder, Diana. "Save the Bay's 'Toxic Diet' Project." *Small Flows Journal* 1 (1994): 3.

Wilder, Robert J. "Building an Environmental Regime Based on Precaution, Pollution Prevention, and Industrial Ecology." In *1995 Reports: Environmental Science and Engineering Fellows Program*. Washington, D.C.: American Association for the Advancement of Science Press, 1995.

————. "Cooperative Governance, Environmental Policy, and Management of Offshore Oil and Gas in the United States." *Ocean Development and International Law* 24 (1993): 41, 43–45.

————. "Is This Holistic Ecology or Just Muddling Through? The Theory and Practice of Marine Policy." *Coastal Management* 21 (1993): 209.

————. "Law of the Sea Convention as Stimulus for Robust Environmental Policy: The Case for Precautionary Action." In *Ocean Yearbook 12*, ed. Elizabeth Mann-Borgese, Norton Ginsberg and Joseph Morgan. Chicago: University of Chicago Press, 1996.

————. "The Precautionary Principle and the Law of the Sea Convention." In *Implications of Entry Into Force of the Law of the Sea Convention for U.S. Ocean Governance*, ed. Cicin-Sain and Leccese.

————. "Prevention Rather Than Cure." *Nature* 369 (30 June 1994): 700.

————. "Sea-Change from Bush to Clinton: Setting a New Course for Offshore Oil Development and U.S. Energy Policy." *UCLA Journal of Environmental Law and Policy* 11 (1993): 131.

————. "The Three-Mile Territorial Sea: Its Origins and Implications for Contemporary Offshore Federalism." *Virginia Journal of International Law* 32 (1992): 681.

Wilkinson, Cynthia, L. Pittman, and Rebecca Dye. "Slick Work: An Analysis of the Oil Pollution Act of 1990." *Journal of Energy, Natural Resources and Environmental Law* 12 (1992): 181.

Woodwell, George. "How Does the World Work? Great Issues of Life and Government Hinge on the Answer." In *Global Warming and Biological Diversity*, ed. Peters and Lovejoy.

Index

abalone, 100–01
advanced energy storage technologies, 114
Agenda 21, 175
Alaska: and Bristol Bay salmon fishery, 46–50; and opposition to twelve-mile territorial sea, 78
alternative energy sources: in California, 117; funding for, 114
Army Corps of Engineers (COE), 170–71
Atomic Energy Commission (AEC), 154

Babbitt, Bruce, 115
Baker, James (U.S. secretary of state), 151
Ball, Milner, 121
Bartley, Ernest, 59
benthic species, 71
Bering Island, and Steller's Sea Cow, 23
Bering Sea, 24–26
"best available technology" (BAT), 166–68
"best conventional pollutant control technology" (BCT), 168
Biddle, Francis (U.S. attorney general), 45, 52–53
biodiversity, xiv, 23, 103–06; and precautionary action, 146; preserving, 69–70
biological diversity. See biodiversity
"bioma" theory, 72
Black, Hugo (U.S. Supreme Court justice), and U.S. v. California, 59, 60
Boomer v. Atlantic Cement Co., 195–96
Boone v. Kingsbury (Calif.), 36

bounded rationality model of decision making, 97–99
bovine spongiform encephalopathy (BSE), 152
Breverton-Holt model, 89
Britain. See England
burden of proof: and OCSLA, 133–34; and precautionary principle, 144
Bureau of Land Management, 130
Bush, George (U.S. president), 136–37
bycatches, 158
Bynkershoek, Cornelius Von, De Dominio Maris, 14–15

Caldwell, Lynton, 155–56
California: applications of DfE in, 181; changes in San Francisco Bay area, 197–98; discovery of oil in, 30; as example of state governance, 99–103; and National Estuary Program, 200–02; oil spills off coast, 33; and regulation of offshore oil drilling, 34–37; runoff problems, 102–03; slant drilling in, 36–37; U.S. v. California, 58
California Air Resources Board, 117
California Coastal Commission, 129
California Resources Agency, 99
Canada: collapse of Grand Banks fish stocks, 88–91; and Great Lakes precautionary action, 175–76

line-of-sight doctrine, 19; as origin of
three-mile territorial sea, 11, 12–13
logging, 94
London Dumping Convention of 1972
(LDC), 169–70, 171
Long, Breckenridge (U.S. assistant secretary of state), 53–54
Louisiana: and state ownership of offshore
oil, 41; Supreme Court decision
against, 62
Lubchenco, Jane, 103
Lujan, Manuel (U.S. secretary of the interior), 112

MacKenzie, Debora, 91
"mad cow disease," 152
Magnuson-Stevens Act, 91, 94, 156–63,
208; failures of, 156–59; and optimum sustainable yield, 95; passage
of, 80–81; and precautionary principle, 157; proposed alterations in,
159–63
March, James, 98
Mare Clausum, Seu de Dominio Maris (Selden),
10
mare clausum. *See* closed seas
mare liberum. *See* open seas
Mare Liberum (Grotius), 9, 14
mare nostrum. *See* "our seas"
marine league, defined, 7
marine policy, "first-generation," xiv–xv
Marine Protection, Research, and Sanctuaries Act of 1972 (MPRSA), 169–72
maximum sustainable yield, 95
Mazmanian, Daniel, 127–28
mercury, 102; successful reduction of, 147
Mineral Leasing Act of 1920, 35; issue of
offshore application, 61; and ownership of offshore lands, 38, 39
Minerals Management Service (MMS),
137; OCS development and, 129–32;
and OCS subcommittee, 137
Montreal Protocol on Substances That Deplete the Ozone Layer, 175
multilateral protections for marine ecosystems, 174–75

National Environmental Policy Act of

1970 (NEPA), 153–56; ESA con-
trasted with, 165; Supreme Court
interpretation of, 155
National Estuary Program (1987), 200–02
National Fisherman, 160
National Marine Fisheries Service
(NMFS), 157; and conservation of
essential fish habitat, 94
National Seafood Promotion Council, 92
natural gas, 139–40
Natural Resources Defense Council
(NRDC), 138–39
Natural Resources Defense Council v. Reilly,
167
Nature Conservancy, 166
nautical miles vs. statute miles, 21
New England: fisheries management in,
91–93; and opposition to twelve-
mile territorial sea, 78; pollution
prevention in, 147–49; results of
overfishing in, 157
New York Times, 158
Norse, Elliott: on marine biodiversity,
104; on responsible ocean governance, 95–96
North Carolina's Areas of Environmental
Concern, 205
northern fur seal, 24–26
Novo Nordisk, 181–82
nuclear power, 142
nuclear waste dumping, by Soviet Union,
170–71
Nye, Gerald (U.S. senator), 41, 42

Ocean Dumping Ban Act of 1988, 170
ocean governance, U.S.: recommendations
for, 210–12; status of, 26–27
OCS development, 113–19; and administration by U.S. Geological Survey,
129–30; and MMS, 129–32;
OCSLA amendments and, 125
OCS drilling, 110–13
OCSLA (1953), 65, 67, 68, 123; and
burden of proof, 133–34; failures of,
163; further changes to, 132; mistakes in, 125; precautionary principle and, 164; proposed alterations
to, 163–64

resistance to, 151–52; and UNC-
LOS III, 172–74
prevention, 143–82 passim, 208; case
study in, 147–49
Proctor letter (1933), 38
prospecting permits for offshore oil, 35
Public Lands Committee, 56

quitclaim legislation, 61, 63–64; passed
in Congress, 65

radioactive fallout, 147
rational-comprehensive model of decision
making, 98
Ray, G. Carleton, 70, 159
Reagan, Ronald (U.S. president): and declaration of EEZ, 81; and proclamation of twelve-mile territorial sea,
84, 86
recessions, U.S., 136
reductionist thinking, 187–89
Reed, Stanley (U.S. Supreme Court justice), and *U.S. v. California*, 59, 60
Regula, Ralph, 127
Resource Conservation and Recovery Act
of 1976, 176
risk management, 167
Roosevelt, Franklin (U.S. president): and
continental shelf resources, 51, 52;
interest in offshore oil, 44–46; interest in salmon conservation, 48–49;
and "inventive genius," 44, 45, 55,
209; and Tidelands Debate, 53
Roosevelt administration: and effects of
Great Depression, 40; effects of
WWII on, 50; on status of submerged lands, 38
rule of capture, 34, 35
runoff, 102–03
Russia: and northern fur seal, 24–26; and
treaty banning pelagic seal hunting,
26

Sabatier, Paul, 127–28
Sacramento River, 198
salmon: Bristol Bay, dispute over, 46–50;
in Pacific Northwest, 195, 198

salmon smolts, 93–94
San Francisco Bay area: changes in,
197–98; and failure of state resource
management, 101–02; and National
Estuary Program (1987), 200–02
San Joaquin River, 198
San Jose Mercury News, 33
Santa Barbara, Calif.: Chamber of Com-
merce position on offshore drilling,
33; and offshore oil, 29, 30, 110–11,
112; oil spill (1969), 109
Santa Barbara Channel: oil reserves under,
112; prospecting permits for, 35
Santa Monica Bay: prospecting permits
for, 35; toxic chemicals in, 102
Sassoferrato, Bartolus de, 5, 10, 11; and
seaward jurisdiction, 5
Saurenman, John, 134–35
Sax, Joseph, 193–94
Scandinavian league, 11–12, 13, 19; as
measure of Denmark's neutral zone,
15
Science, 176–77
Sea Fisheries Act (1883), 22
Sears, Paul, 189
Selden, John, 20; and defense of closed
seas, 10–11; *Mare Clausum, Seu de Do-
minio Maris*, 10
Senate Bill 2164, 41
Senate Foreign Relations Committee, 56
Senate Joint Resolution 208 (S.J.R. 208),
41–42
Senate Joint Resolution 20 (S.J.R. 20),
63–64
Senate Public Lands Committee, 42
Seward Convention of 1867, 25
Shultz, George (U.S. secretary of state),
85
Signal Oil Company stock value, 60
Silent Spring (Carson), 144
Simon, Herbert, 98
six-mile territorial sea, 75
slant drilling, 36–37
source reduction, 176; EPA funds spent
on, 177; EPA's "33/50" program for,
179
Source Reduction Clearinghouse, 178

oil from Summerland, 30; on owner-
ship of oceans, 43–44; scientific ori-
entation of, 129–30
U.S. Navy, and concerns about twelve-
mile territorial sea, 83
U.S. Supreme Court: decision in *U.S. v.
California*, 58, 59, 62; decision in
U.S. v. Louisiana, 62; decision in *U.S.
v. Texas*, 62; interpretation of NEPA,
155
U.S. tuna fleet, 71; and claims by Latin
American nations, 72–73; and
twelve-mile territorial sea, 78
U.S. v. California, 58, 60, 120; decision in,
62
U.S. v. Louisiana decision, 62
U.S. v. Texas decision, 62
Ubaldis, Baldus de, 11; and seaward juris-
diction, 5
UN Agreement on Straddling and Highly
Migratory Fish Stocks (1995), 174
UNCLOS, 75–76
UNCLOS I (1958), 76–77, 172–73; fail-
ure of, 76–78
UNCLOS II (1960), and twelve-mile ter-
ritorial sea, 77
UNCLOS III (1982): as basis for fisheries
management, 87–88, 94–95; and
EEZs, 173; negotiations leading to,
78–82; and precautionary action,
172–74
UN Conference on Environment and De-
velopment (1992), 175
UN General Assembly Drift-Net Resolu-
tion, 175
United Nations Conference on the Law of
the Sea. *See* UNCLOS
United States: adoption of twelve-mile
territorial sea, 82–86; and convening

of UNCLOS III, 78–79; as distant-
water fishing nation, 71; position on
twelve-mile territorial sea, 74; and
three-mile territorial sea, 17–20;
and treaty banning pelagic seal hunting, 26
USSR. *See* Soviet Union
UV-B radiation, 193

Van de Kamp, John, 134–35
veto/clearance points: burden of proof
and, 134; for OCSLA, 132–33
volatile organic compounds (VOCs), 102

Washington, George (U.S. president),
97, 98; and three-mile neutrality
zone, 17–18
Washington (state): and Bristol Bay
salmon dispute, 48, 49; and opposition to twelve-mile territorial sea, 78
waste management, 208; as business, 144;
under PPA, 176
Water Alliances for Voluntary Efficiency,
179
Watt, James (U.S. secretary of the interior), 112, 133
whaling, 105; regulation of, 175
Wheeler, Douglas P. (Calif. secretary of
resources), 100
whipstocking, 37
Wilson, E. O., 166
World War I, 41
World War II, 50, 71; Soviet Union
after, 73
Wright, Judge Skelly, 154

zero-emission vehicles (ZEVs), 117
zinc, as pollutant, 148–49

South Pole, 193

Soviet Union: and Chernobyl nuclear plant, 194–95; and convening of UNCLOS III, 78–79; and intelligence advantage of three-mile territorial sea, 83–84; nuclear waste dumping by, 170–71; position on innocent passage, 73–74; position on straits passage, 74; position on three-mile territorial sea, 73; and support for twelve-mile territorial sea, 73

species diversity, 103–04

species extinction, 192–94

sport fishing, 162

St. Louis Post-Dispatch, 57

Standard Oil Company, 36–37

State, U.S. Department of: and Bristol Bay salmon dispute, 46–47, 48–50; and continental shelf resources, 51–52; and fisheries conservation treaties, 54; position on Magnuson-Stevens Act, 81; position on ownership of submerged lands, 65

state governance of marine environments, 99–103

statute miles vs. nautical miles, 21

Steller's Sea Cow, 23, 24

Stettinius, Edward (U.S. secretary of state), 55

straddling stocks, 174

straits passage: Soviet position on, 74; and twelve-mile territorial sea, 83

submarines, and innocent passage, 83

Submerged Lands Act of 1953 (SLA), 65–67, 68, 123

Summerland, Calif., 30–32

Supreme Court. *See* U.S. Supreme Court

Sustainable Fisheries Act, 94

Swartztrauber, Sayre, 10, 17; on northern fur seal controversy, 26

Sweden: refused innocent passage by Soviet Union, 74; and Scandinavian league, 12

terrestrial diversity, 104

Territorial Seas Treaty (1958), 76

Territorial Waters Act (1878), 22

Texas, 65; and state ownership of offshore oil, 41; Supreme Court decision against, 62

"33/50" program, 179

Thomas, Lewis, 189

three-mile territorial sea, xiii; California and, 34; demise of, 70–86; early American application of, 17–20; England's implementation of, 20–22; formal appearance of, 15; Frankfurter on supremacy over, 60; Ickes on control of, 38; as issue at UNCLOS, 75–76; navy appeal for submerged lands in, 42–43; northern fur seal and, 26; oil claims beyond, 43–44; origins of, 11–16; paramount rights to, 58; Soviet intelligence advantage of, 83–84; Soviet position on, 73

Tidelands Controversy. *See* Tidelands Debate

Tidelands Debate, xiii, 22, 29–68 passim; and claim jumpers, 39; Ickes and, 38; political pressures regarding, 53

Toxic Diet Project, 177

Toxic Substances Control Act (TSCA), 168

Toyota, 118

Truman, Harry S. (U.S. president), 56; and Ickes's resignation, 57; position on federal ownership of submerged lands, 58; on S.J.R. 20, 63–64

Truman administration, Mineral Leasing Act of 1920 and, 61

Truman Proclamations, 53–62, 67; effect on Tidelands Debate, 56; Latin American nations' view of, 72; long-term effect of, 80

twelve-mile territorial sea: Soviet support for, 73, 75–76; U.S. adoption of, 78, 82–86; and UNCLOS II, 77

200-mile territorial sea, 79–80

U.S. Fisheries Conservation and Management Act. *See* Magnuson-Stevens Act

U.S. Geological Survey: and administration of OCS development, 129–30; Conservation Division of, 129; on